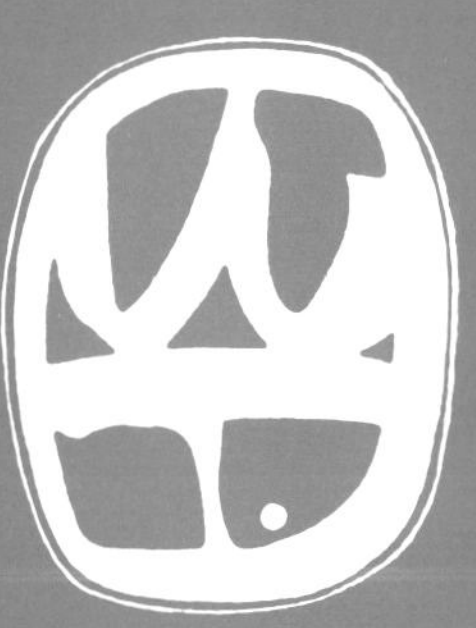

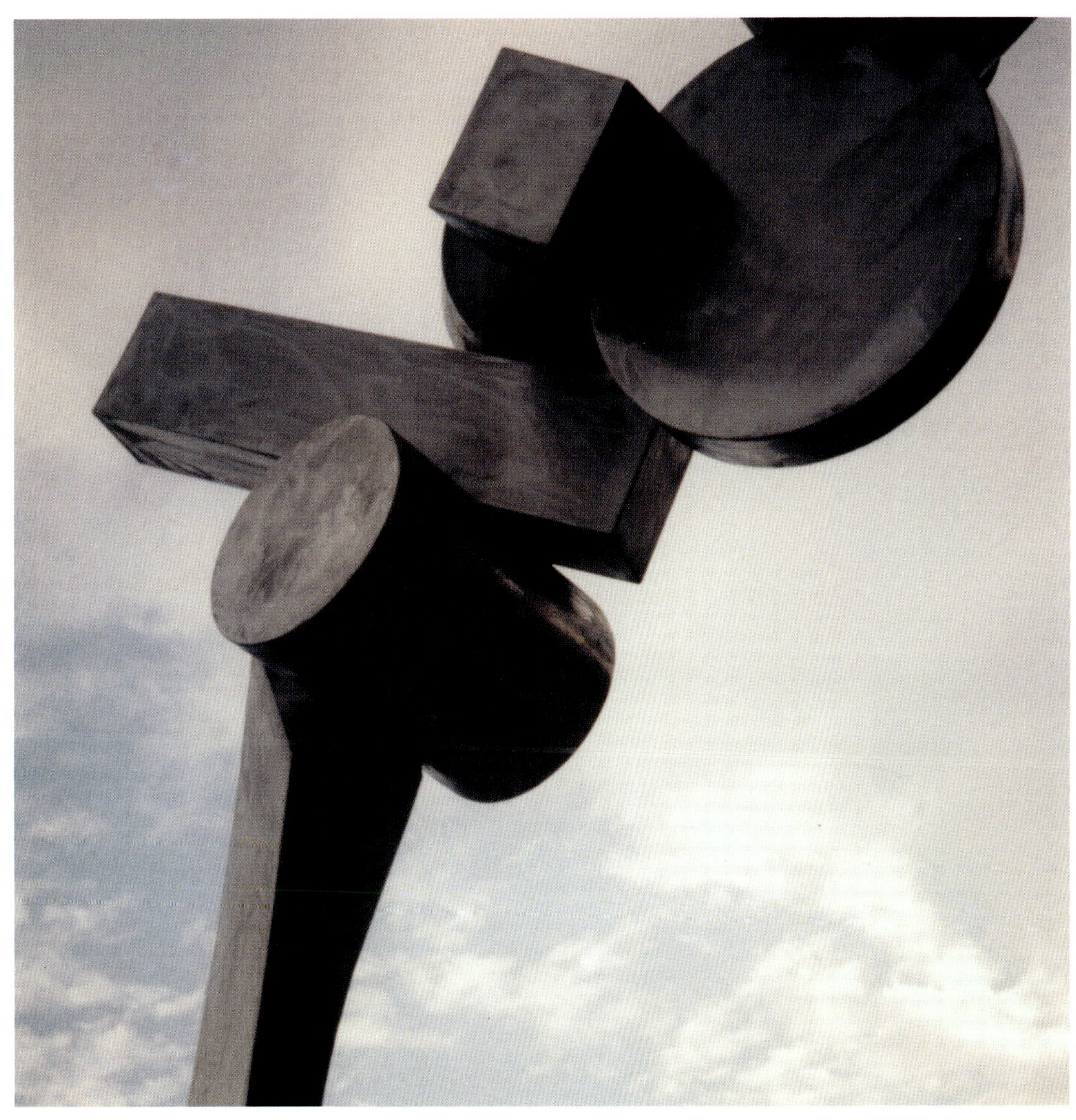

WAYNE TRAPP

The Journey of a Sculptor

EDITED BY DEBORAH MAYHALL BRADSHAW

WAYNE TRAPP
The Journey of a Sculptor

ISBN 1-879802-02-3

Published by Dancingfish Press,
Valle Crucis, NC USA

Research: Kathleen Trapp, Lou Penfield, & Scott Burns
Photography: Frederica Georgia, Michael Siede, & Friends of the Artist
Designer: Deborah Mayhall-Bradshaw
Printed & Bound in Korea by Pacifica Communications

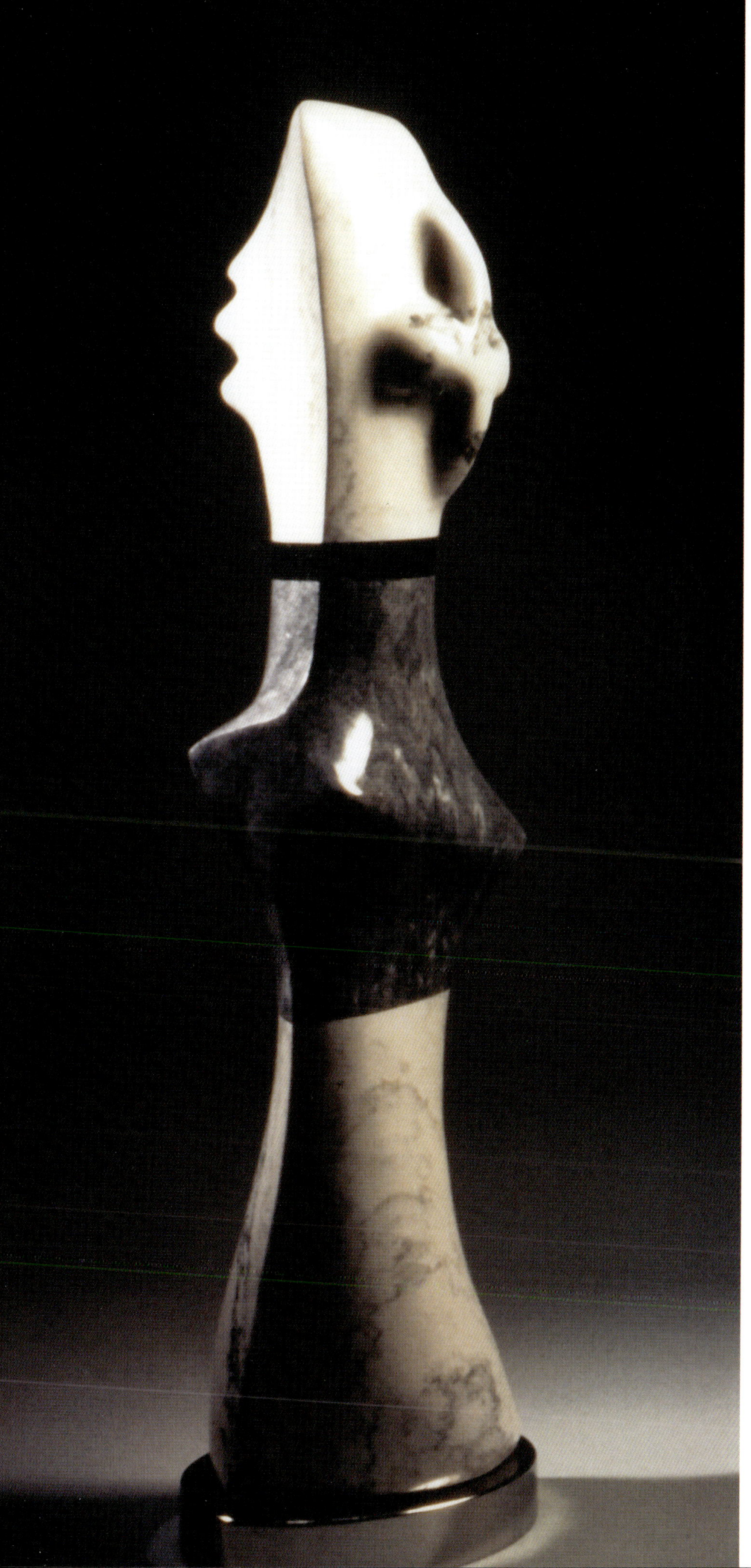

CONTENTS

It is a rare event that allows us to look behind the curtain at what really motivates an artist in any field of work, often without notice and recognition, to communicate their vision of what order or reason underlies our existence. Where does the impulse to pronounce meaning into the world come from and what are the rewards and costs in an individual's pursuit of awareness and expression? In this book some of these questions are answered and many more are posed.

As we advantage this opportunity by reading the text deftly selected by the editor from the artist's journals and investigate the evolution of important images both large and small, we start to get the sense of the artist's presence deep within himself. We feel his driving insecurities in the material world and his sensitivities in the spiritual one. Trapp's definition of himself is "workman" but his work is object poetry. The artist is ever seeking the right phrase, the right gesture and color or the right story to tell us to push us hard to live now. We are "to dance", as he says, in the furious light of temporal being. Time is running out. Do what you can now, enjoy what you can experience now, because that is all the beauty that we can have in a world of sense.

But doesn't the artist's work leave a mark, and doesn't the work stand as witness on and on after our being is transformed by death? Of course, and that is the reality of art and this desire to make things that last. Intensity refines craft.

The life that drives the flower to bloom, the force that grows us from child to adult, the energy that pushes the song from the bird and the fish into the net, is all one.

Wayne spends little time analyzing this. After all, the mortal clock ticks away and Jacob must continue to wrestle the angel.

This book is a form of truth. It is the revelation of the man behind the artist and a trenchant statement about what it is we do here. Look, read carefully and then get to work.

Steve Ferguson
Artist & Critic / Appalachian State University, NC USA

For

Frederica Georgia
    … whose beautiful photography
    can be found throughout this book

Luke Schoenigner

Kathy, and daughter Devon Trapp

Lois Hinrichs

Amy Farris

EDITOR'S NOTE

The journal passages are not
presented chronological order.

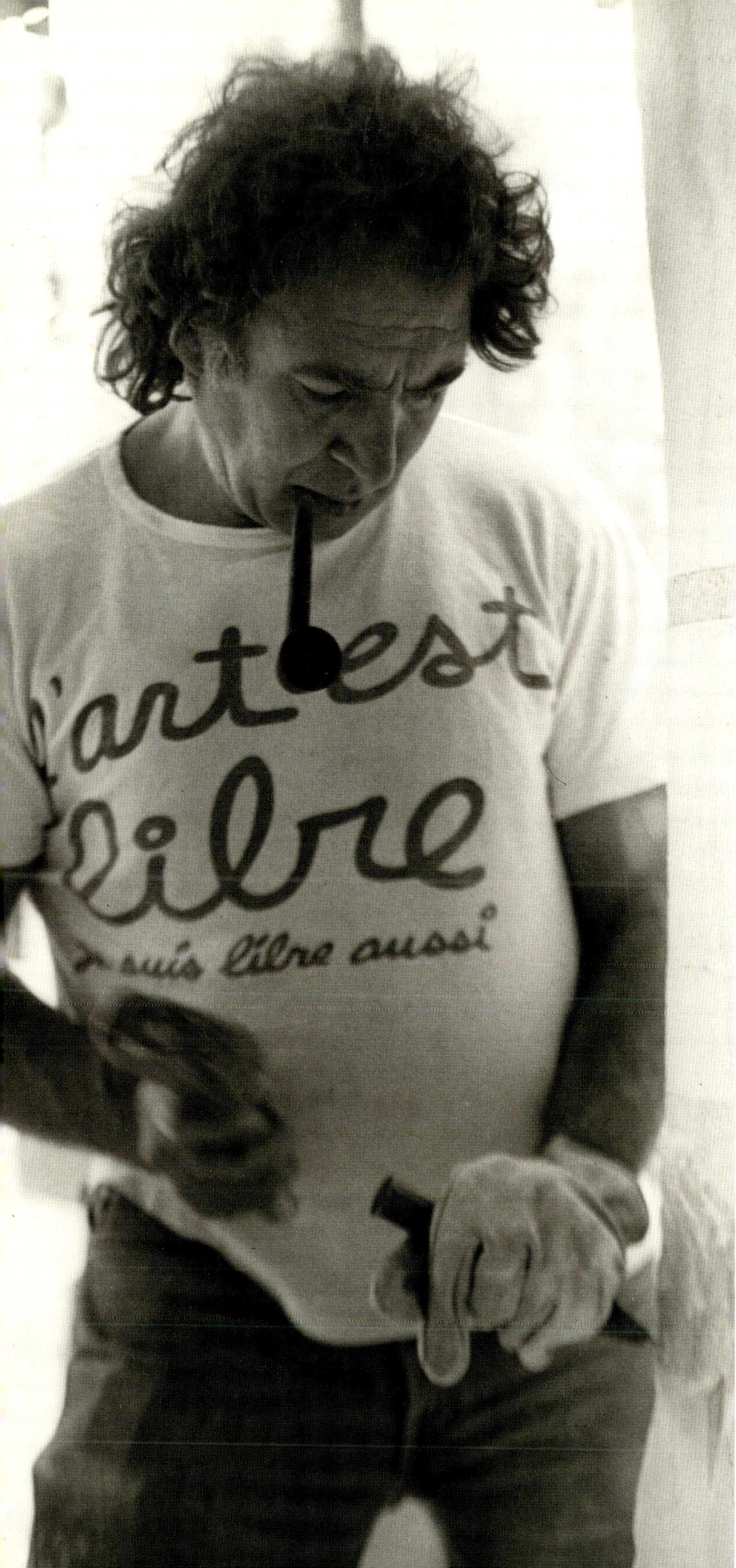

INTRODUCTION

Part Bohemian, part country gentleman, Wayne Trapp takes each hour, each sunset, each season wholly and embraces the daily work that is the heart of all he creates. With a shameless lust for life and art and a knack for stoking the fire of enthusiasm and spontaneity in other artists, galleries, and collectors, he amounts to a magician of sorts. Trapp, a veteran listener, brings a sense of wonder and care to any dialogue, making the most ordinary chat special. Ever the dreamer and a man of grace, he is contagious, and the listener, wanting to catch what he has, hangs on for transfusions of information and enlightenment.

The celebrated sculptor has worked in stone and steel for years, creating lavish, even colossal outdoor pieces for corporate clients and smaller more particular pieces for the private clientele. His hands, his shoulders are sore, sensitive, the scars of sculpting, but he can no more give it up than he can give up breathing. He avows that now he sculpts only by commission, but if a fine piece of stone presents itself or a flash of metal catches his eye or a woman turns her head just so, or if the moon is right, well . . . the dance begins.

Trapp the painter, emerged full-blown from the stone carver, took what he could not say in bronze and marble and let go with it in oil and ink on canvas and paper. His oils deliver to the eye a feast of color and stroke saturated with childlike curiosity and adult confidence. Not for the meek, or the abstinent, his work aimed at the alive and well, begs appetite, thirst, and desire. Wine, women, and song. His fabled nudes in ink and wash on handmade paper are simple lines curving and dipping and soaring to become women of sophistication and style, women with secrets, women you've known or would like to know.

With unbridled energy and an insatiable passion for everything that crosses his path, Trapp forever seeks interchange, new ground, and a good time. The man, by any standard, is an artist for the millennium.

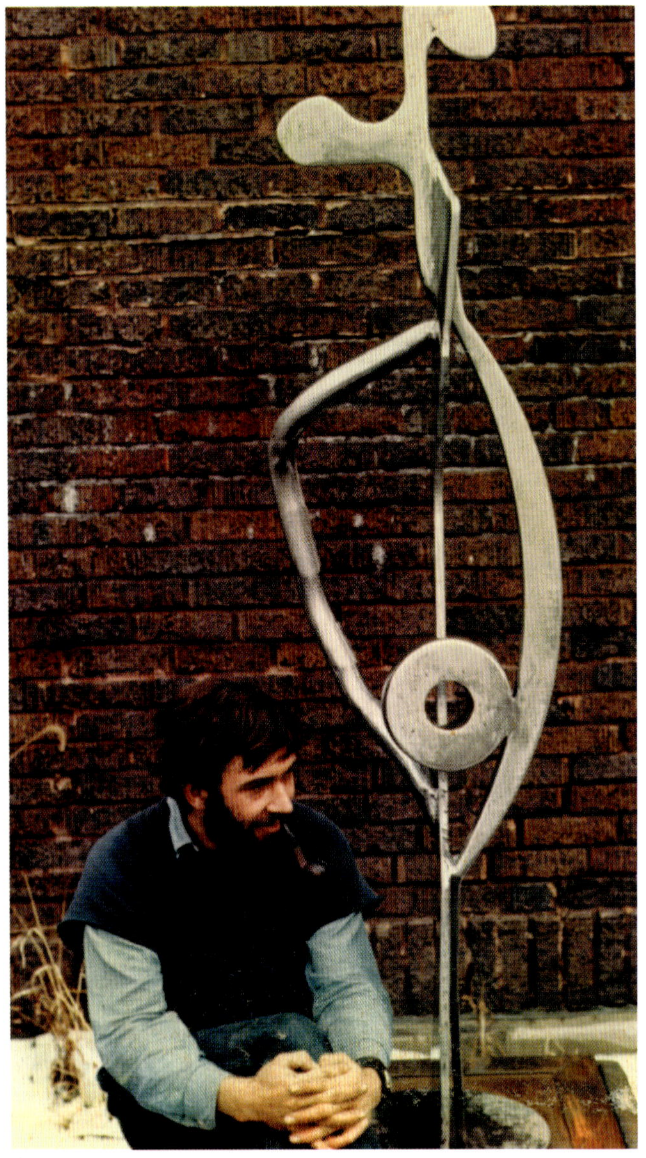

1

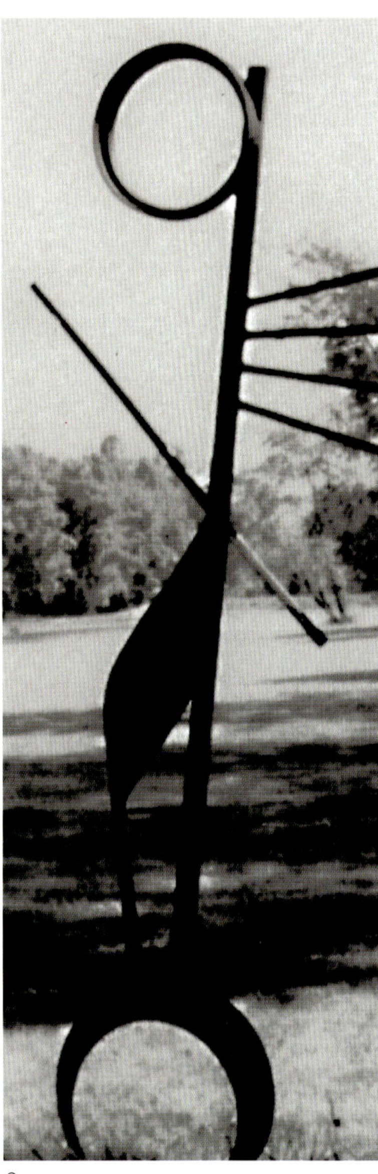

2

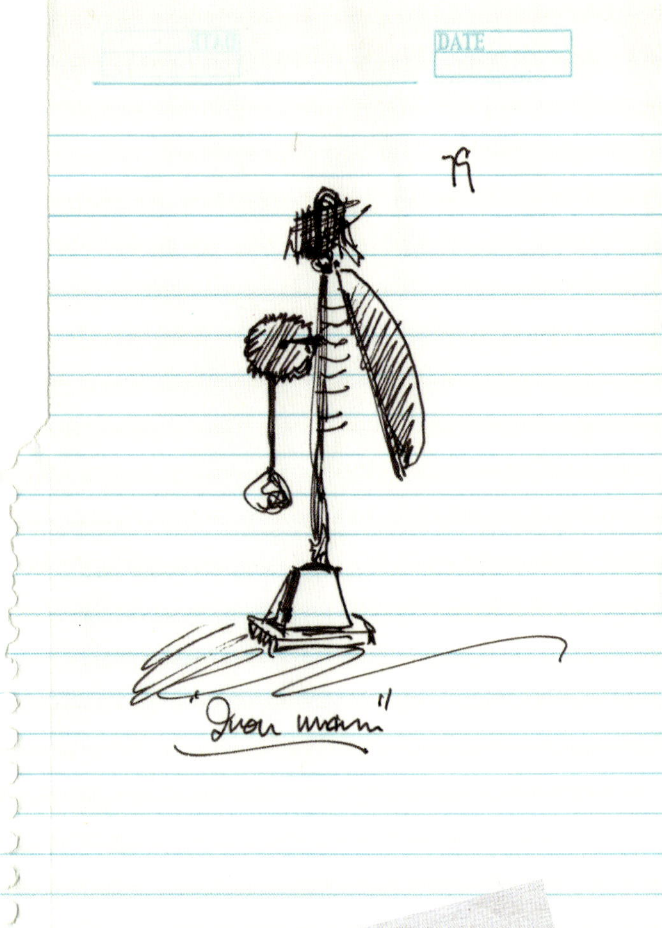

I'm at a slight standstill again with sculpture. It is virtually impossible for me to go on, to continue with new ideas in this present mental and economic state. Have to continue with drawings and clay for the time being. Don't even have the money to buy more paint or canvas. Can draw and think about future pieces I guess, but it is difficult to prime myself under the present conditions. Need to send out more slides, but have no money to make them. I keep hoping that the mail will bring good news, or the phone will ring with something positive. I have been working nearly a year now on hope and self conviction. I believe that what I am doing is right, but I have had very little help and support by anyone.

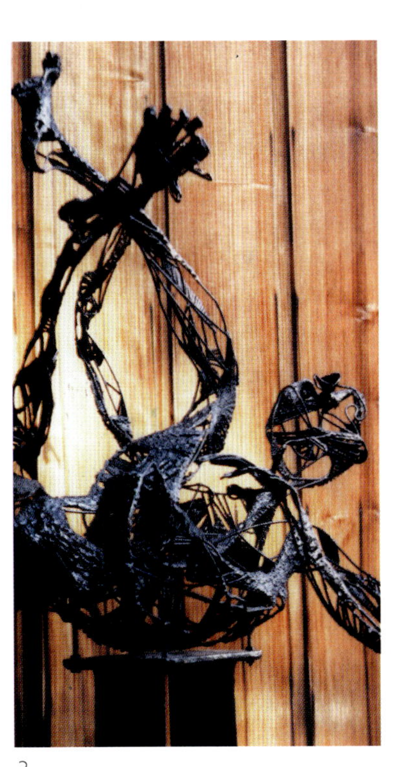

3

. . . the end of the year. A perplexing year in many respects, and yet a year of many rewards — rewards in the sense that Steppenwolf considers rewards to be — those things that the establishment considers non-rewarding. The plan for this year is to fill this journal, and more if possible, with thoughts, ideas, and responses to completed sculptures . . .

question is — what is it in man's psyche that causes this to happen — this wild advance of skill in so short a period of time, and secondly will it continue to be progress or will there one day become a safe plateau upon which to rest? I can't imagine at this point, but the significance is that progress, is so few months, has been phenominal. I feel badly about having sold the early works—

Ah! the bird, "Vision of daedalus" and the "fallen man" were both sold — With schoiniger, I agreed to also give him the seated lady, to put in his field near the pond. Both of these pieces were accepted at Brainsfreus — don't know if it will take prize or not but it did get accepted.

And now it's Sunday morning, I didn't think I was going to see today. Last night I ran a high fever, the pain was fantastic and most of the night was spent tossing. I had hallucinations most of the time. I recall part of them. I had built some sort of organic structure (house size) other people work on it. It was the color of animal bones and I recall finding upon its completion the same thing I wrote about (above) — a sort of peace with myself — a knowing about life and about man. A confidence and a serenity combined. It all ended abruptly when the police came and took me off to jail for creating obscene structures the rest of the time was spent defending

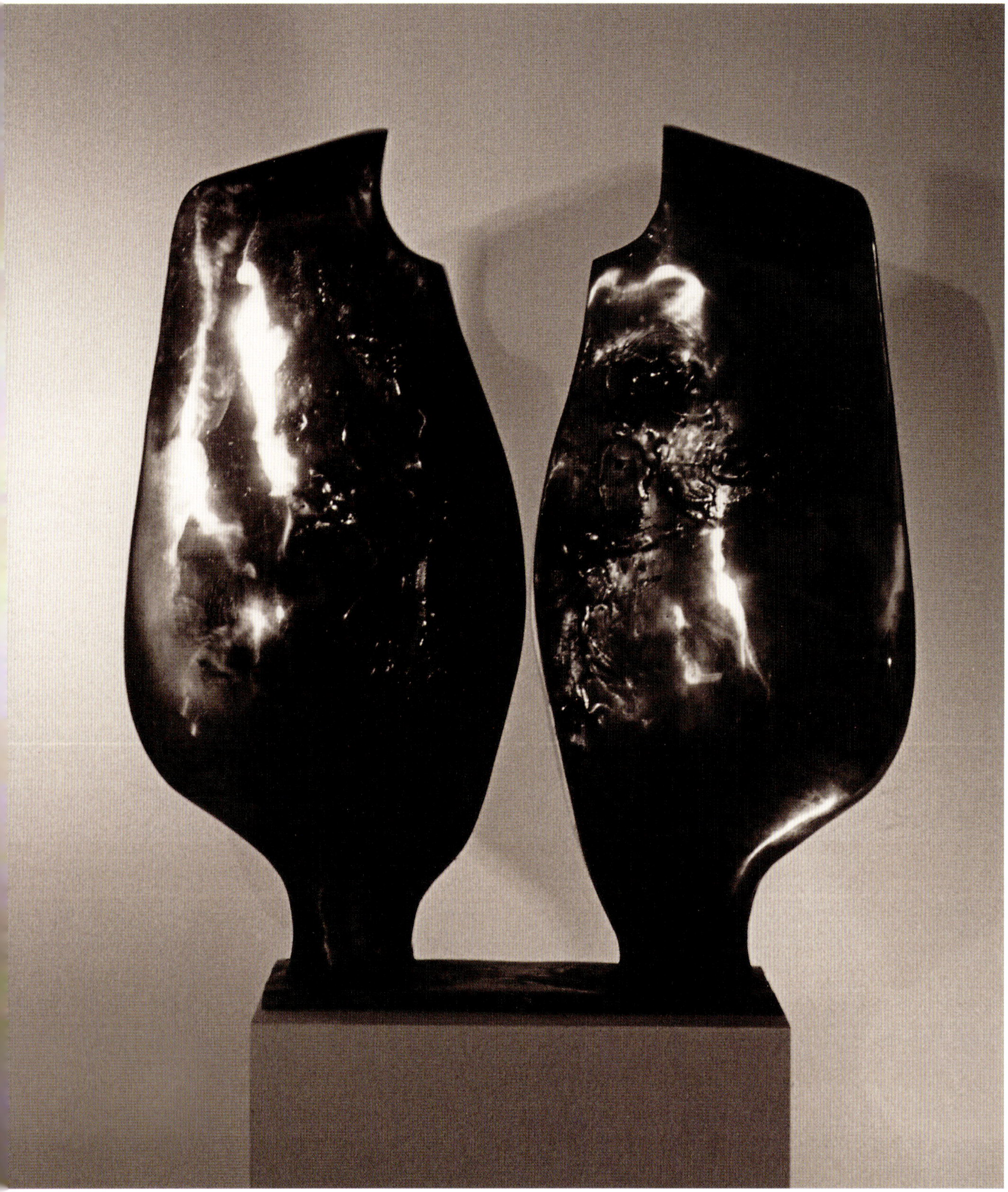

As I concentrate, art images of the past pass before my eyes. Most I reject as I did when viewing them for the first time. Again they pass before me, one after the other – Rodin, Klee, Van Gogh, Noguchi, Arp, Brancusi, Goya, Baskin – all are marching before me. Some forms stop briefly, then continue with the parade. Connell, Aska, Evans, Niese. I've been working now for 71 hours. Will try to go outside to work again, keep awake, drink more coffee, breath more air. Chest hurts, my heart still pounding. Oriental paintings and gardens now join the parade. The courtyard trees remind me of Japanese prints. An illusive wind blows forms past me in a game of charades. Dominos stand, then fall one by one.

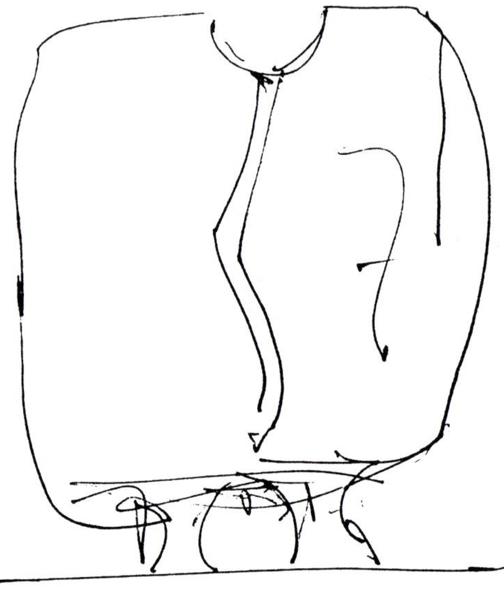

4

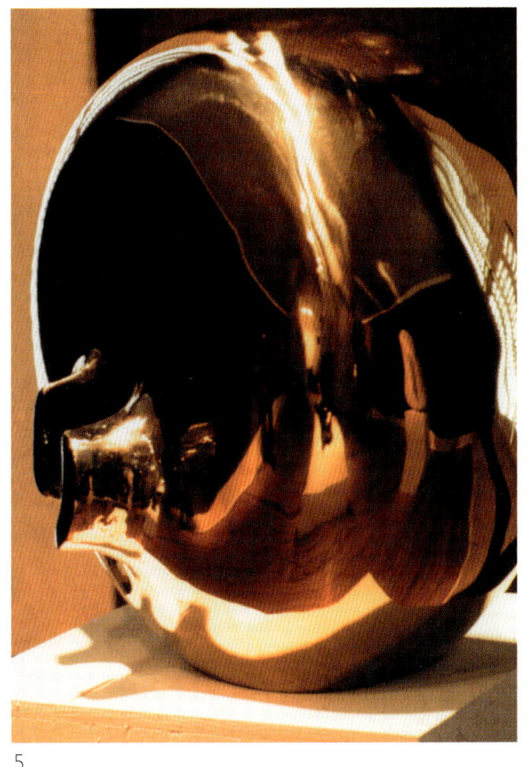

5

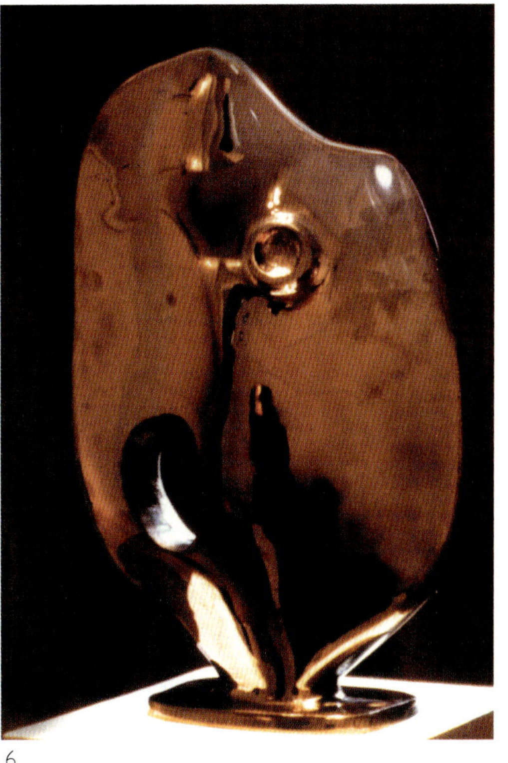

6

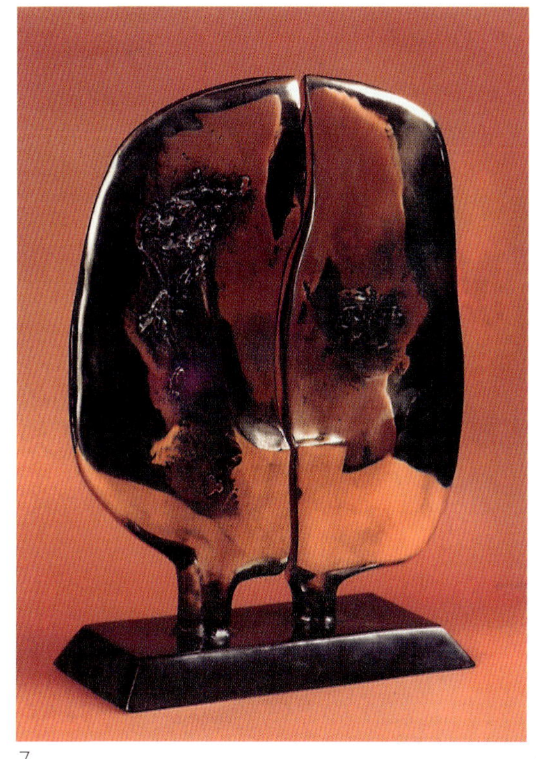

7

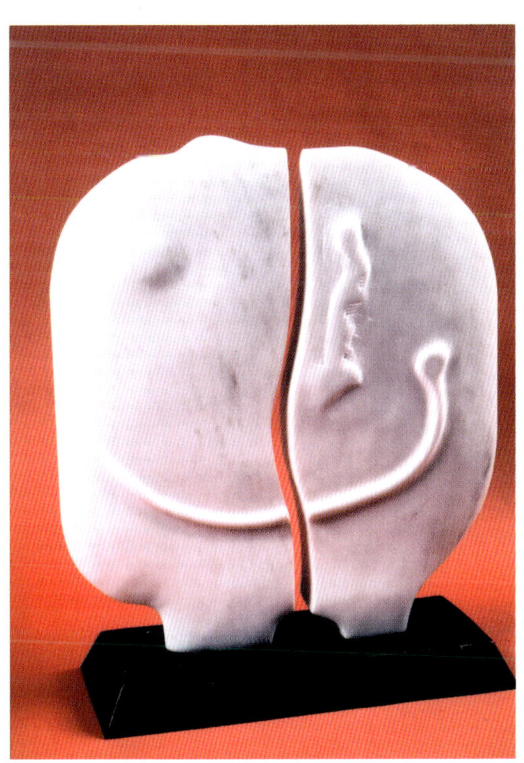

8

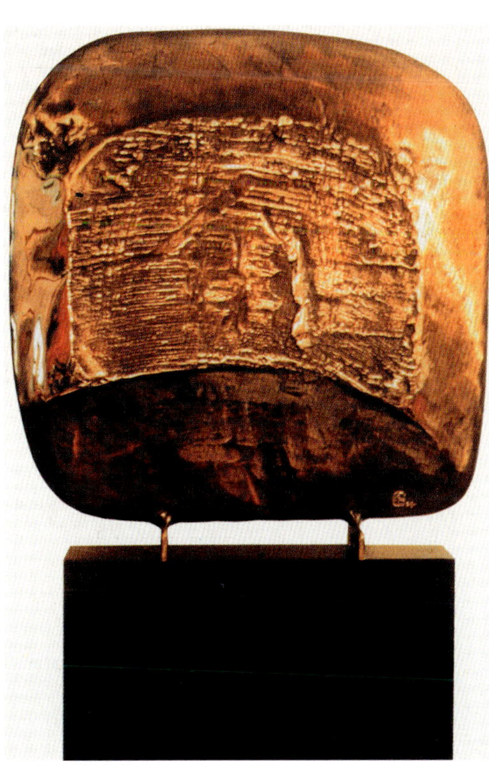

9

… after the museum, went to the zoo to draw. The new home for the bears was incredible – made of fero cement and very sculptural – will open up new thoughts for sculpture … why not split the disk! – let the empty space be a new object?!

Yabba-dabba-doo!

Flintstones-like home still has people gaping in Concord Twp.

By Karen Far...

The house on Cascade Rd. in Concord Township has been called an anthill, a serpent and the Flintstones' residence. It was built nearly 10 years ago, but people still drive by to gape or ask for a tour.

The free-form concrete structure was built by Wayne Trapp in 1970. Trapp, a sculptor, worked with 20 college students to build the 2,200-square-foot dwelling for a Mentor family of 10.

Trapp, who had never built a house before, worked from a set of blueprints that needed little revision as the building progressed. There are 16 rooms, a guest house, two tunnels, an observation tower and an indoor-outdoor playroom, all of which stretch 145 feet along the base of a hill.

"Wayne felt that a person really doesn't comprehend sculpture unless you can walk around it and live in it," said Louis A. Penfield of Willoughby Hills, an art teacher who watched the construction and became friends with Trapp.

Trapp and the students, who earned $25 per week, all lived on the site during construction.

The house, with rounded rooms and no corners, was made with curved steel bars covered with wire mesh. Concrete was troweled over the mesh and the inside was sprayed with insulation, which then hardened.

All the beds, shelves and desks are formed of concrete. Skylights and odd-shaped, tinted windows provide light.

Architects and engineers from around the country came to study the house during and ing in. "We have been here for 3½ years, and though people still crawl on the roof and knock on the door at all hours, it has quieted down," Mrs. Page said.

The original family lived in the house less than a year because the parents separated, Mrs. Page said. The house was then rented until the Pages bought it. "We put up a split-rail fence and a chain across the driveway to keep out unwanted visitors," she said.

The Pages completed construction by spraying a concrete-like substance on the interior walls, painting them white and repairing cabinets and other fixtures.

Although the house resembles a large cave, it is light inside and ceilings reach 18 feet in the living and dining rooms.

Megan, the Page's 1½-year-old daughter, enjoys the house. "She had to learn to walk quickly because it is hard to crawl on concrete," Page said. Only the kitchen and master bedroom are carpeted.

Trapp and students who helped him still come by to visit. "During the holidays and summer, people who were involved with the house when it was built come by to see if it is still here and to remember how it was when they worked on it," Page said.

"The kids who worked on the house loved the place," Penfield said. "They didn't like people stopping and making derogatory remarks, but Trapp would tell them to 'let them look and learn something.'"

The house has been photographed by many

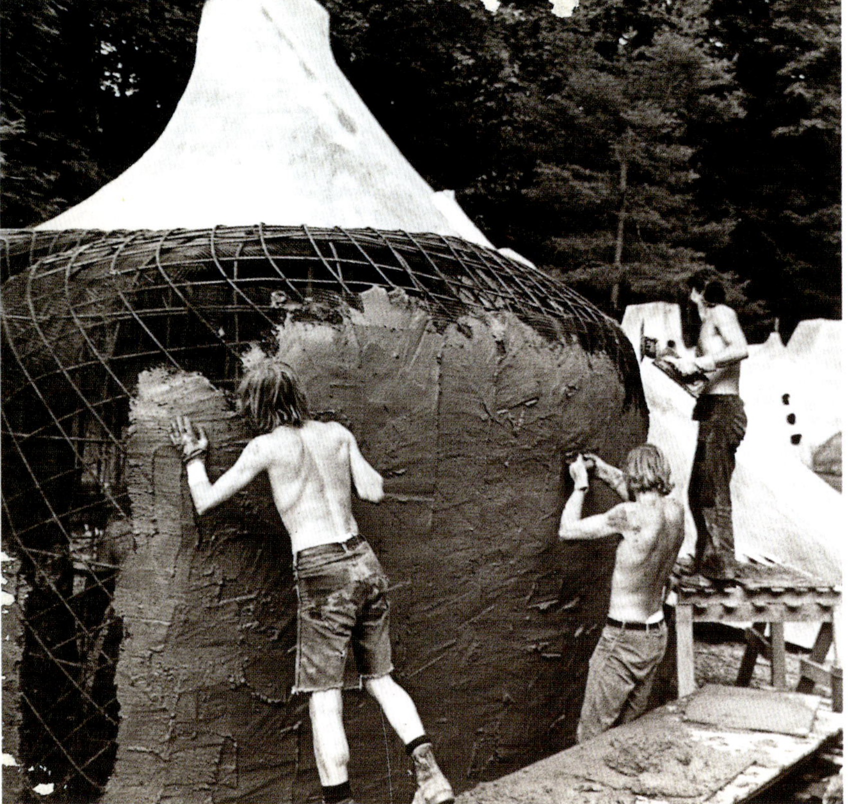

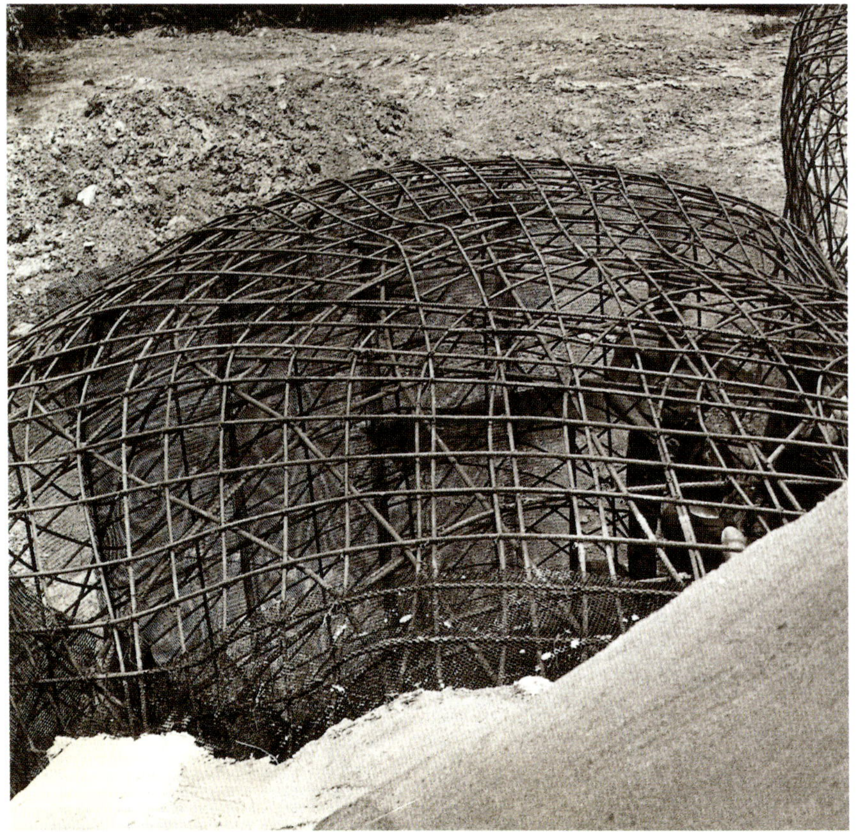

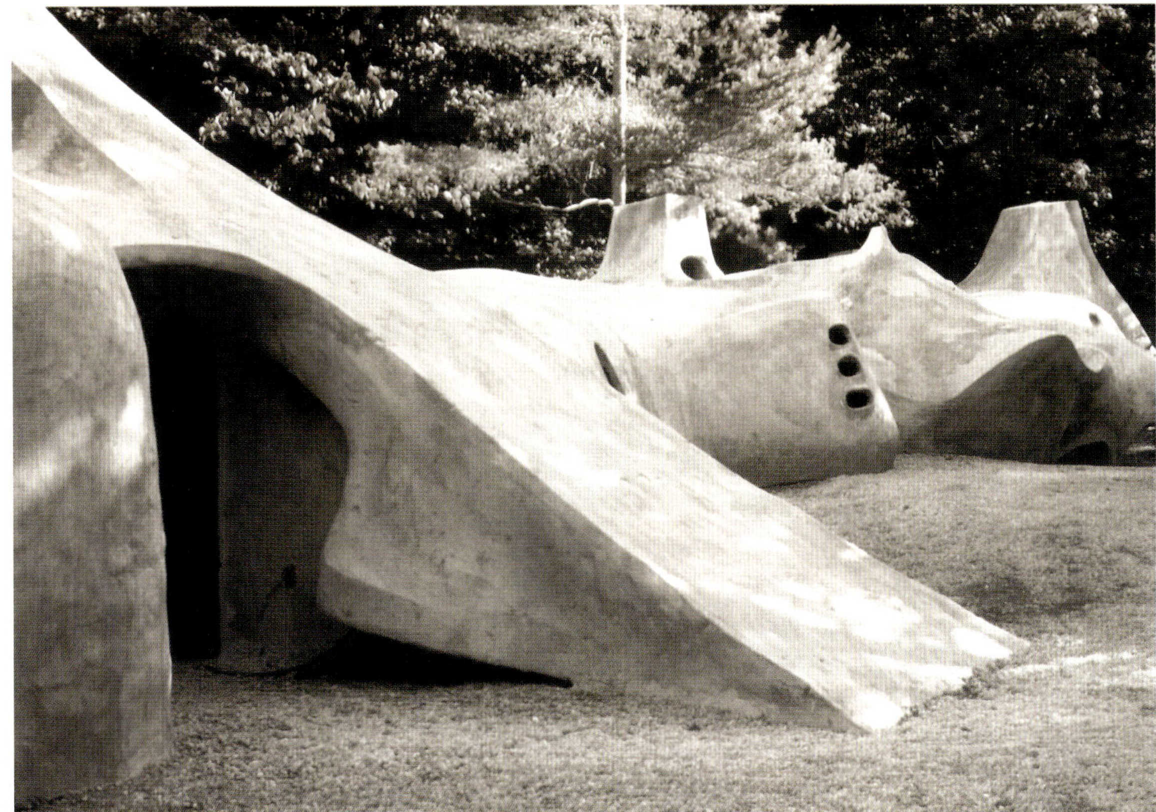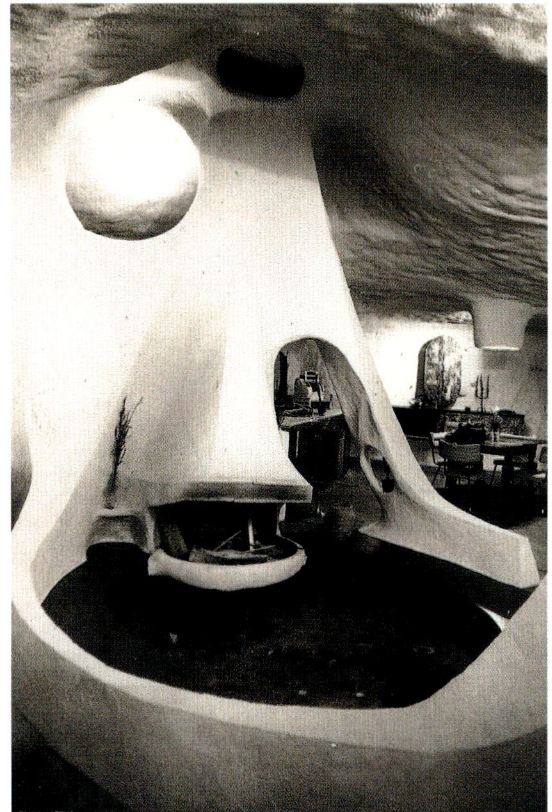

God, I've created a monster . . . what's going on here? None of the crew (now over 25 from all over the country, Germany, Spain, and France) have a clue as to my real madness. This whole project borders on insanity.

The last of the footers have been poured – the overall length is over 145 feet. Tons of rebar, tons of concrete, and too many nights without sleep. Another newspaper was here to do yet another story. With each passing day, more curiosity seekers show up. Have had to limit public days and charge a dollar admission (no child rates). I hope they write what I said in my words, not theirs – yet, who gives a damn, anyway.

I just need to get away, listen to Greek music, drink Mextaca and dance - alone! Some neighbors down the road bring food on the weekends and home-made wine. Will invite them to completion party if that ever happens.

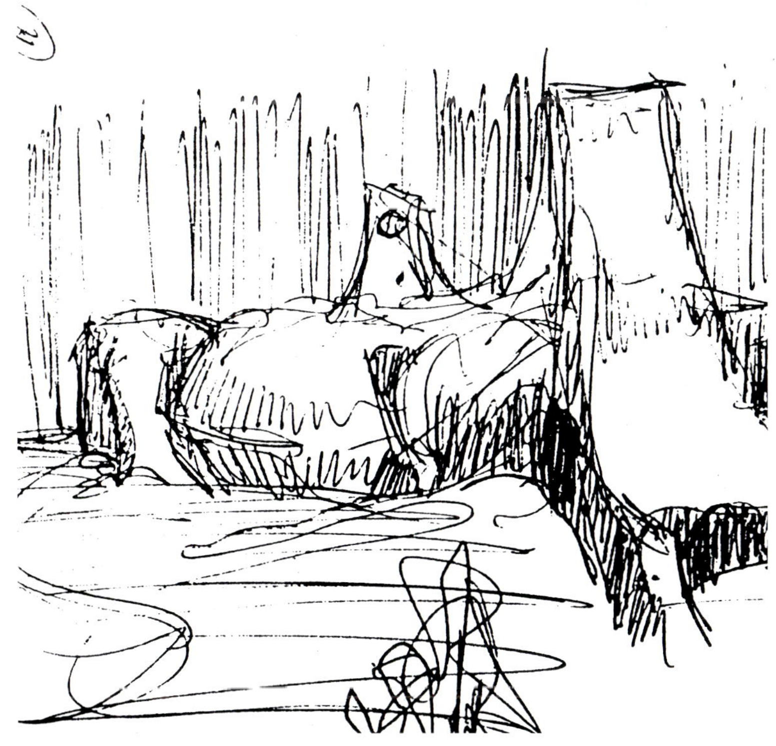

The good: everyone getting along and in good spirits, and still within budget. I'm just tired of solving problems as this house grows out of the ground.

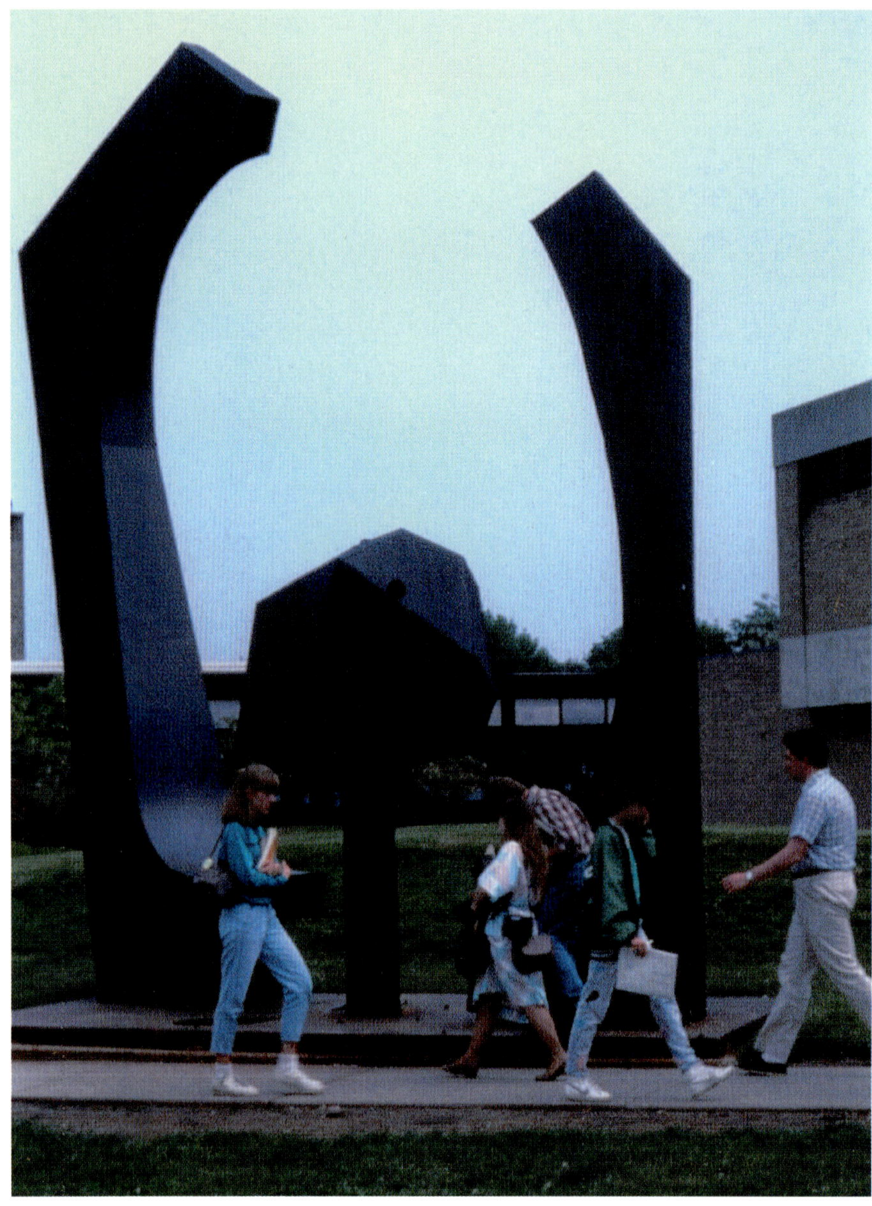

10

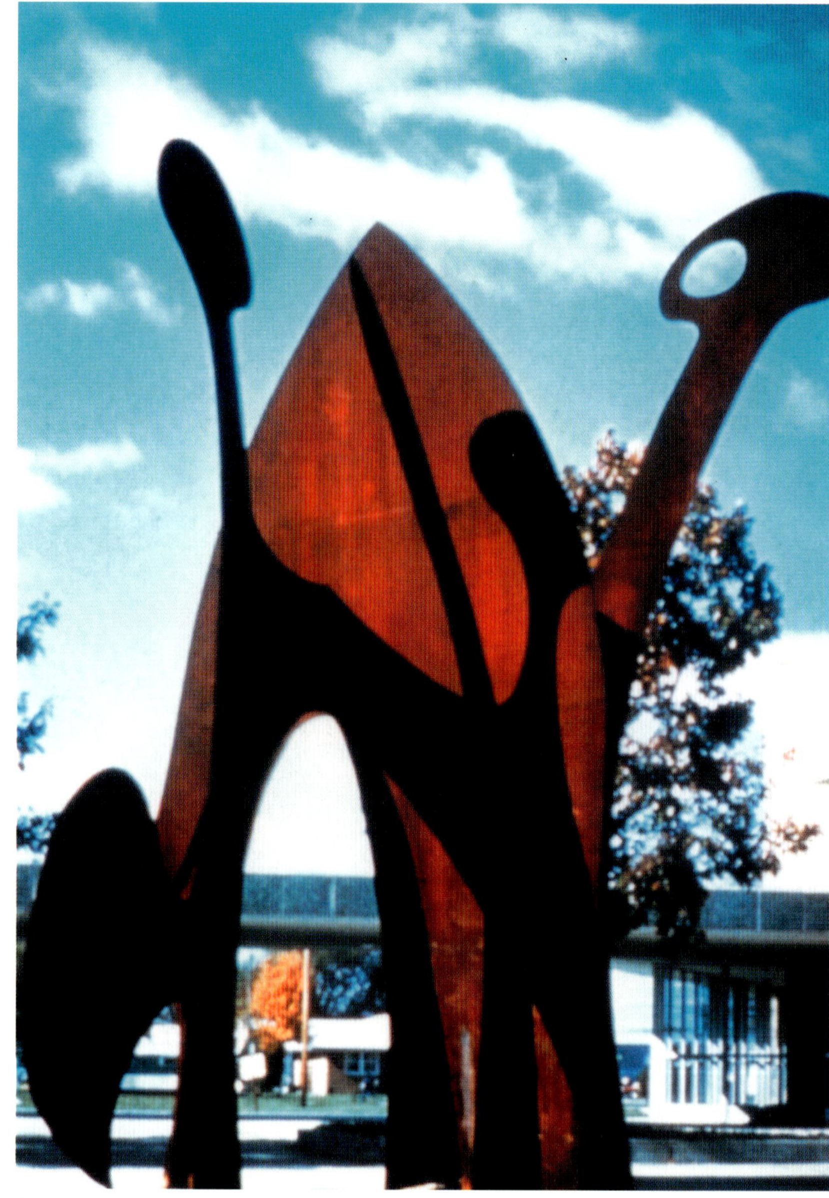

11

Am at Andy Capp's again – a good place in that it has a European feeling about it. There it is again (Europe). At any rate, I sit drinking Mextaca in my coffee and wondering exactly what the ideal studio would be.

As I look back to the second floor of the Carriage house, it wasn't free. Bad memories and restrictions, also not enough space. Ok to paint there, but so small and always cluttered. From there to the Courtyard, ok except for rain. Outside had a good feeling, especially at night with the trees and sky over me. The work stood out in space there – as it should. Then to the big warehouse. Too much space? No, it was perhaps the best of all. Space to work, warm, high ceilings, room to set pieces when complete. Room to look at them. The crane was good, lights good, not livable though. Couldn't control the space and yet the space was good to have around me. The big door space had a good feeling about it – ample room to enter or leave with just about anything of any size. And outside there was plenty of things to photograph .

From there to the smaller warehouse. A fine place. Table, white walls, high ceilings – not enough space – but it had the best feeling of all. And the heat was good!

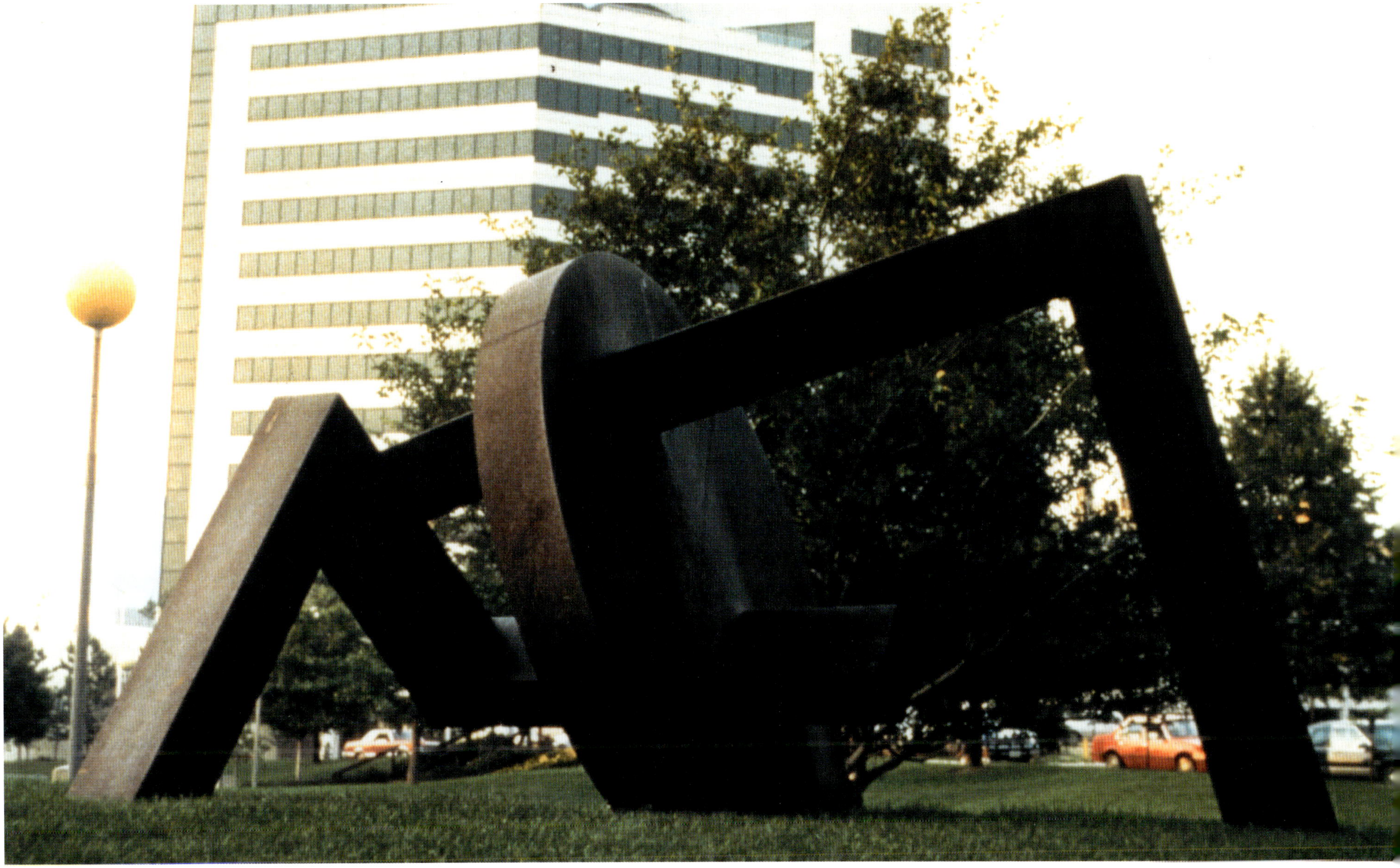

12

13, 14

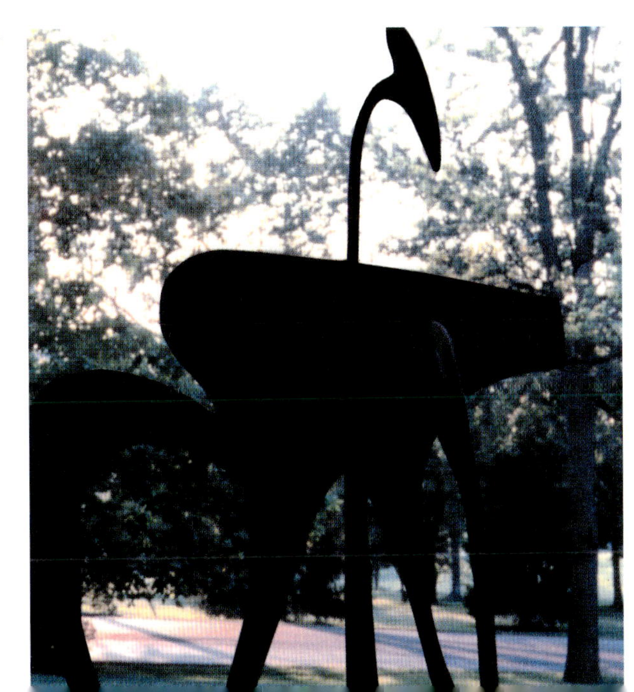

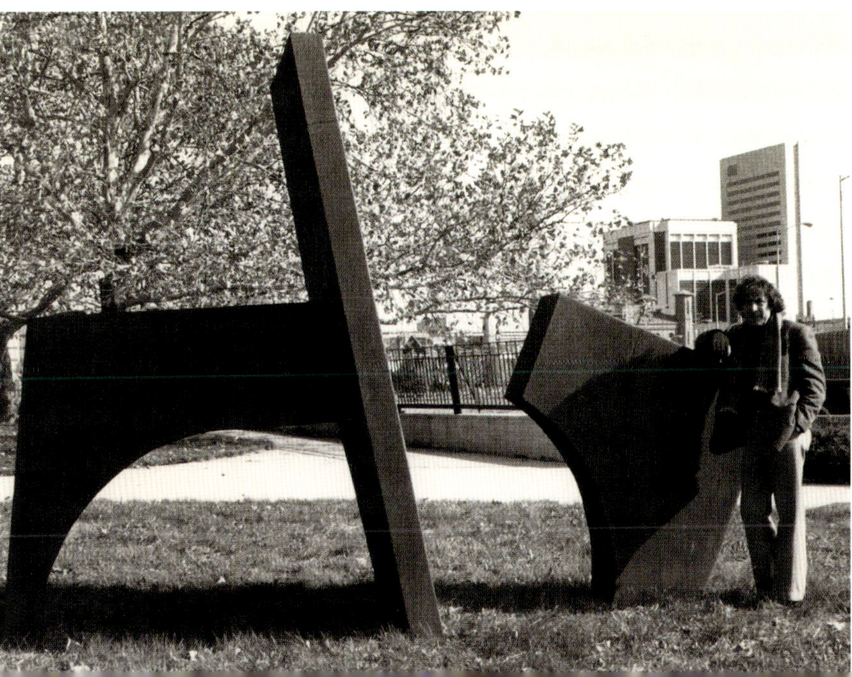

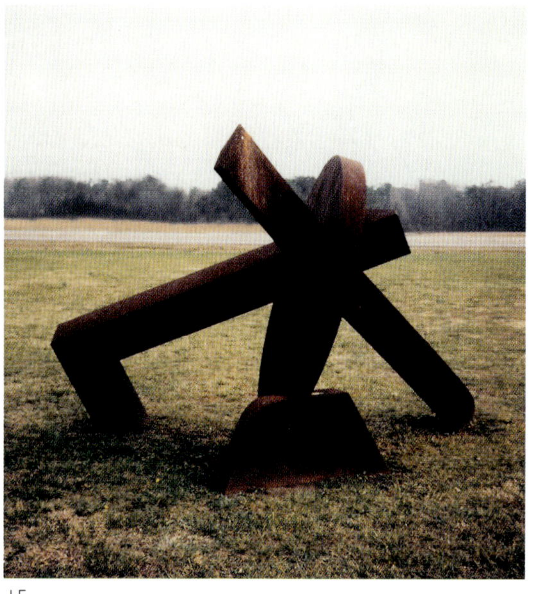

15

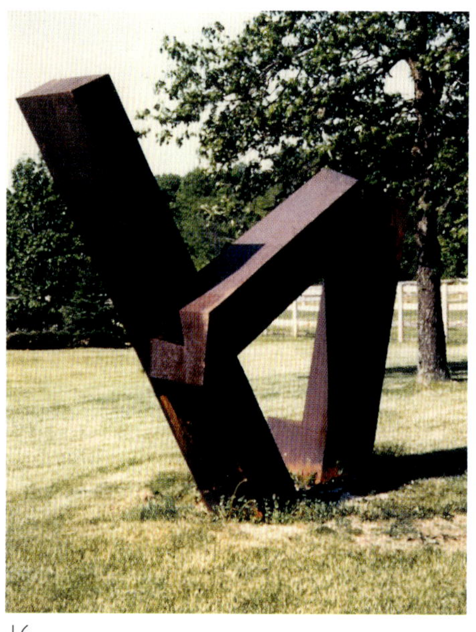

16

There is a direct relationship – birth and art – together they form the greatest lie man can tell about man.

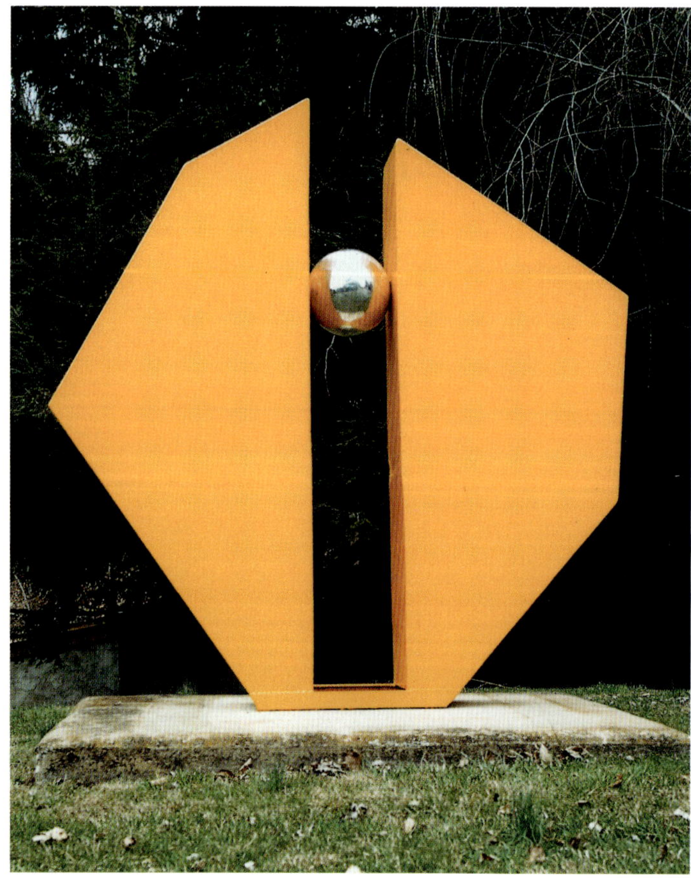

17

Perhaps if I resolve that problem at the Schoolhouse where I'm at now, I'll be Ok. Everything is there. The walls still need to be painted white, but everything else is fine – ceilings, lights – though it does need a new door. It feels good now that it is mine and that I will be there alone. Good things should happen in the next few months.

Want to take another orange to Luke.

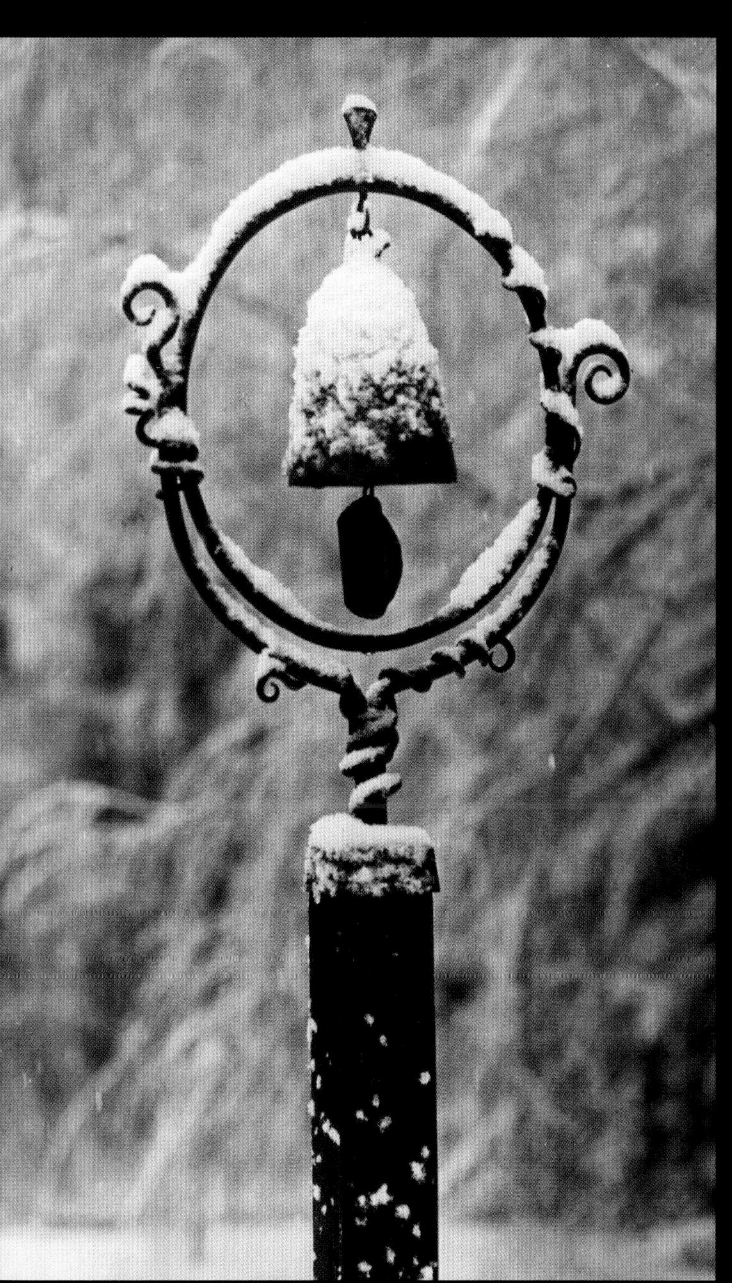

October Snow

The first snow just
after the start of fall.

It's not that I don't want it,
it's just that I'm not yet
saturated by autumn-fall-color.

It's uncomfortable when
things start without me.

A man needs time
to plan and think – prepare.
Some days begin without me,
but not an entire season!

No time for ceremony.

The leaves are still green.
Flowers still bloom.

Why?

Vermont...
an unanticipated hiatus from art

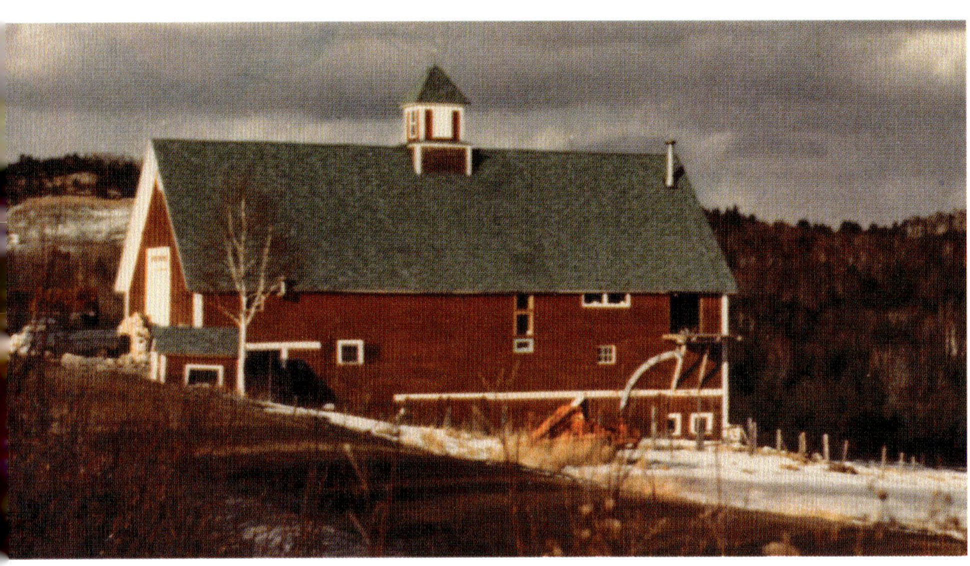

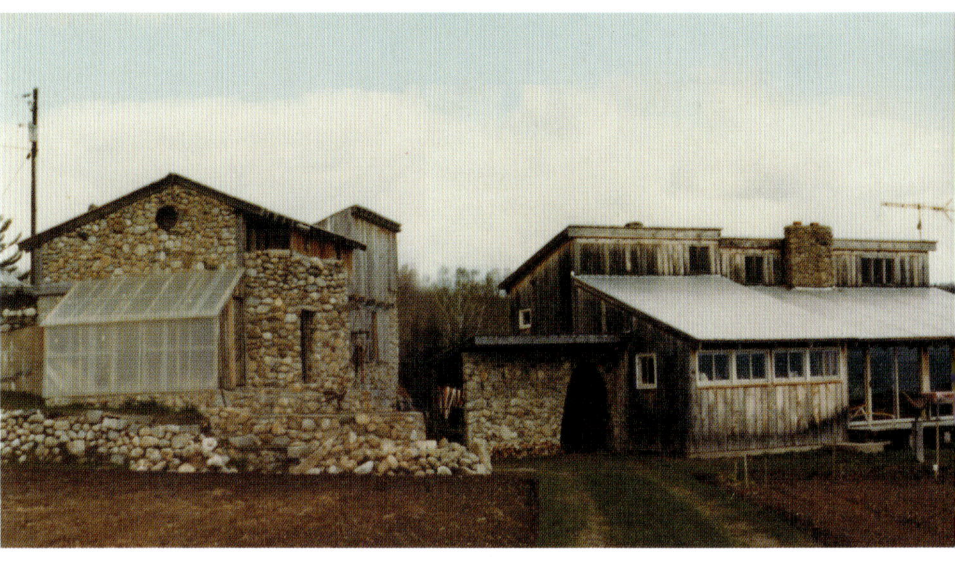

BEFORE THE FIRE   **...AFTER THE FIRE**

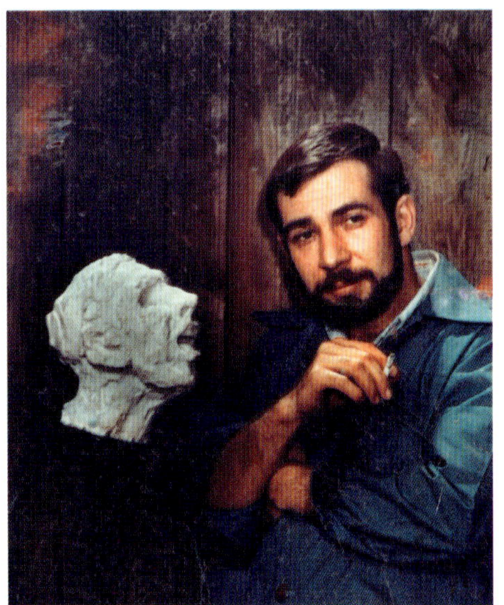

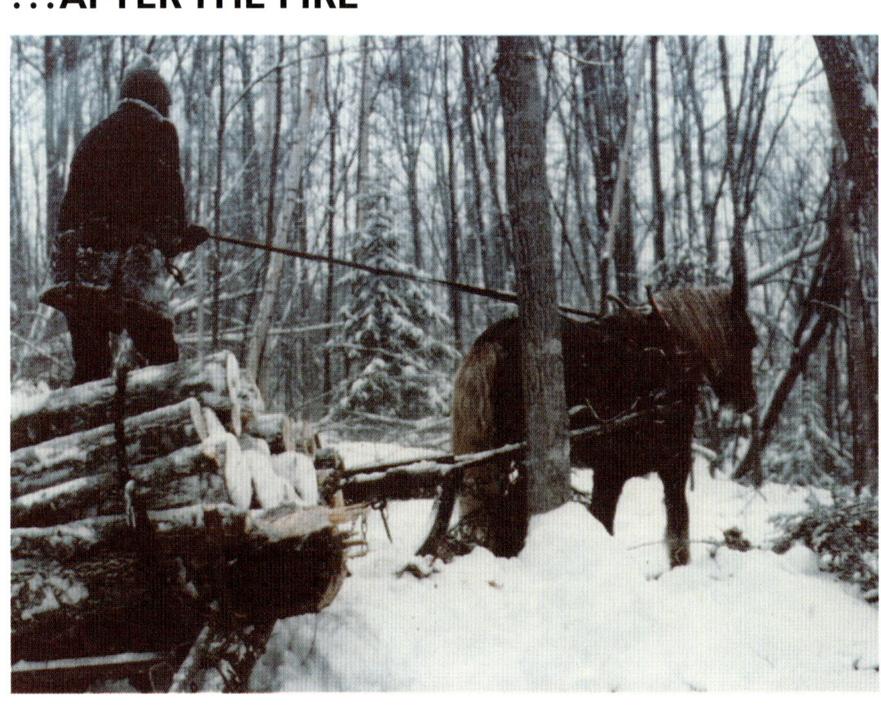

It is significant, I think, that each year prior to Vermont I filled at least one full journal book with thoughts, happenings, etc. Since I've moved here it has all been condensed into one book – seven years of little energy, no real creative thoughts, months of just being, or getting through winters. No productive time toward art, and even more important, the complete questioning of art. The environment here, the people, the cost (in terms of energy output just to survive) leaves little time to make, let alone think of, art. How has this complete turn-around taken place? This and other thoughts is what I will complete on the remainder of this journal's pages . . .

I feel it is interesting that I haven't written often. Also, it is important that the subject of poverty hasn't entered this journal either. Perhaps the exchange of art for money/security was needed. Unfortunately, there are less emotional highs and lows by having that security. The other factor in this non-artist world is the type of people surrounding me in contrast to those who were around me when I was making art. The people in this Vermont countryside spend almost all their time just surviving, getting by, making ends meet.

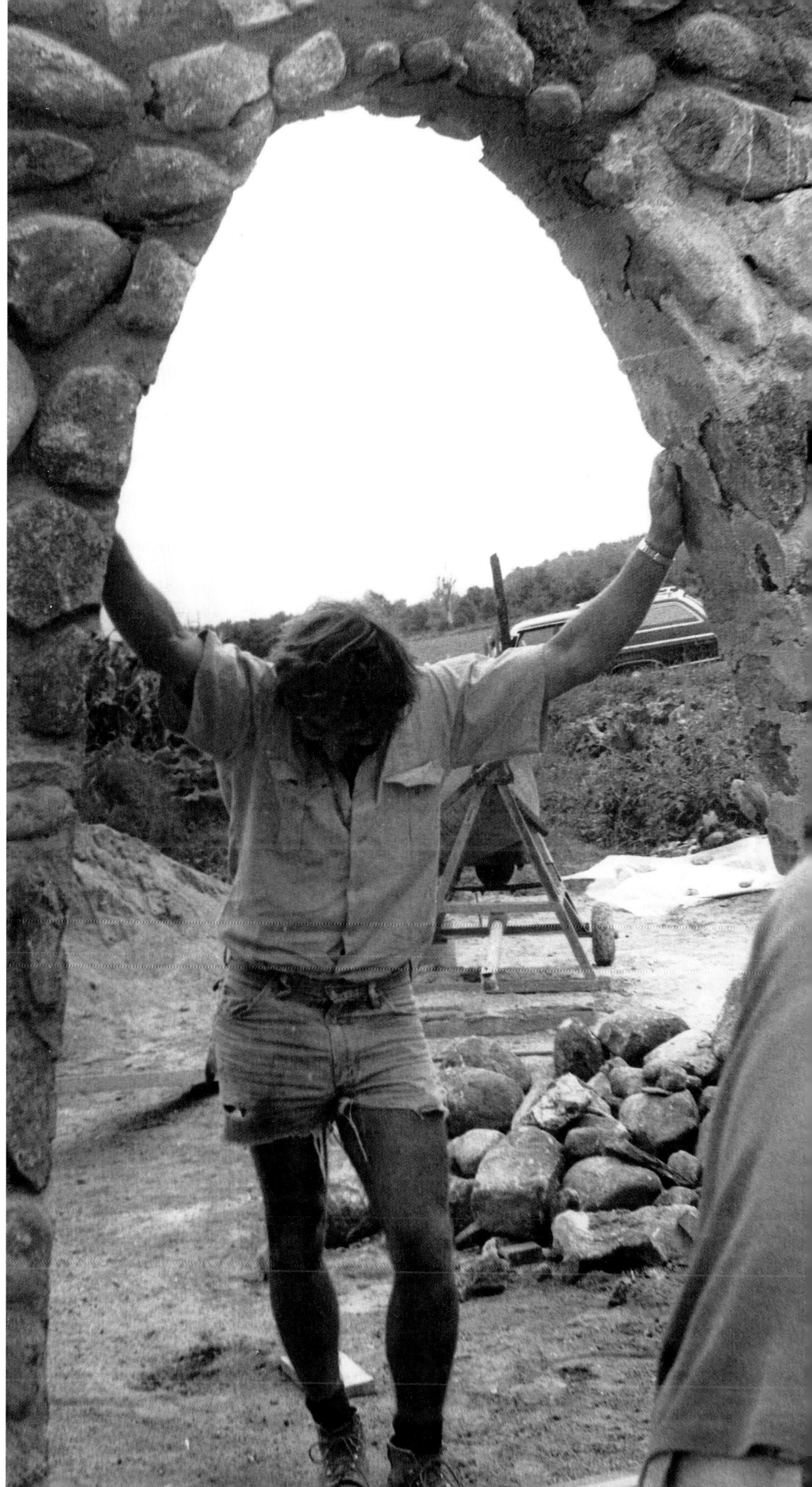

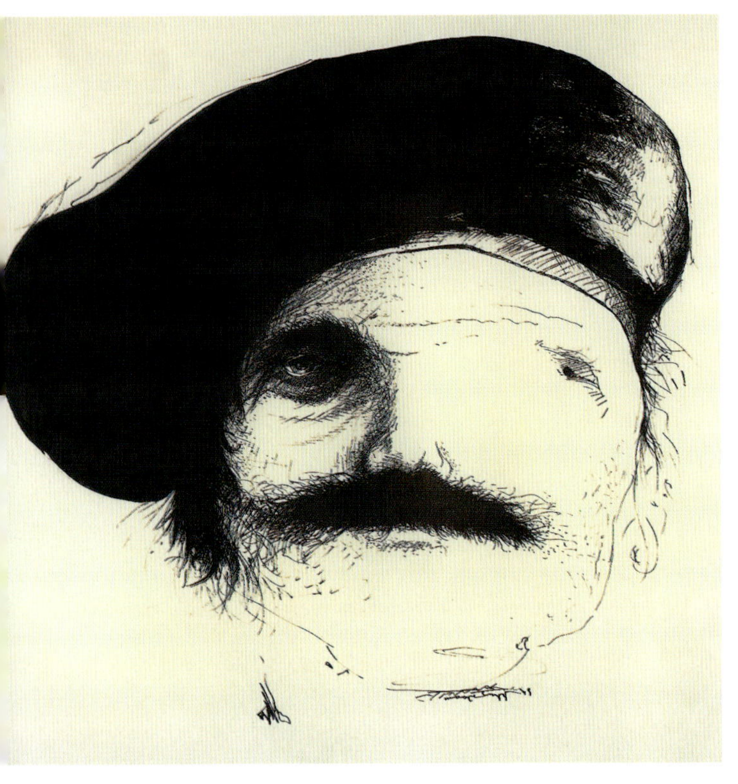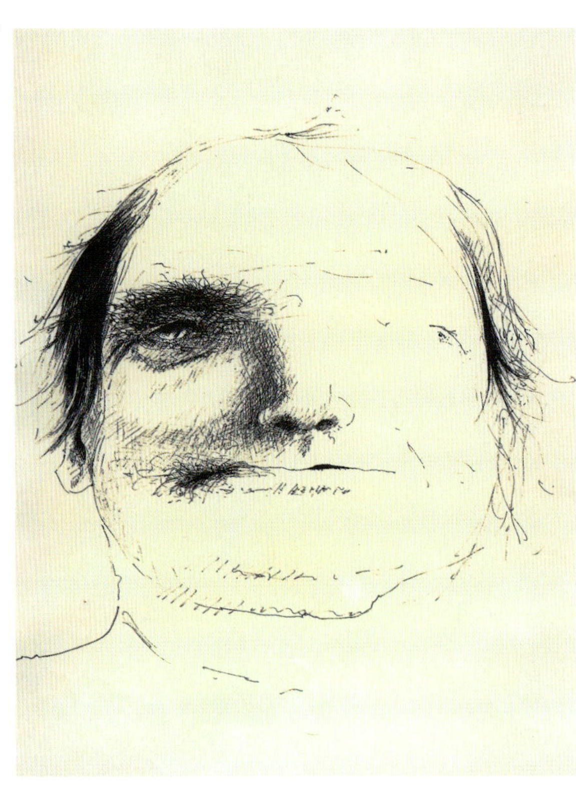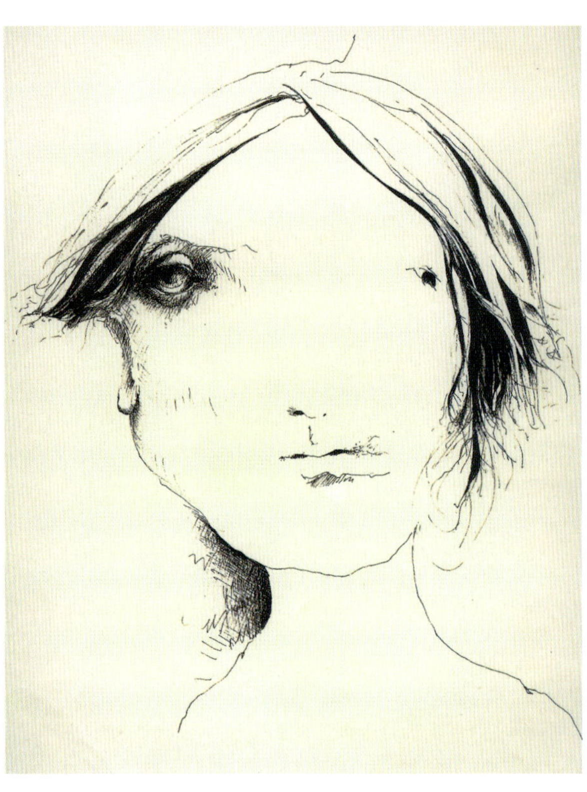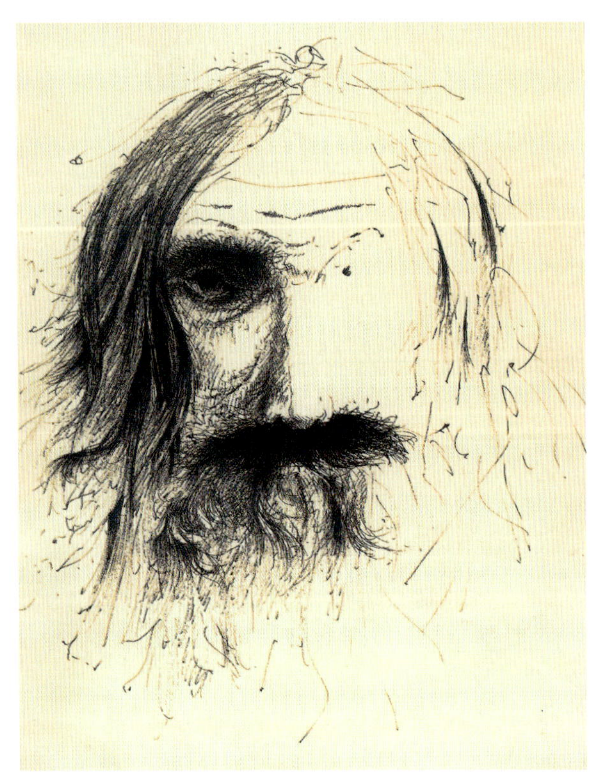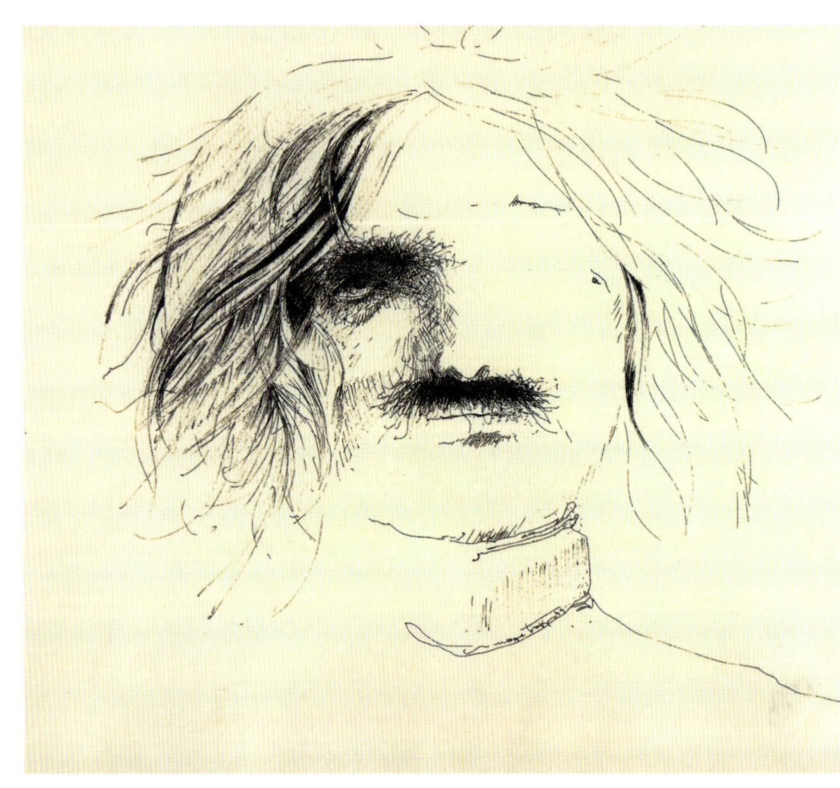

the long winters of Vermont ....

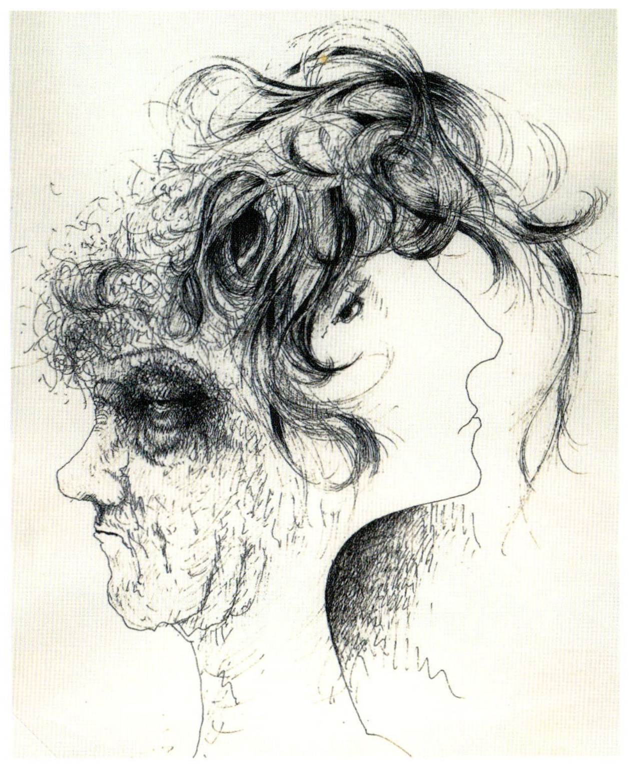

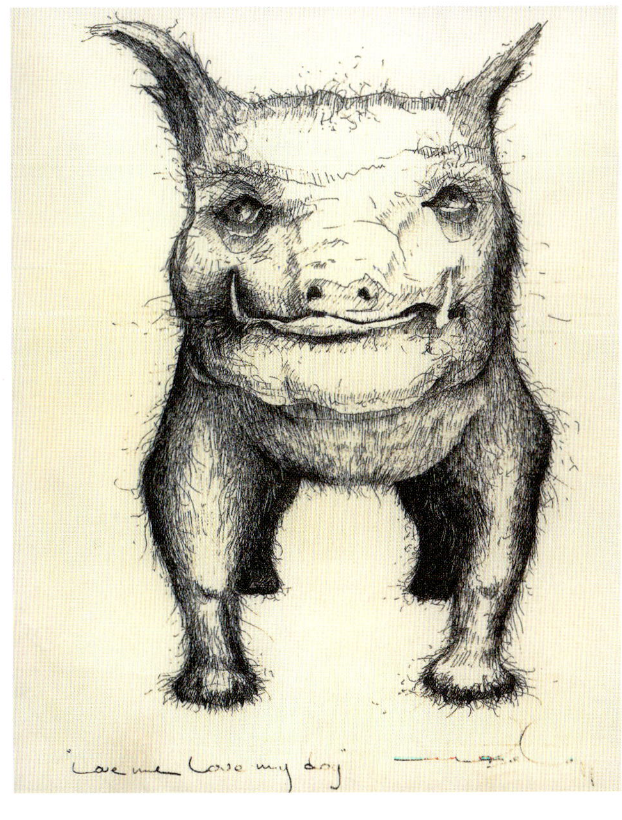

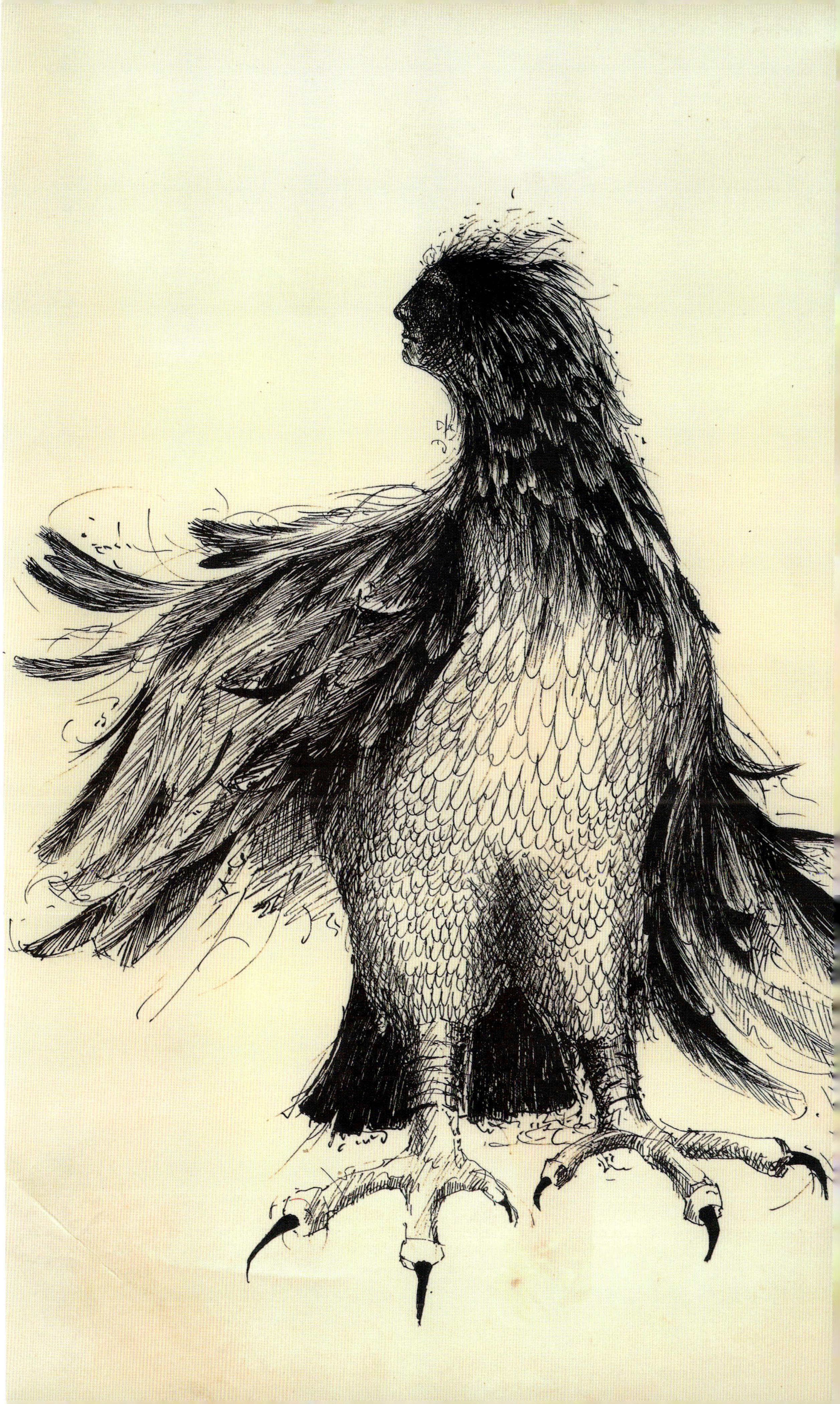

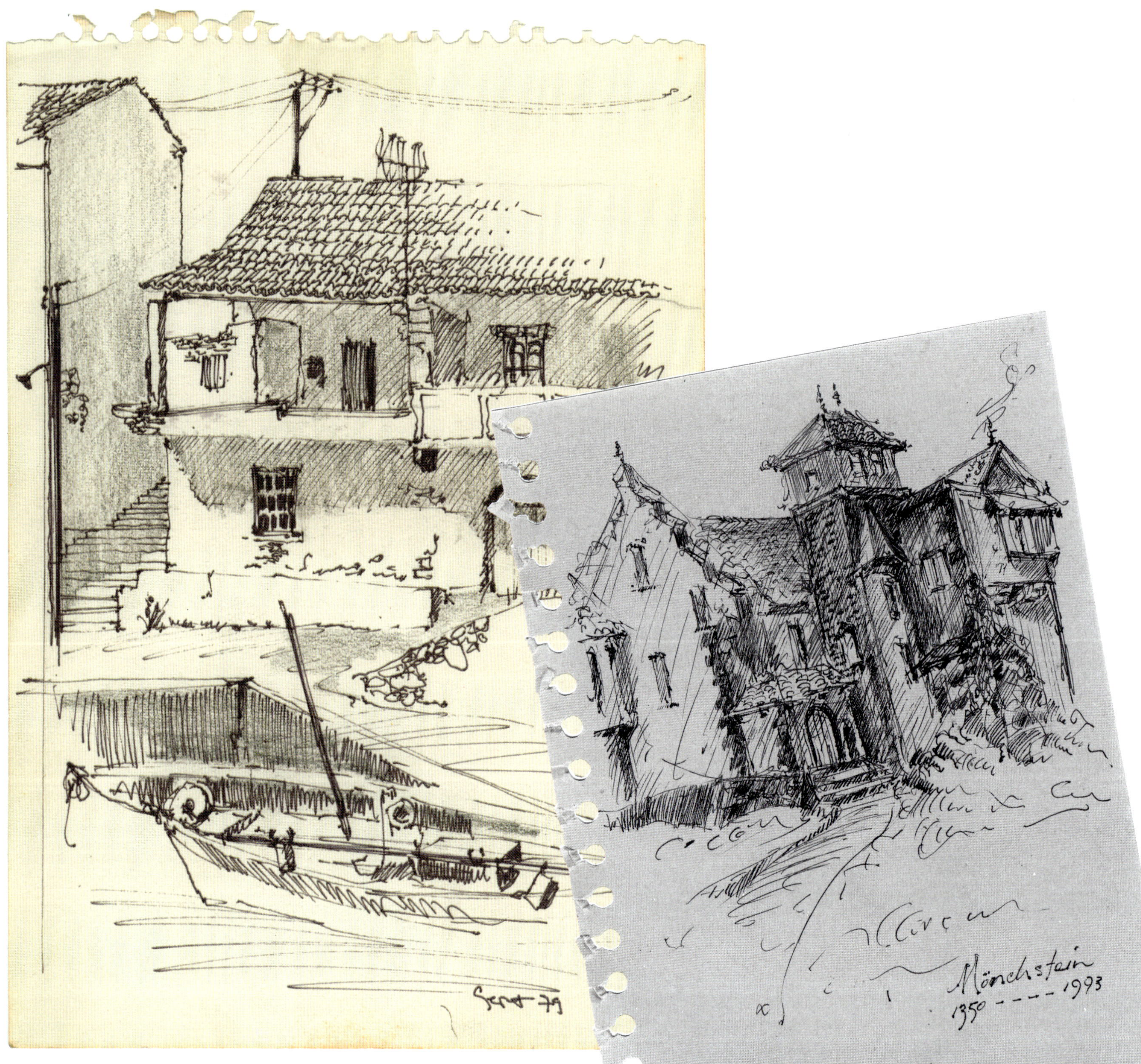
Gert 79
Mönchstein
1350 ---- 1993

In Luxembourg at the hotel, as well as here at the house in Bonn, all of the lights (most) are simply light bulbs — and each one is on a single switch so that when you need a light you can have one where you are and no where else. At the hotel, the key for the room was a large one. Attached to it was a solid bronze casting about 5-inches long. It was a sculpture in its own right. Contrast this with America — a plastic key ring and lots of lights that burn day and night. The designs of the door handles everywhere are totally functional, something to grab hold of easily. They WORK. What else does one need?

Traveling on the train from Luxembourg to Bonn up the Rhine we passed walled vineyards. The entire hillside — everywhere was Bach! No space was untouched. Order reigned in vines and walls. Order as in Bach. The small towns we passed through had the same order. Houses and barns, partially destroyed by bombs, had been repaired with unmatched stone or brick yet a sense of order prevailed. Visually, the new/old materials and mixed textures 'worked', as if intentionally orchestrated into the German 'symphony'.

In downtown Bonn I stood by a Cathedral that was started in the year 800 AD and completed in 1200 AD. At the far end of the plaza was a bronze bust of Beethoven. At the other end a modern, polished steel sculpture. The cobblestones underfoot were laid down by Roman legions. Amazing how such a juxtaposition of cultural styles and textures exist in such harmony.

For some reason, perhaps the mathematical mind of the Germans, their art is very angular. Rounded forms don't seem to fit in anywhere. Don't know why this is. Man is rounded. How then can they sculpt him in linear/angular form? 1 plus 1 equals 2 — I guess it is the 1 plus 1, the visual aspect of that at least. The clothes, the uniforms, the machinery, trucks, cars, the whole architectural concept is 1 plus 1, sometimes 4 plus 4 — but rarely 3 plus 3 or 6 plus 6 (more French or Italian).

Everywhere was a high sense of order … as in Bach!

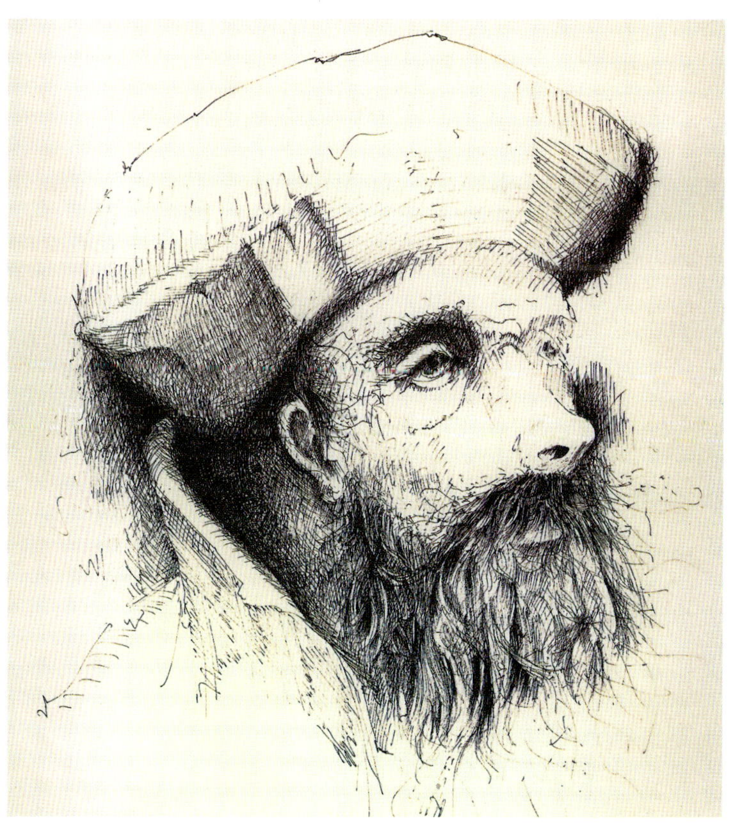

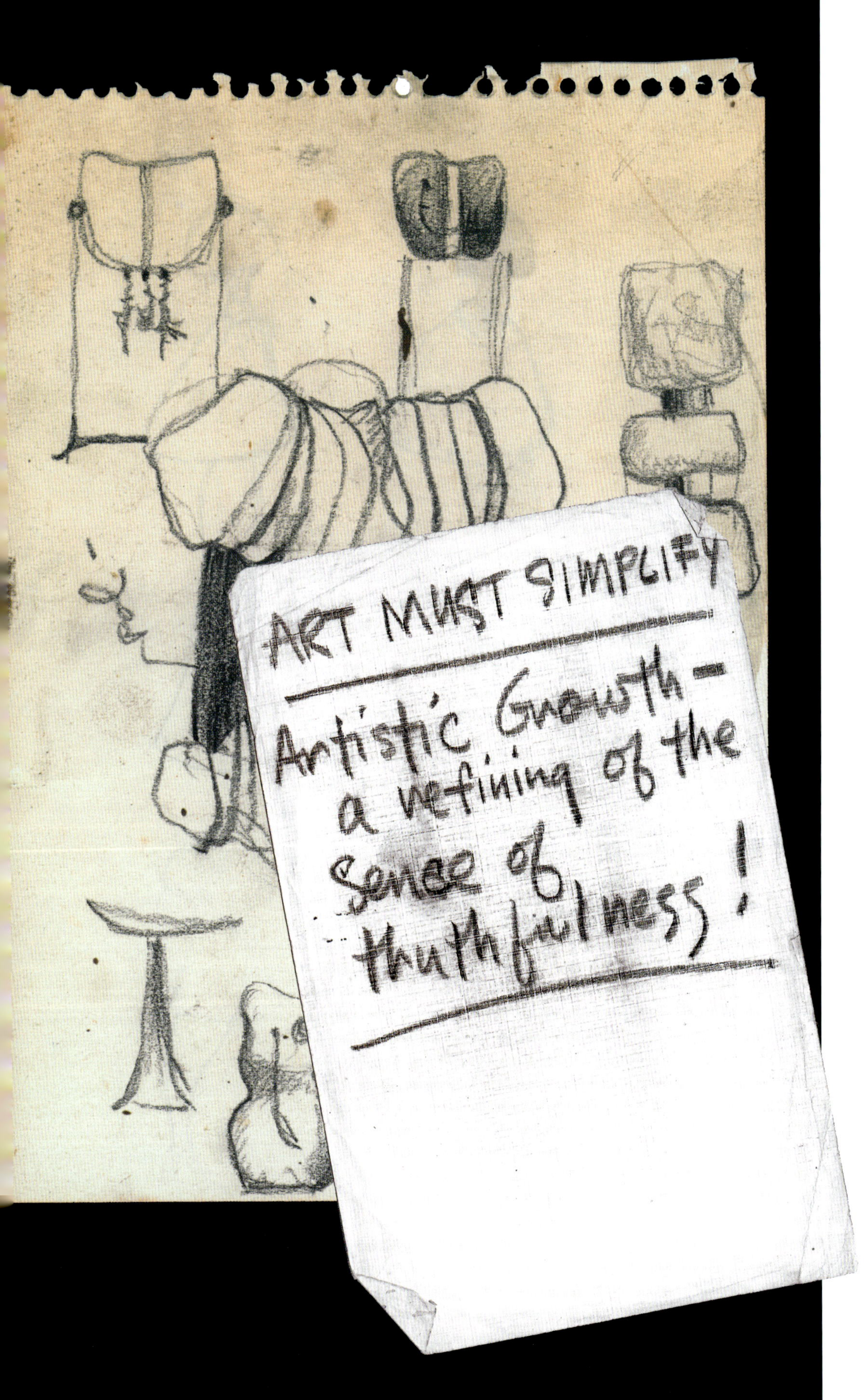

Late last evening a rich society lady came to the studio. She was high. Walked casually about my space dragging her long fur coat behind her. She said she had heard about me. We talked into the morning drinking vodka from a bottle. There seemed to be a closeness and yet it didn't feel real. I can't explain it. As we talked I kept trying to figure out how I could explain my level of poverty and ask for financial help at the same time. I knew only that those who appear successful get help. The conflict made me crazy. By the time she left I was so drunk I couldn't make it to the house. When I woke I decided to clean the studio for Christmas . . . and found hundred dollar bills under three of my sculptures. Miracle on 42nd Street! But as I reflect on this, I wonder why she didn't buy one of my sculptures instead and allow me my dignity . . .

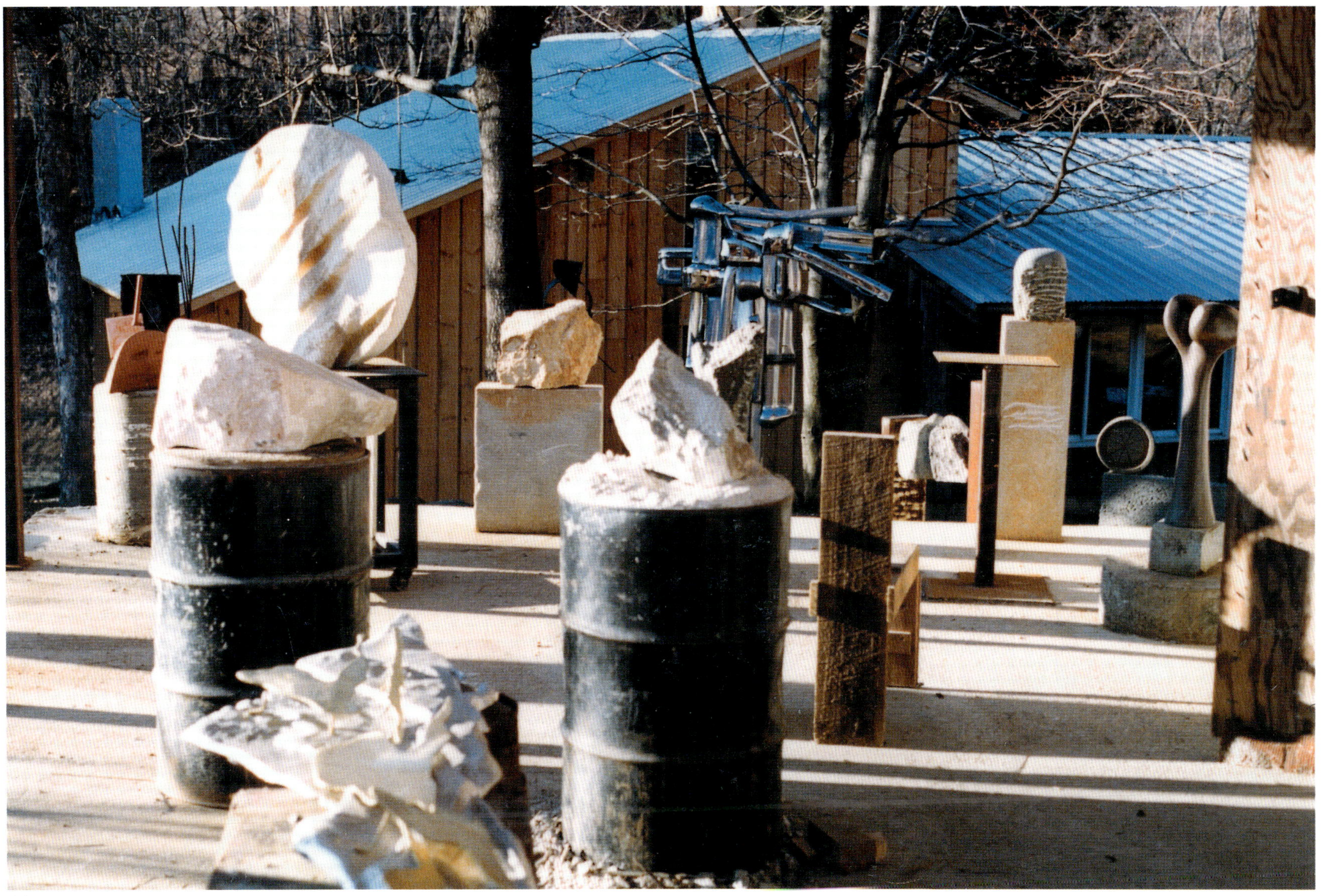

The North Carolina Years

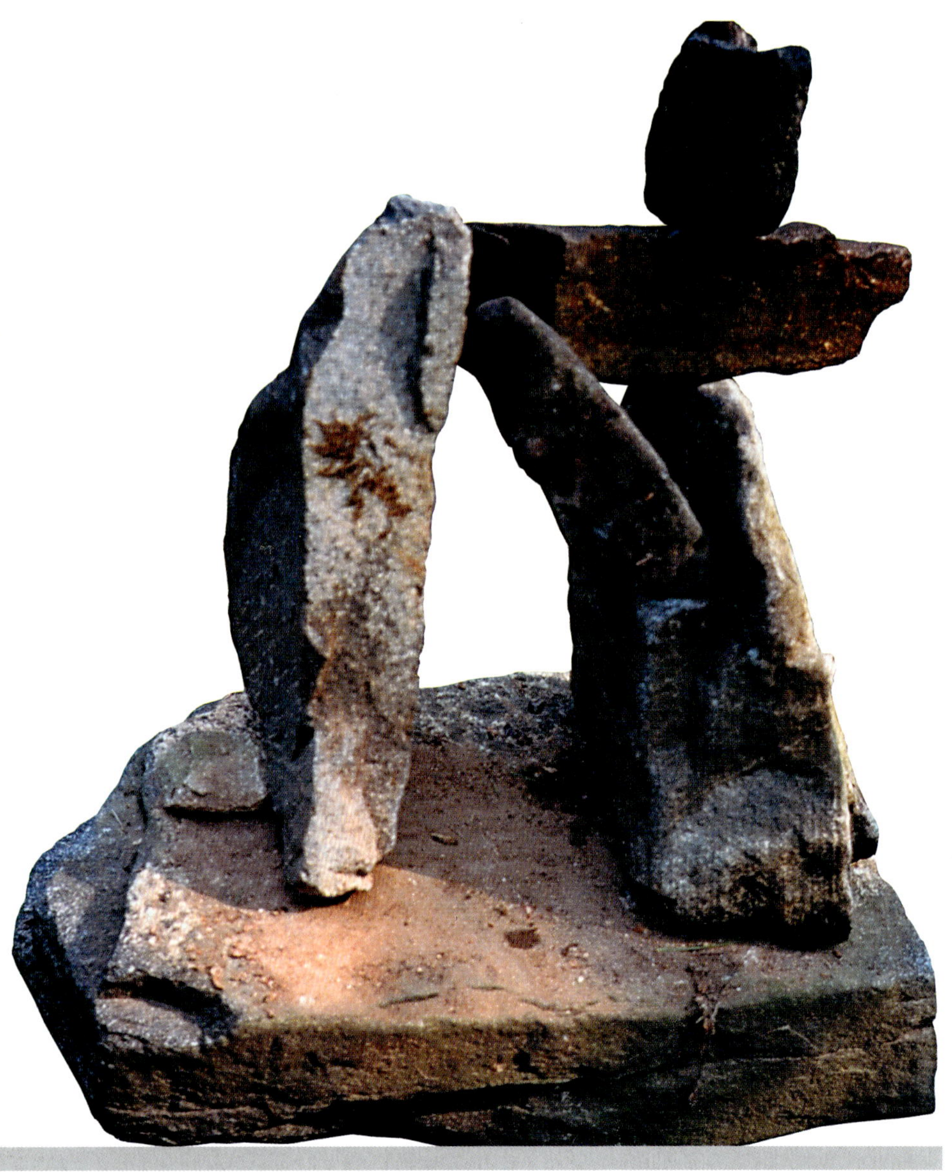

"Reason tempered by passion
is the ideal human state."

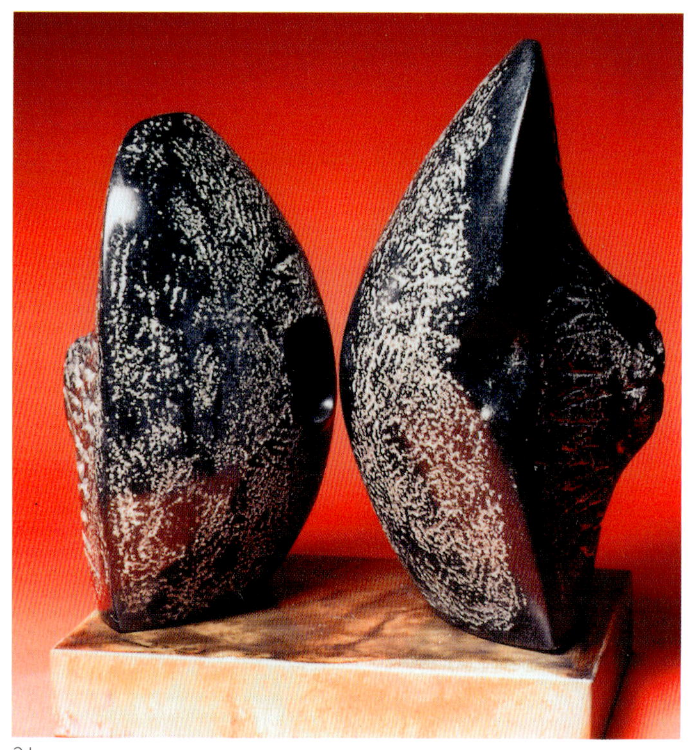

21

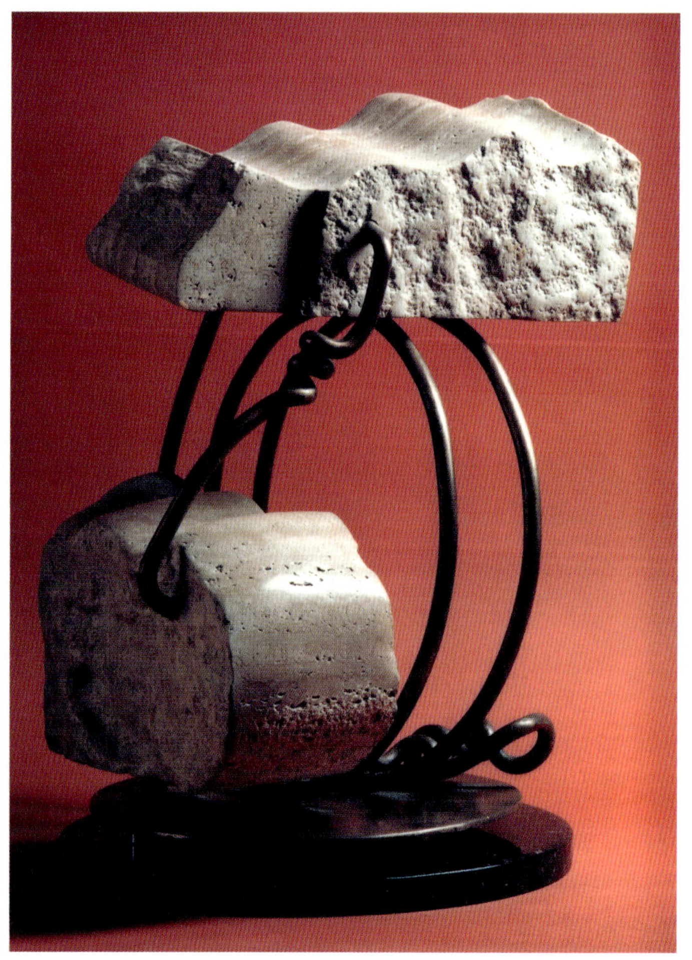

22

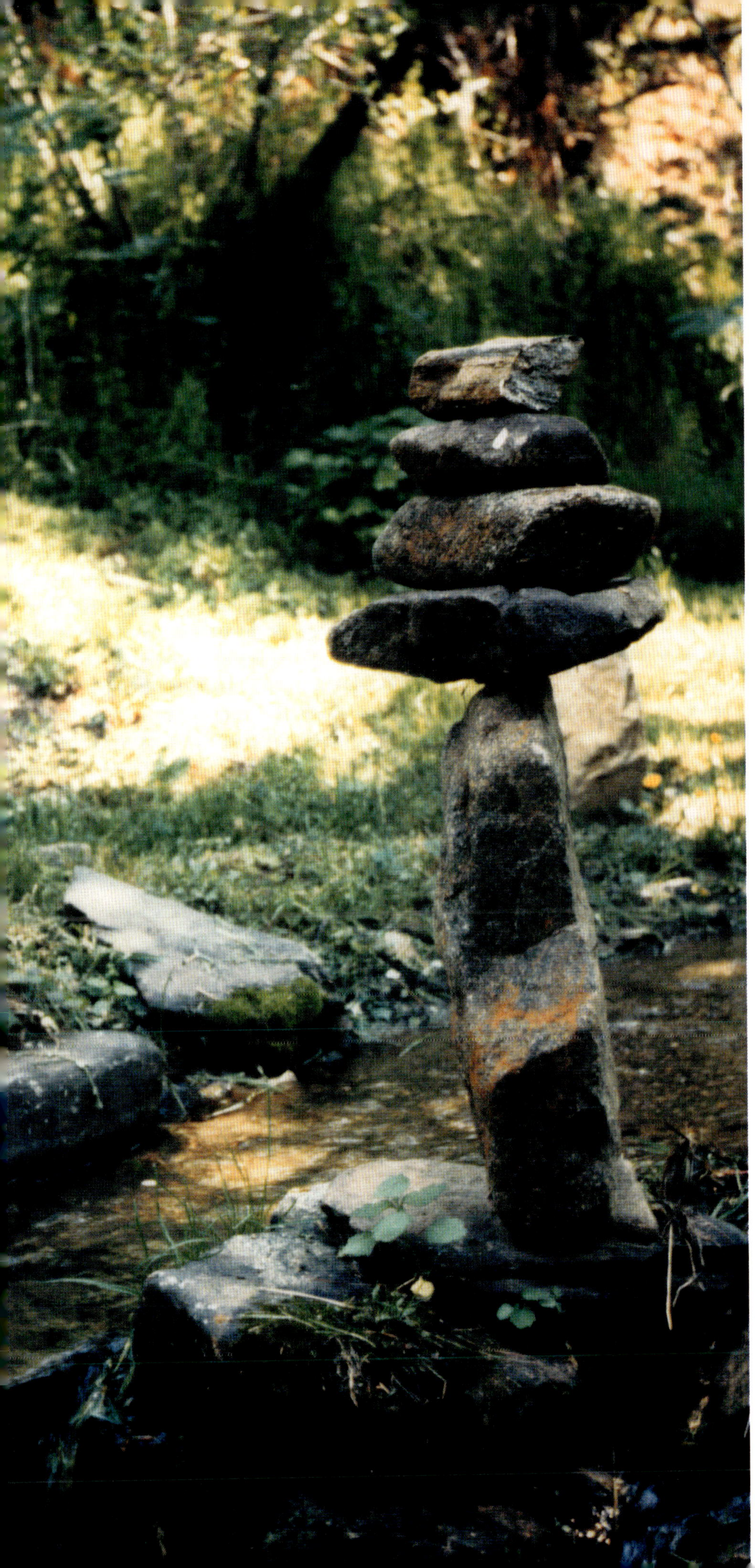

And in the protected silence of the forest I came upon a stream (the steep sloping hills on either side having suggested its existence). Its determination to flow in spite of winter's deep freeze and summer's drought amazed me . . . it flowed in a rhythm of its own, rippling sounds challenging all.

I decided to stop this for the moment. And with sticks and stones, and mud and leaves, I began persuading it to cease. First here, then there, small dams of leaves and rocks began to discourage the flow. One by one the exits were blocked, prohibiting its natural course. Muddy whirlpools behind the dam began spinning. Searching perhaps, wondering at least — why? Crawfish began shooting to the surface to find out who or what molested their comfort.

And finally it was complete — the network of tiny outlets secured. The natural rhythm interrupted. The noise of tumbling water halted. Silence prevailed behind the dam.

And I wondered, as the rising water reacted in a clouded swirling whirlpool . . . would it wait until the dam was full, or would it see a vulnerable crack between two rocks?

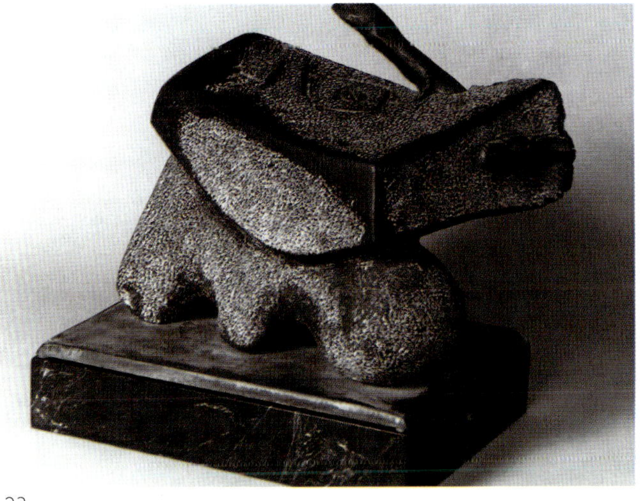

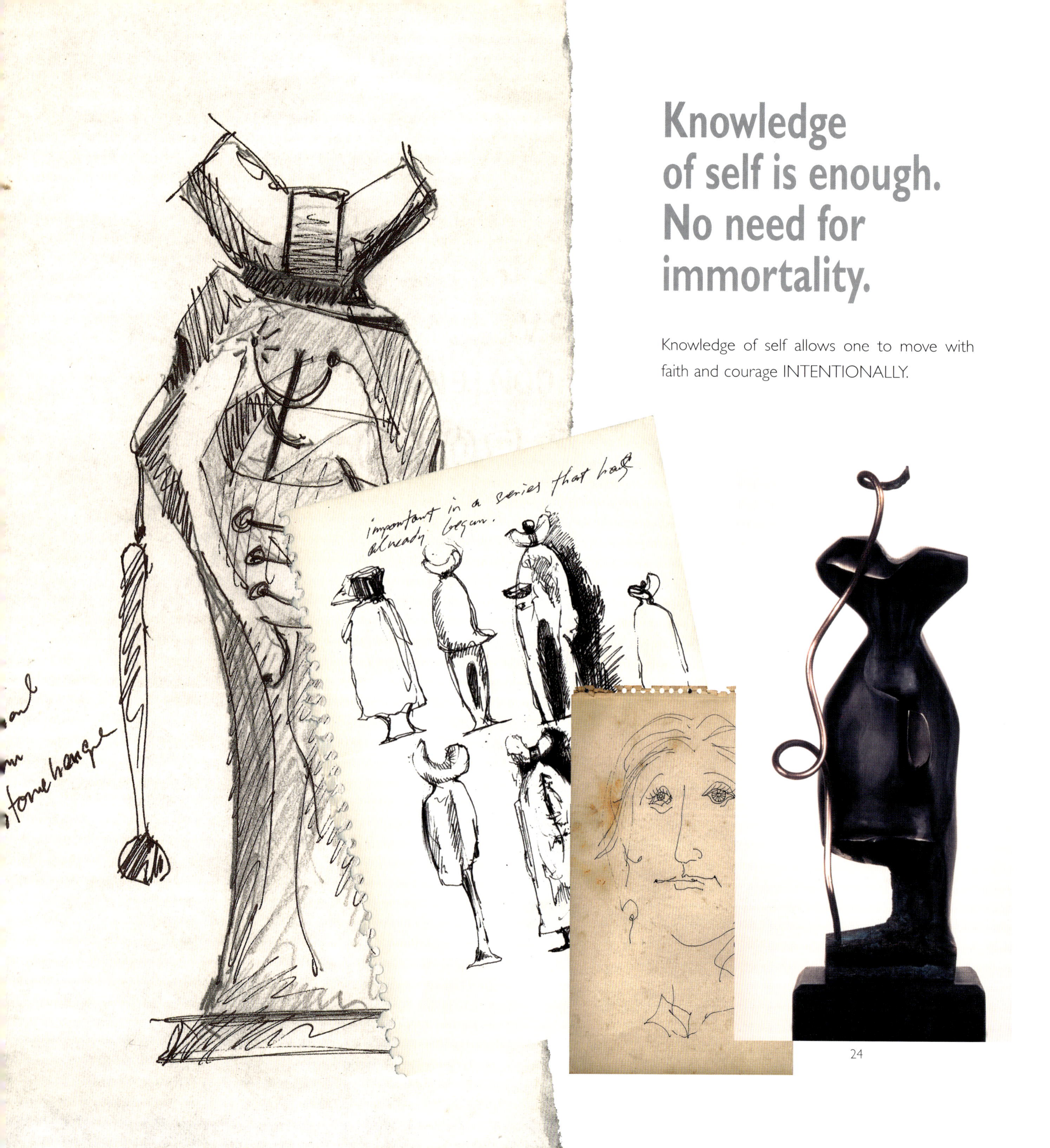

Knowledge of self is enough. No need for immortality.

Knowledge of self allows one to move with faith and courage INTENTIONALLY.

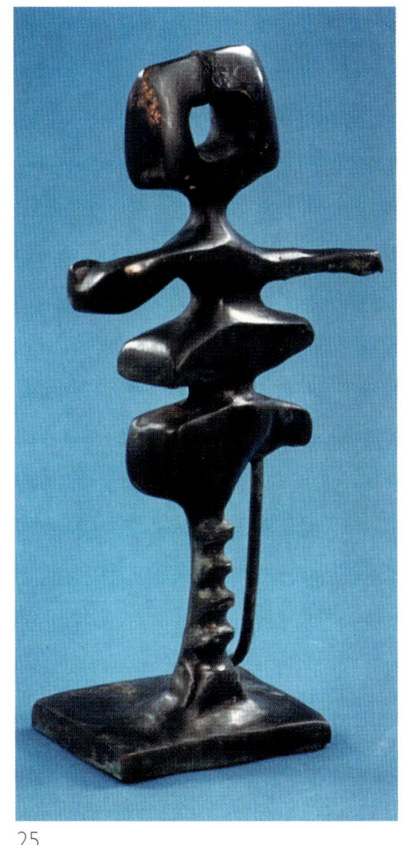

25

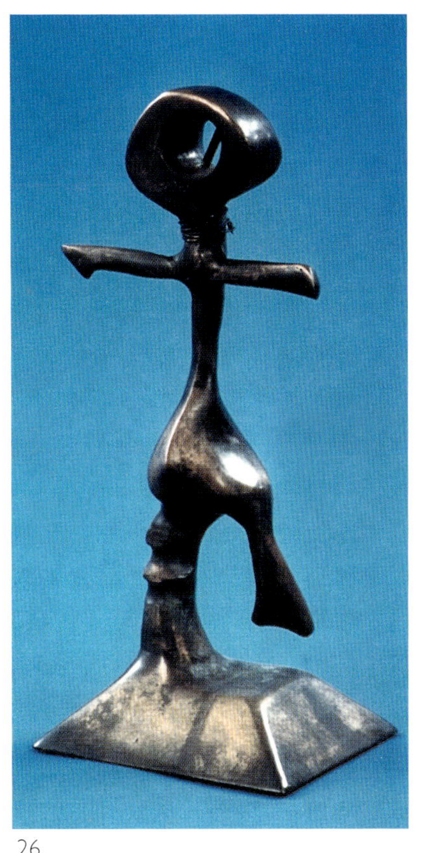

26

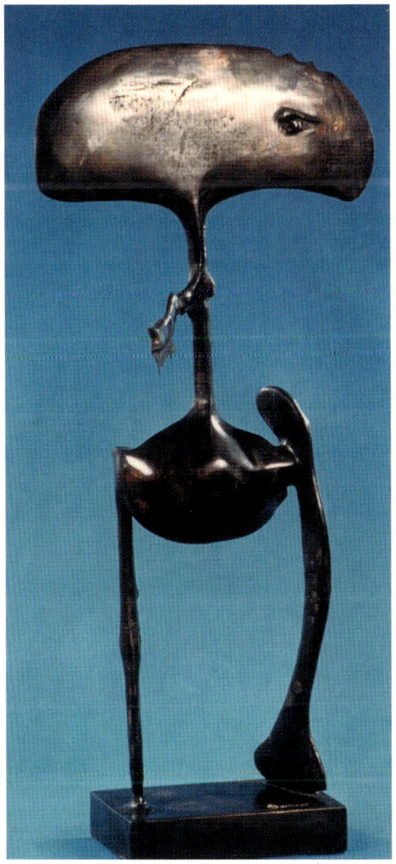

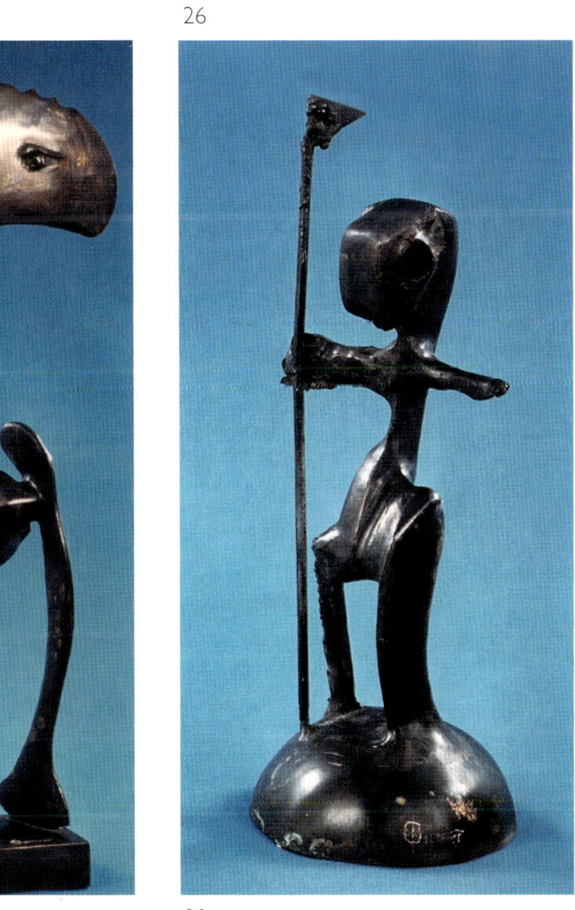

27

28

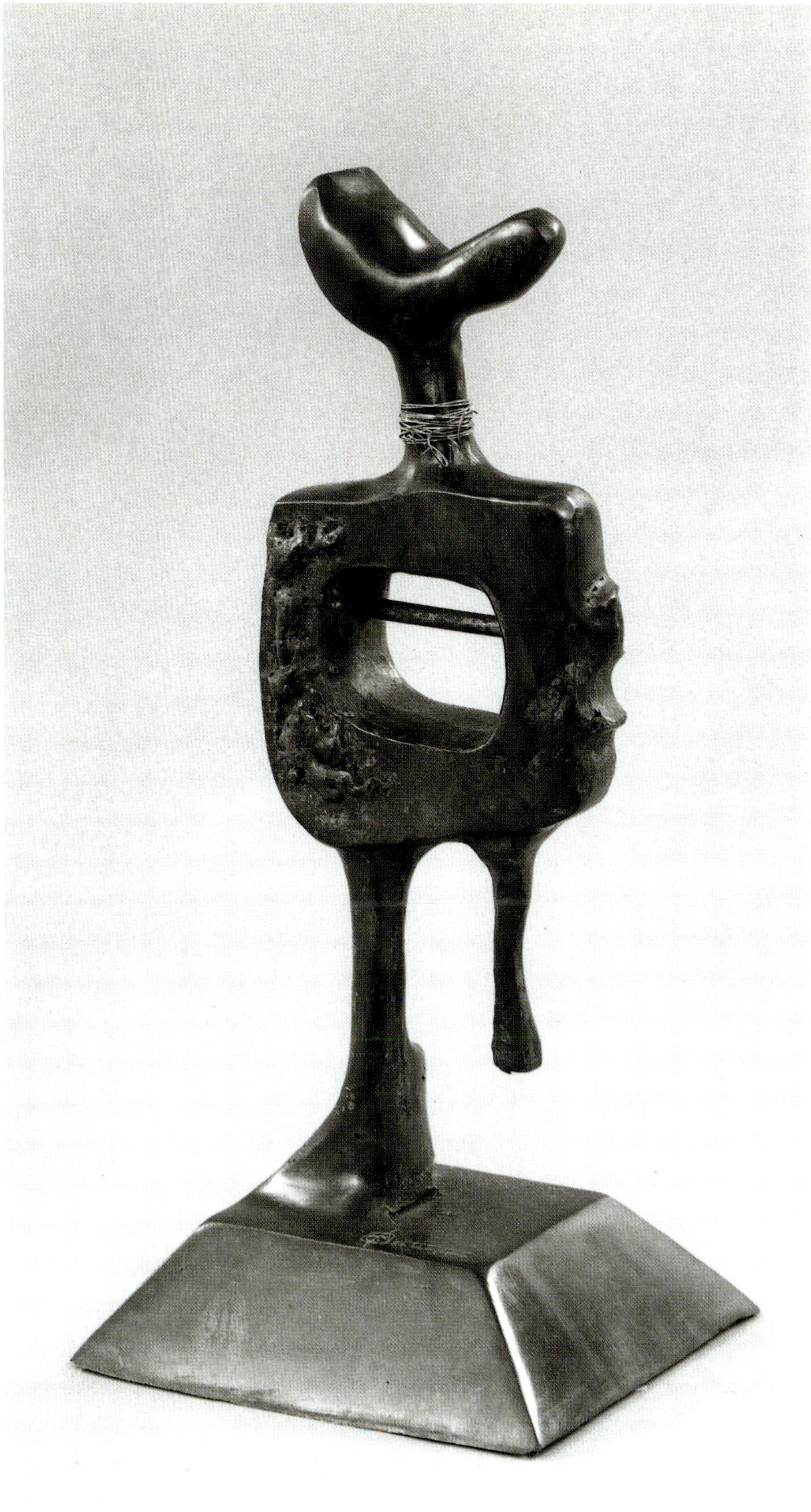

29

look at the watch it tells me the date is 23 Jul
nother silent evening in the woods. Spent the earl
rt of it having dinner with Mrs. Williams and gra
oud sounds and loud conversation. Now the woods
eace. (A plane is overhead the noise breaks the mood
s but this evening, there will be many riots in the citys
iolence causes me to wonder why are we here, w
an't human beings cooperate - is the freedom of de
ay too great a responsibility for man to cope w
ce of pain and suffering and I wonder if th
im to bring out in my work. Is that the
tist? Should he show what is happening
t of it or should he consider what
to happen to man, To show harmon
many races but I can't see as that
me. the book... (can't remember na
s that man must have war always - ca
? perhaps when the strong of mind begin
he weak.

productive - hot yes but I did not stop all
time at this pace for the remainder of th
k (7-5:00 pm) should almost complete the pi
name ___

Williams

winged victory
man and
winged vertibrae

30

Sorting. The choice of what is to stay is a product of experience. The things that are chosen determine the worth of the artist.

I wish now, tonight, that I were capable of writing in more detail so that I could capture all that is in my mind. But as I write I sculpt. I do the work of sorting out. That is the role of the artist — to eliminate the extras, keeping only what is important. The choice of what is to stay is a product of experience. The things that are chosen determine the worth of the artist. If his artistic sensibility is right, then his statement will also be right. To achieve this requires a vast amount of input — experience, words, actions, emotions, thoughts, failure, success, doing. Then sorting. Then doing.

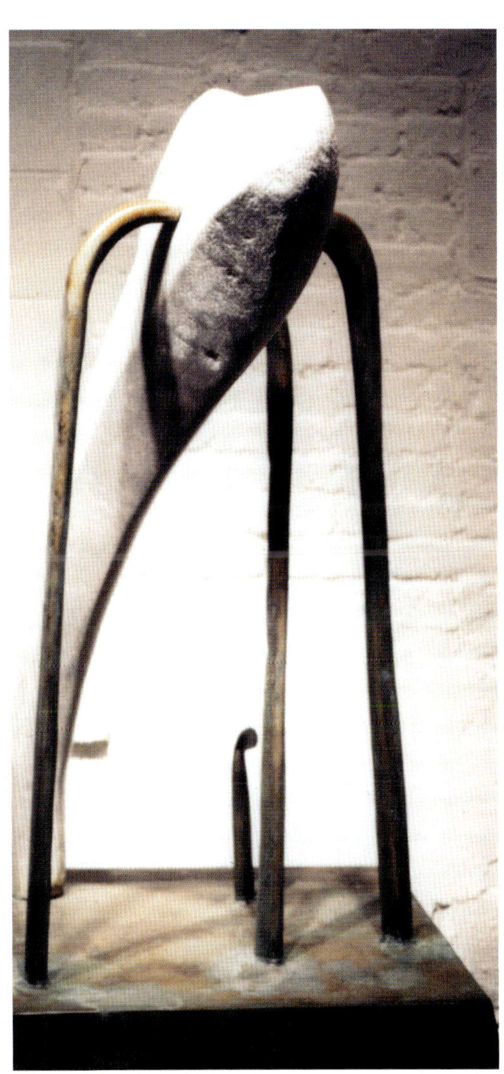

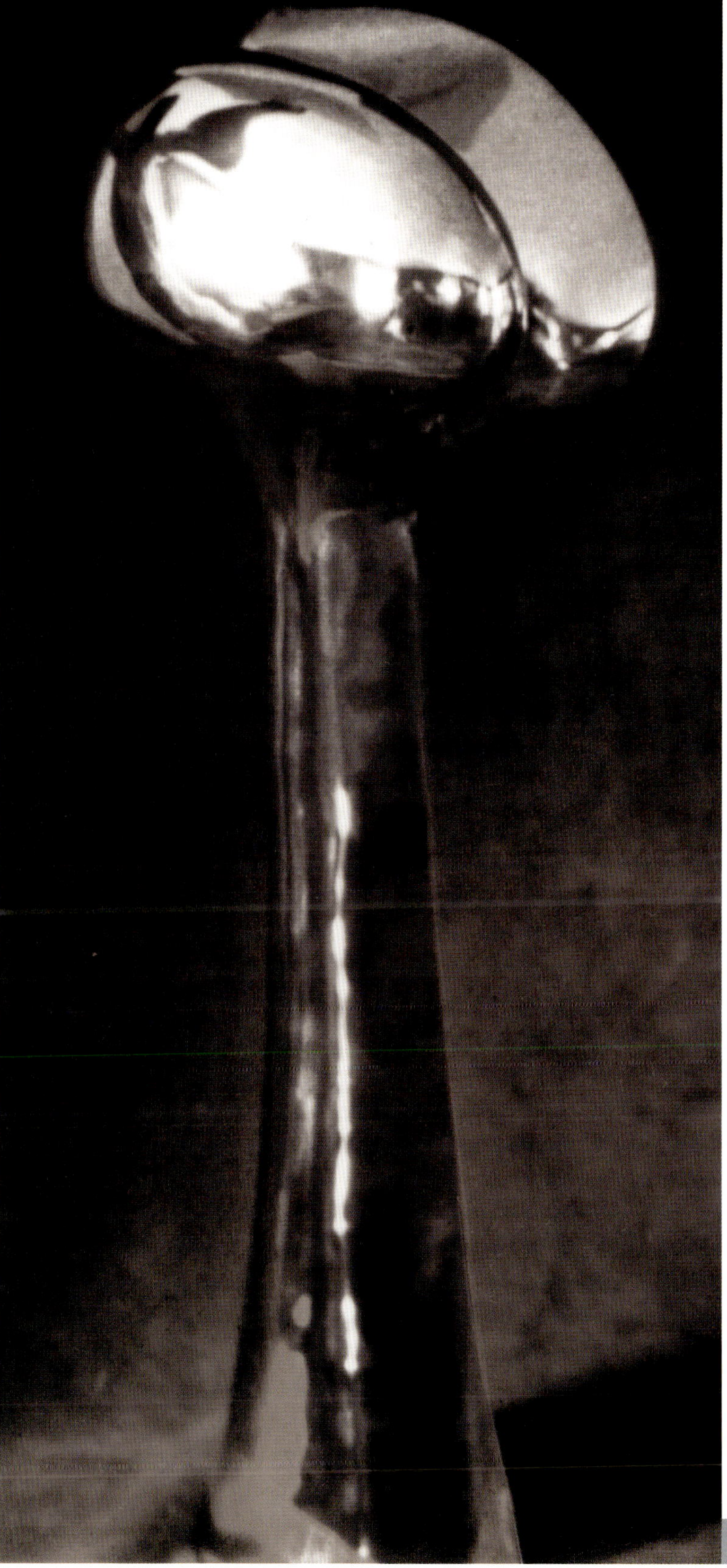

Finding what conventions of form work, and
and what detail one can do without while preserving
the spirit of the whole – that is the task.

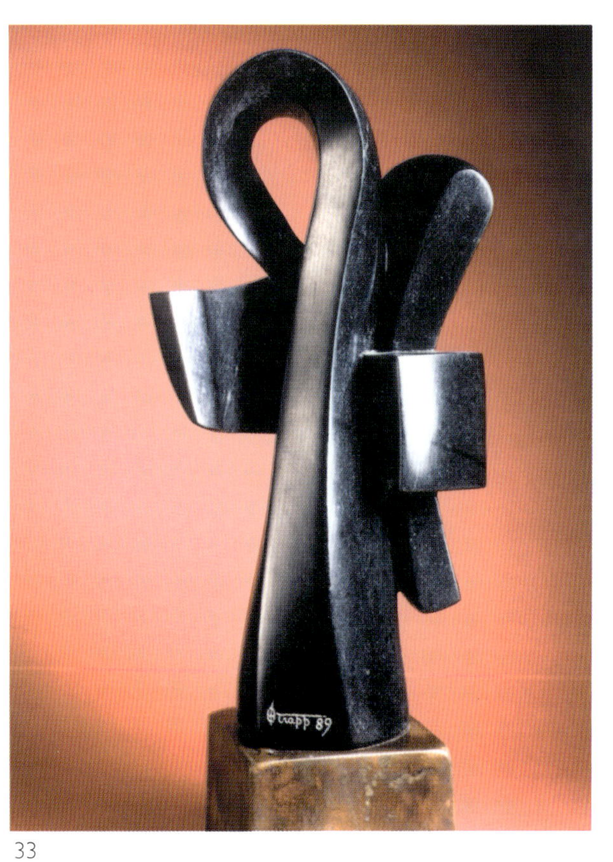

33

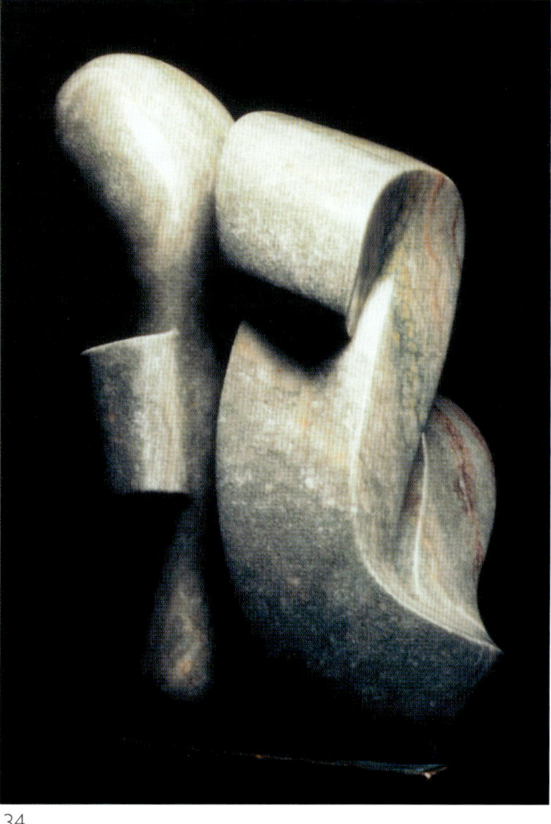

34

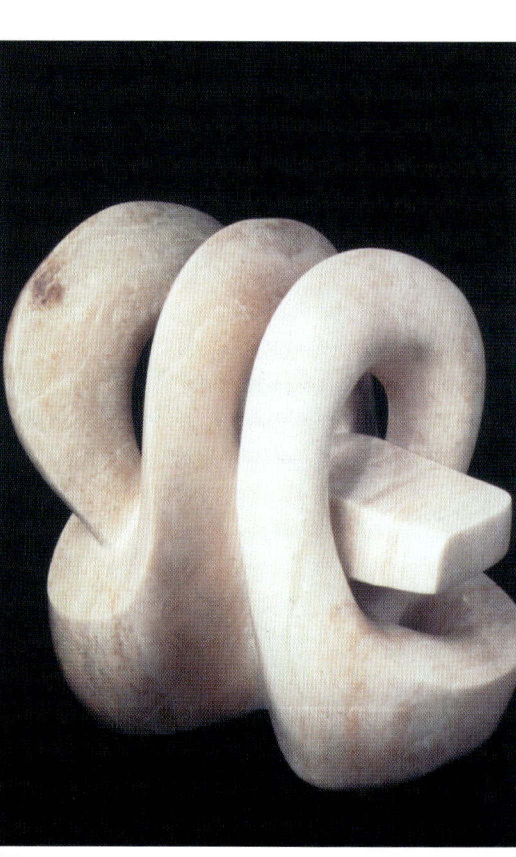

35

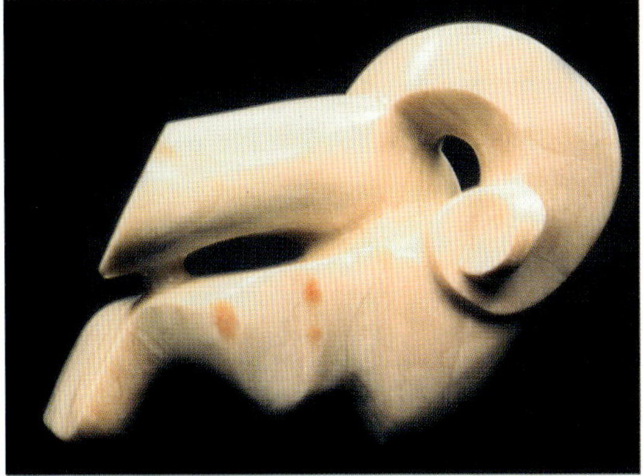

37

I don't need more stimuli. I need to unleash the part of me that overflows – to put the overflow into solid form. I need to work until nothing is left – then rest – then restore the energy to begin again.

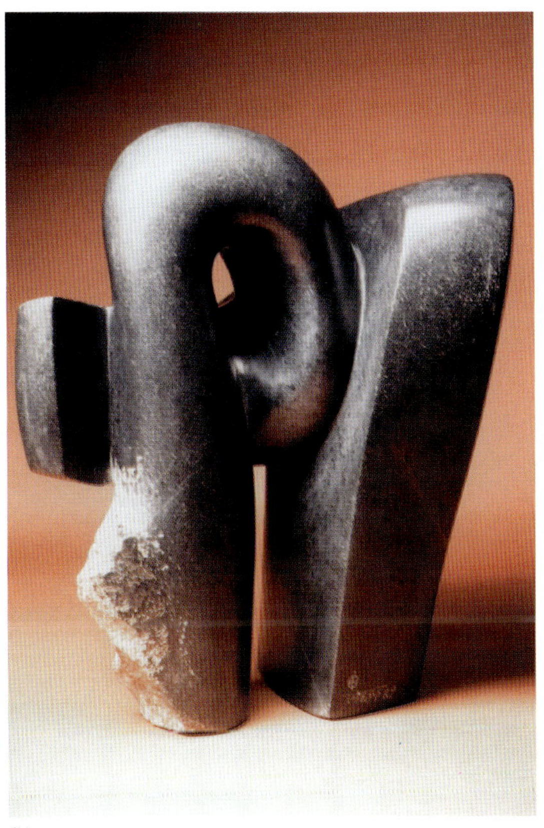

36

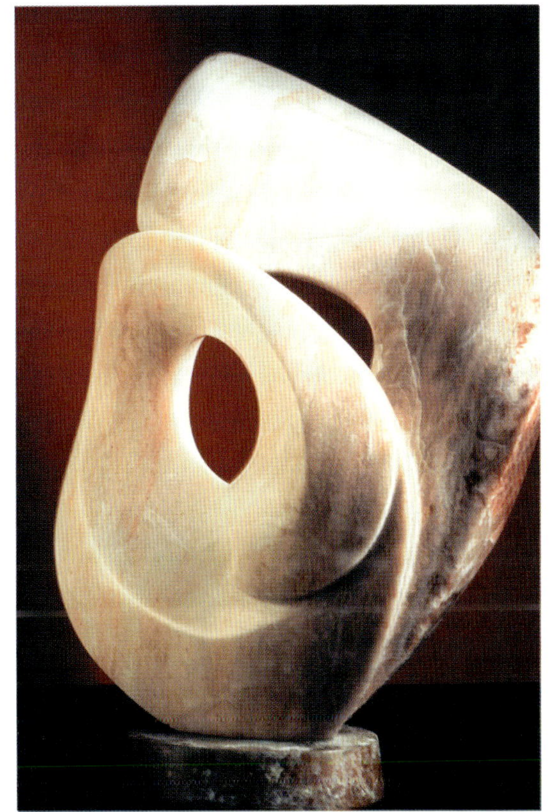

38

It is slowly getting light. A beautiful time of day. Trees are a spring-soft, young green – tender and bursting with eager life that rejoices in the survival of winter. The softness of the trees in the courtyard, in this light, is unlike any experience I have ever had. Very soon the machine of the city will begin and it will break the softness. I must sleep. Head is tired, body shaking, thoughts but no thoughts, once more chest is hurting, heart pounding worse than ever. Dope causes depression which is fought off with physical torturing of self (pain justifies apathy) which justifies dope. Have to stay out of that environment – it will kill both me and my spirit.

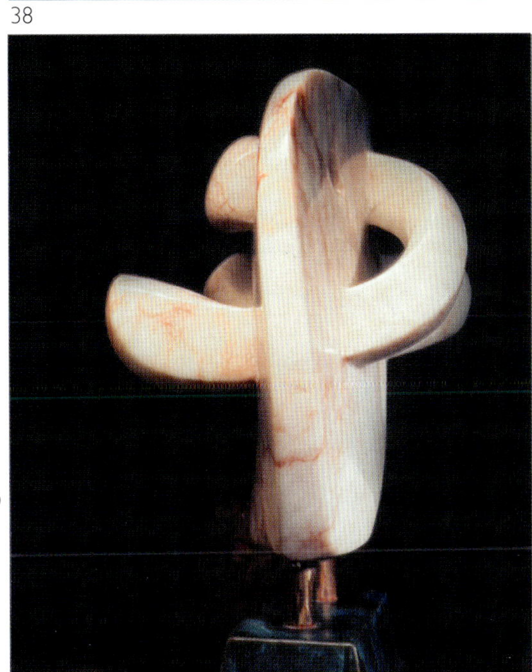

39

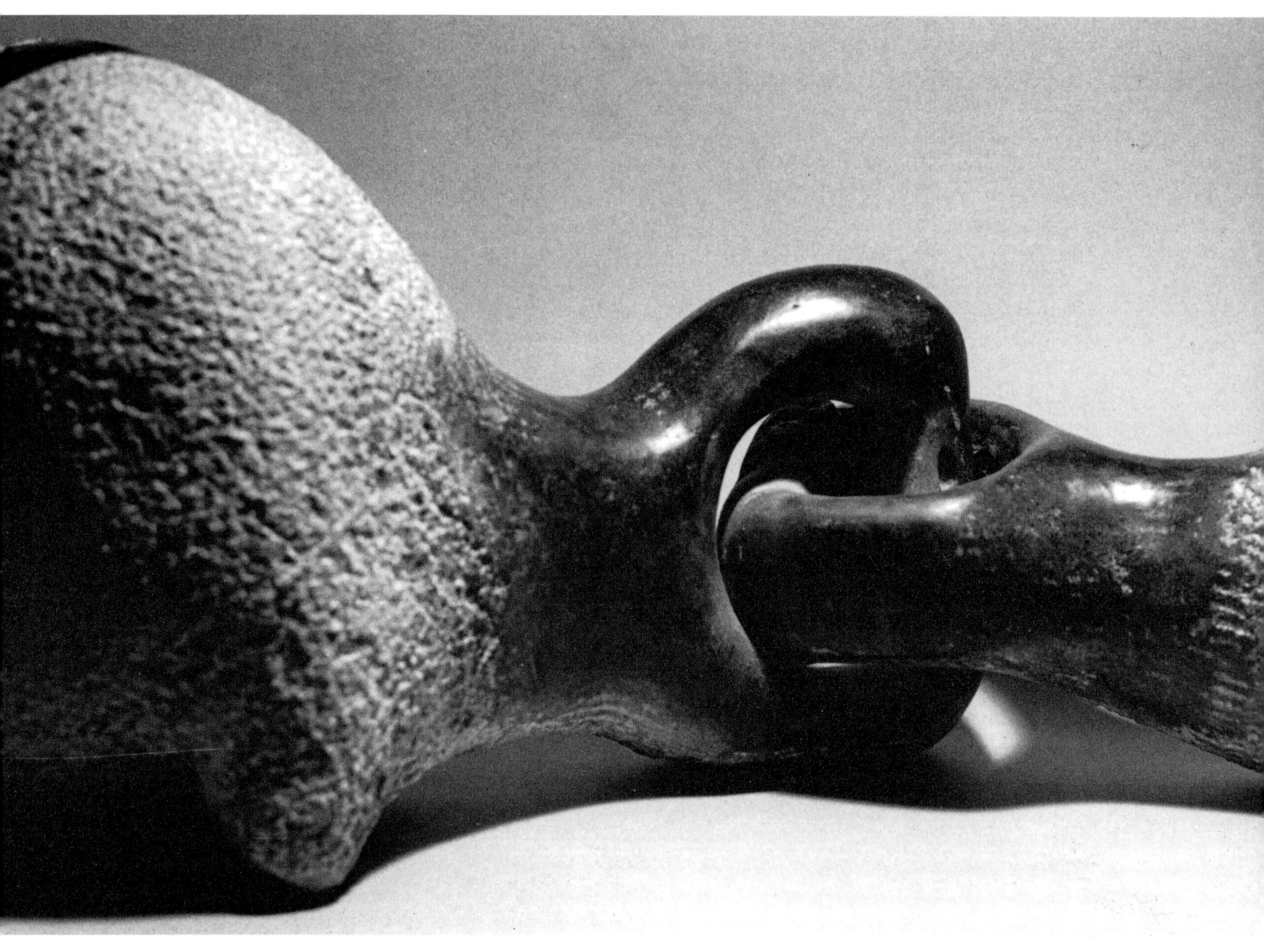

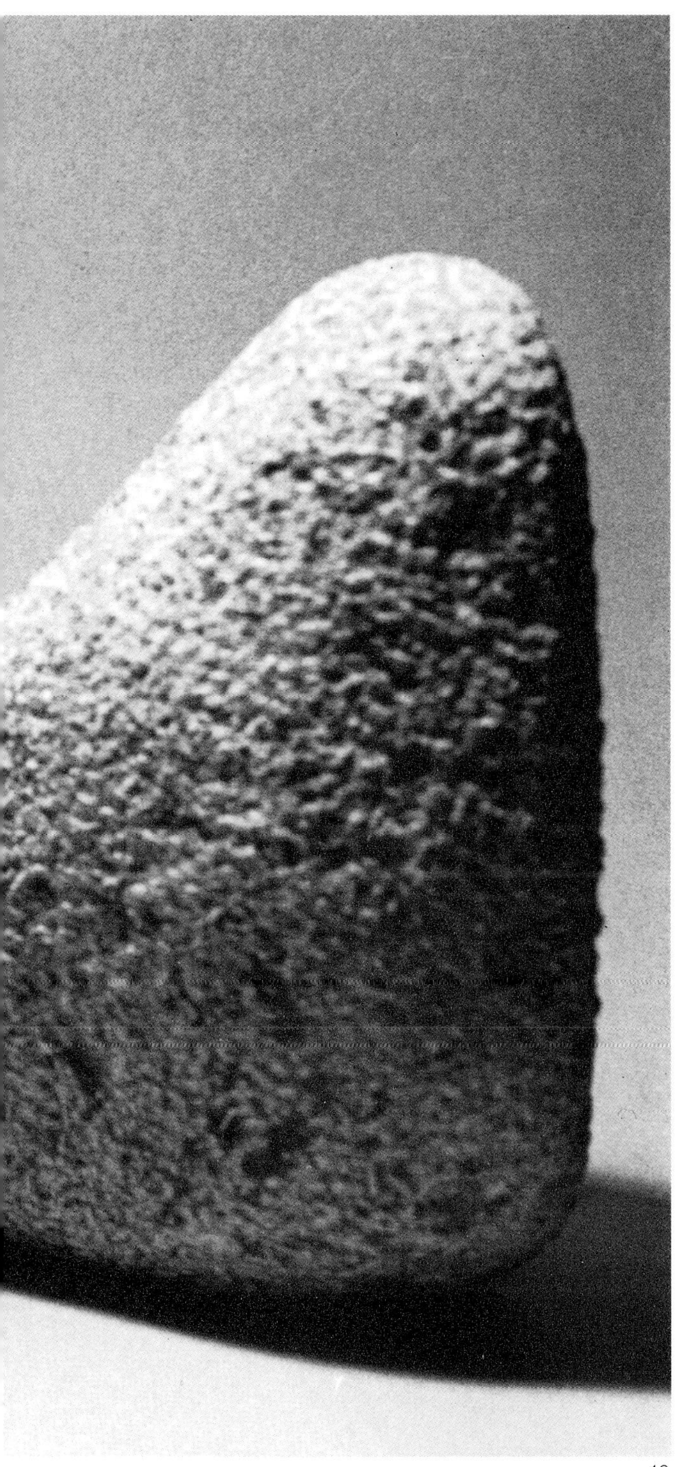

ART MUST SIMPLIFY

The goal for the new year is to do away with as many fears as possible and to pull my inner life together. Do I have to be alone to accomplish this? I don't know – I hope not. The secondary goal is to find land and surround myself with space and nature. Will the cost be too great to be able to produce the things I'm trying to create? The fight for simplicity is so complex.

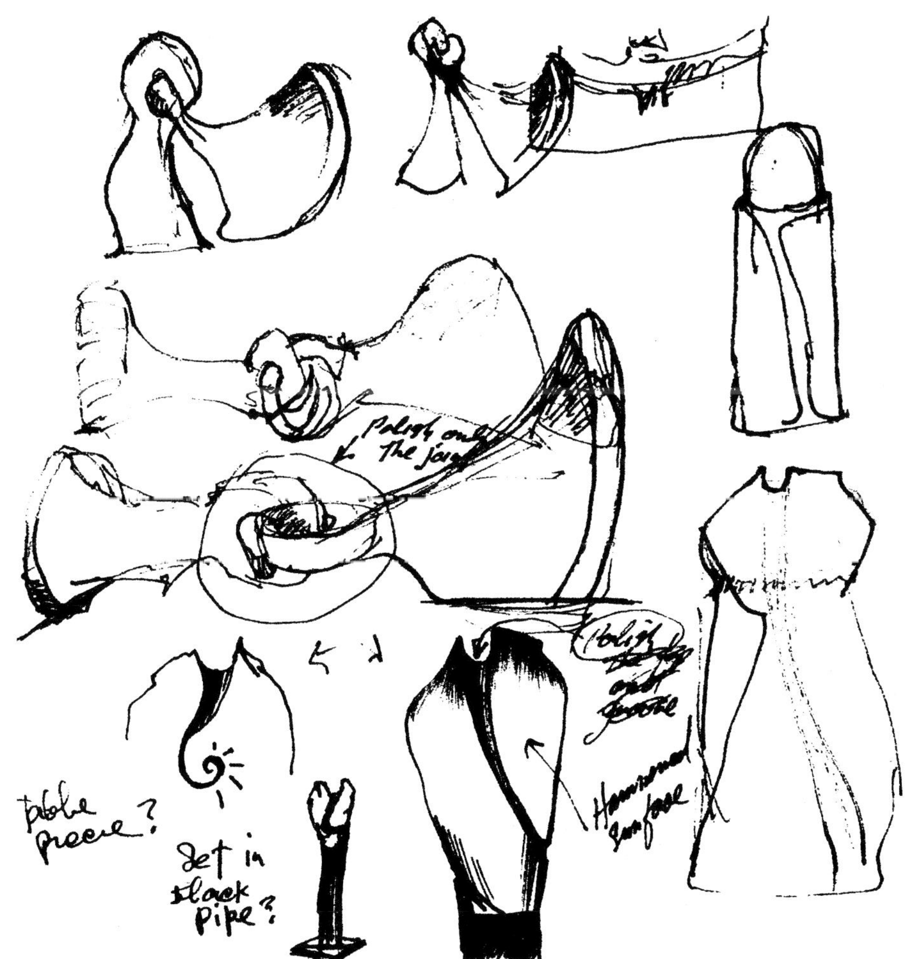

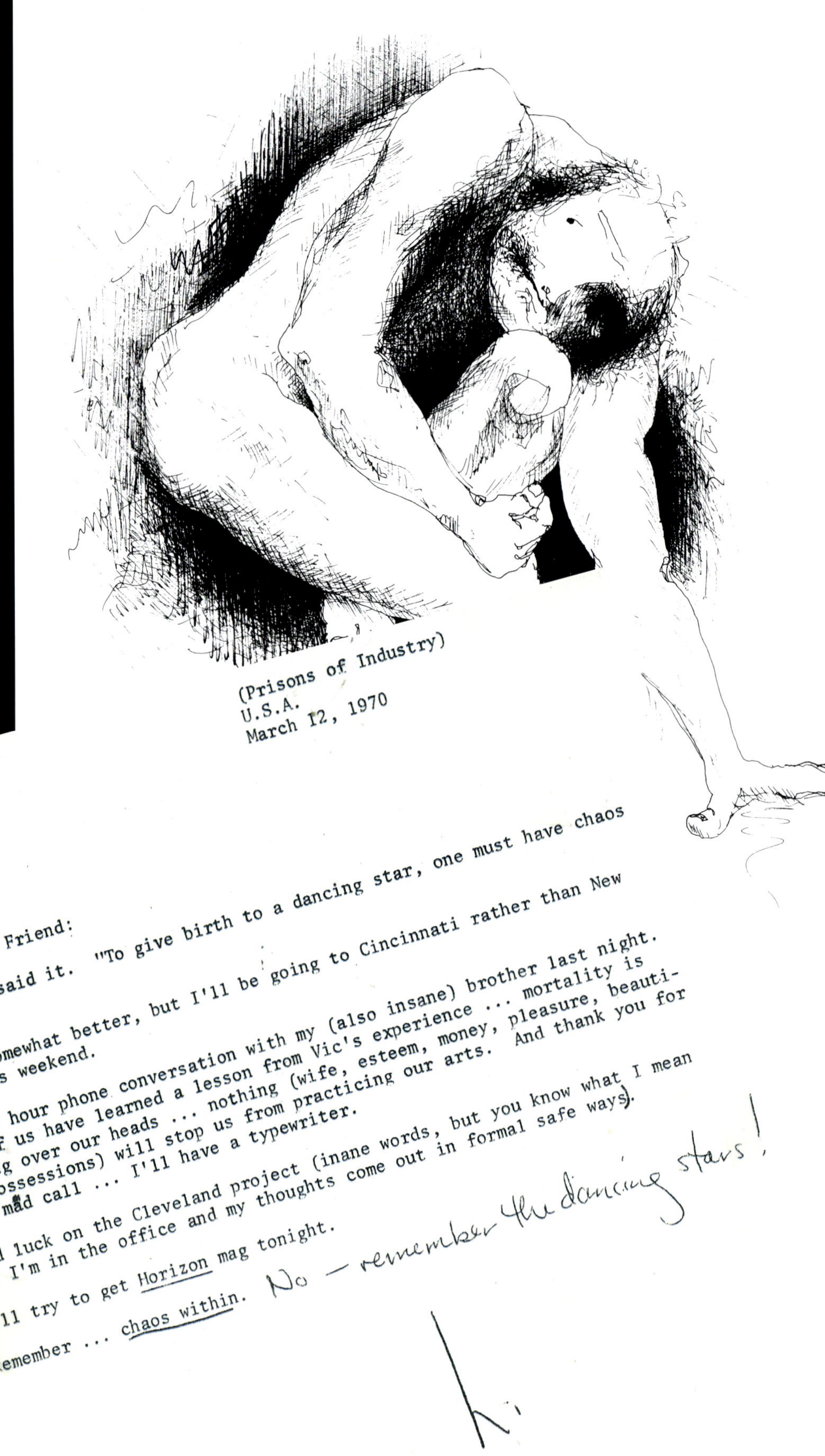

(Prisons of Industry)
U.S.A.
March 12, 1970

Dear Insane Friend:

Nietzsche said it. "To give birth to a dancing star, one must have chaos within."

Vic is somewhat better, but I'll be going to Cincinnati rather than New York this weekend.

Had two hour phone conversation with my (also insane) brother last night. Both of us have learned a lesson from Vic's experience ... mortality is hanging over our heads ... nothing (wife, esteem, money, pleasure, beautiful possessions) will stop us from practicing our arts. And thank you for your mad call ... I'll have a typewriter.

Good luck on the Cleveland project (inane words, but you know what I mean ... I'm in the office and my thoughts come out in formal safe ways).

Will try to get Horizon mag tonight.

Remember ... chaos within. No — remember the dancing stars!

Without the calm, there could be no art in my life. Without the hype, there could be no madness. It is vital to have both. Art is madness – a game we create to pretend meaning or reason. It is the ultimate insanity. To know, and to know that you know. It makes one laugh all the time at all things – becoming serious only if we need them to be serious things. A crisis is only such if we need it to happen. Joy and happiness should be the natural way, but just the opposite happens. There seems to be no reason or purpose to life without a struggle. I have never understood this, and now I understand it less.

I want to scream, to run, to be free of everything that hampers me. I have changed, but there is still a madness inside. When I get involved with my work I want to run, to work harder and faster, to meet people, to fuck, to drink, to dance, to be free. I must. The alternative is death – and if I die, my work will die with me. How do I find the balance between madness and work?

I absorb more now than ever. It takes little to fill my senses, to intoxicate me, to make my whole system dizzy. Once it starts I want to take all the images, conscious and unconscious, and make them into solid form – into sculpture. The forms I see I want to remake, to change, to revise, to make my own.

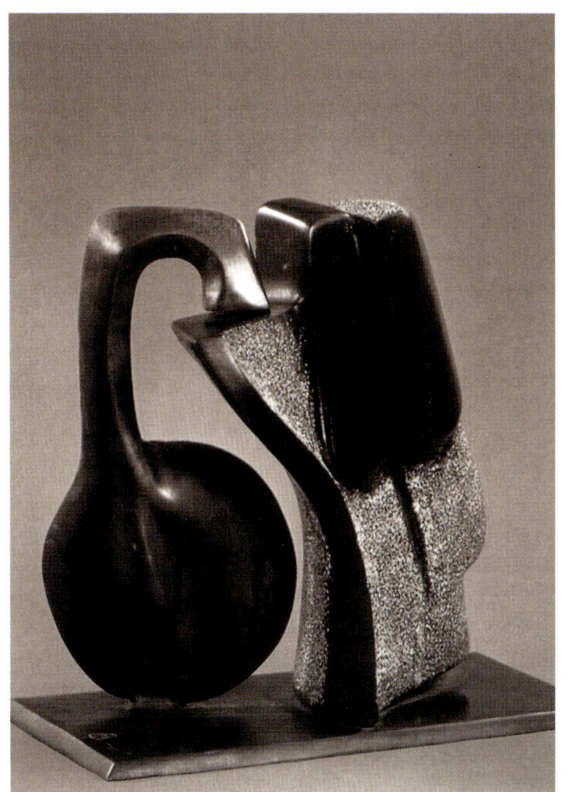

41

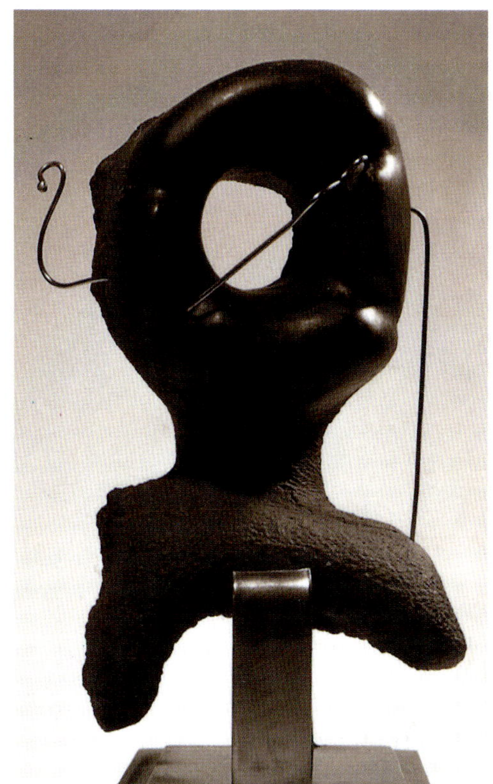

42

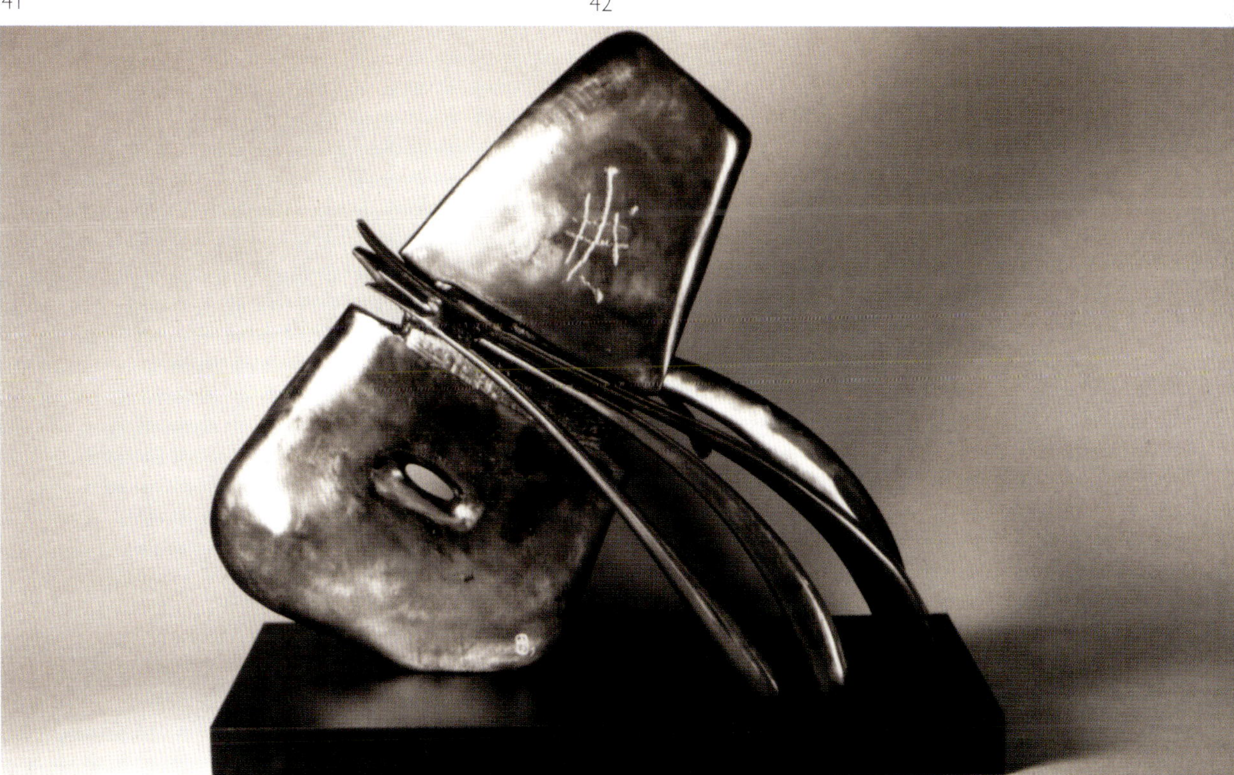

43

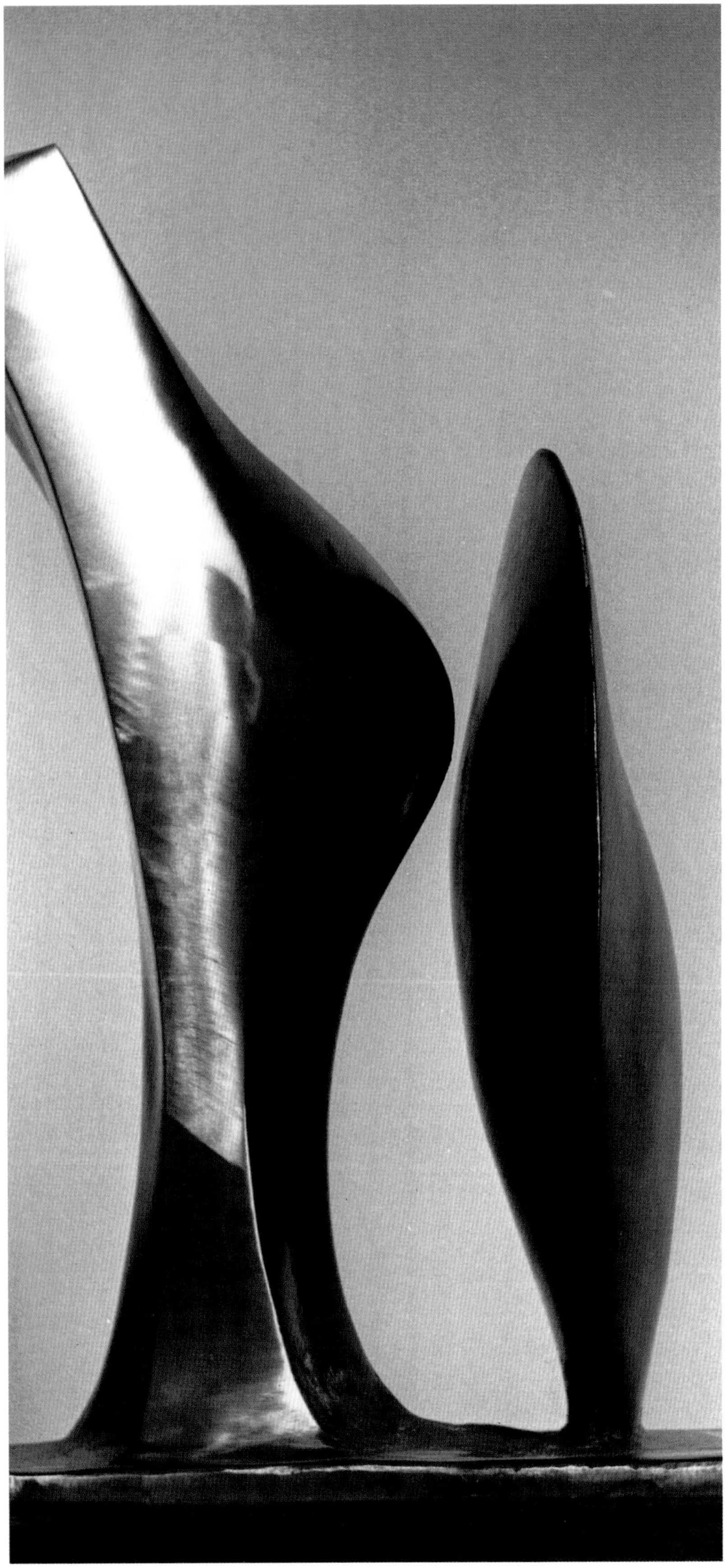

my SELF. the new sculpture is the best ever.
Am finally casting in Bronze, doing Brancusi
type forms. Very refined, true, sophisticated.
my own at last. Have worked day and night
for 2 weeks now am tired but can't sleep
forms keep coming and going, I snatch at sum
then refute most. One out of hundreds.
comes into being. Am having show in Cleveland
end of Sept. Should have 20 sculpts 10 draw
quick sketch of ones so far.

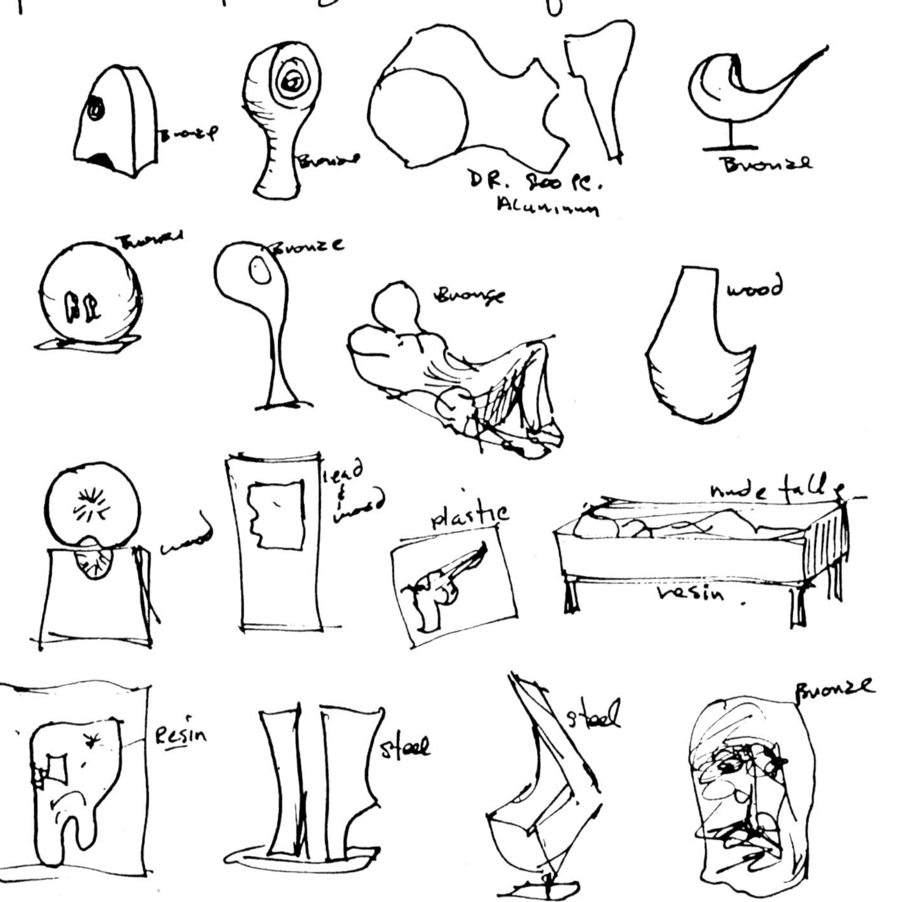

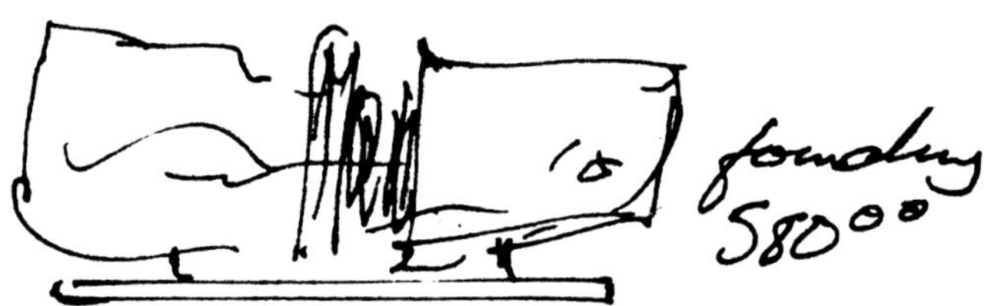

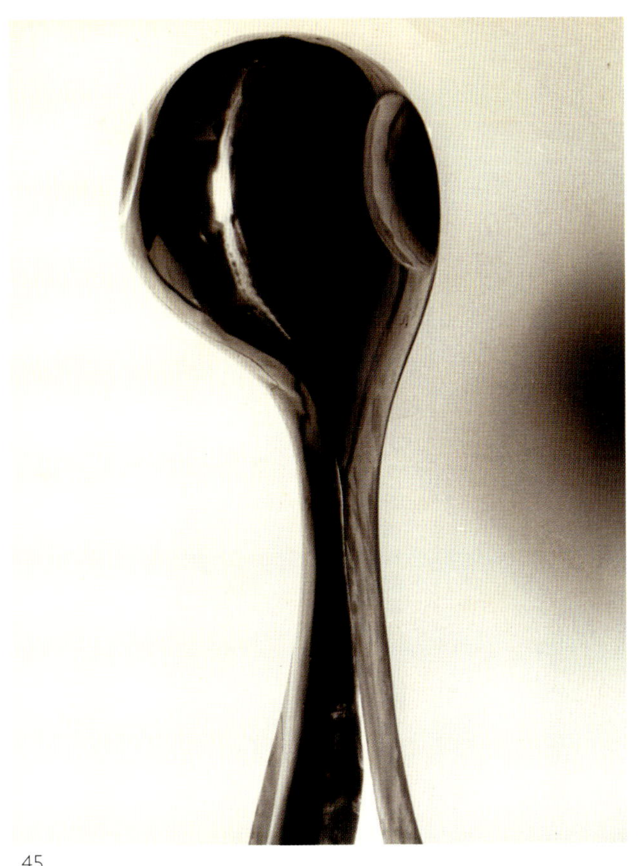

45

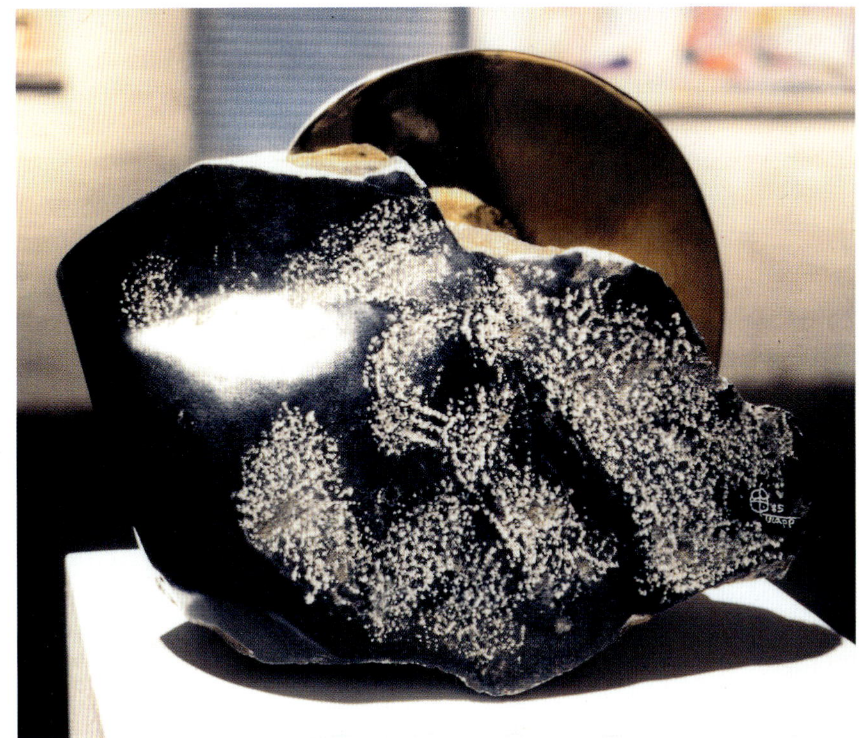

46

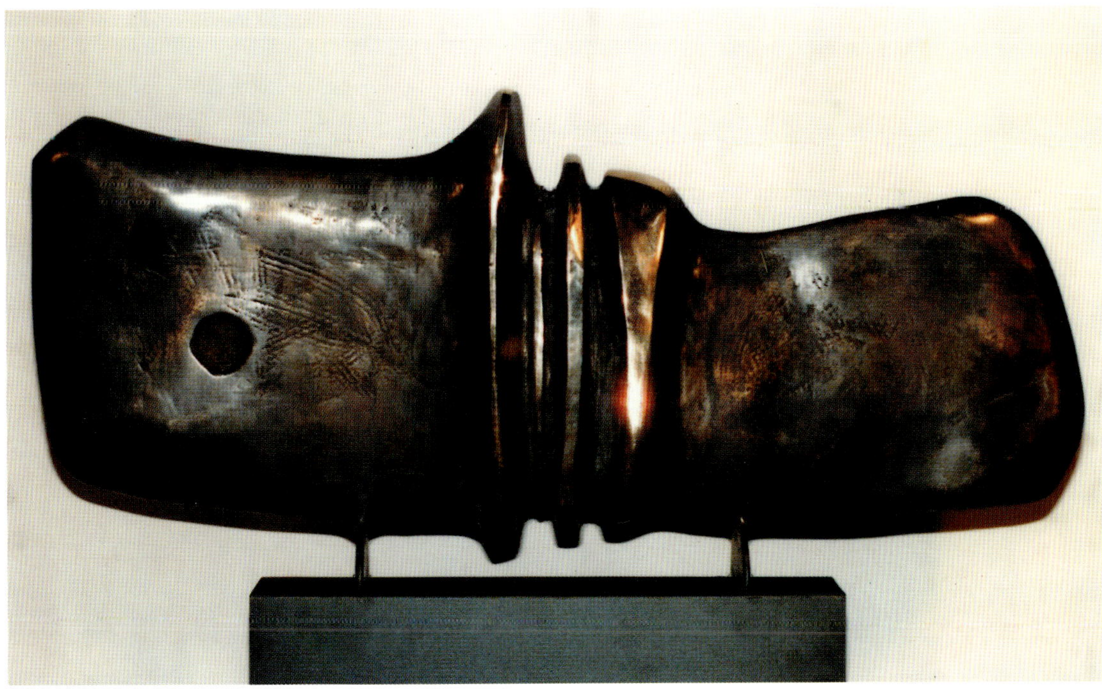

47

This evening I sat in the field, like a primitive man, watching the moon come up over the mountain – and wanting this moon to make life a little different.

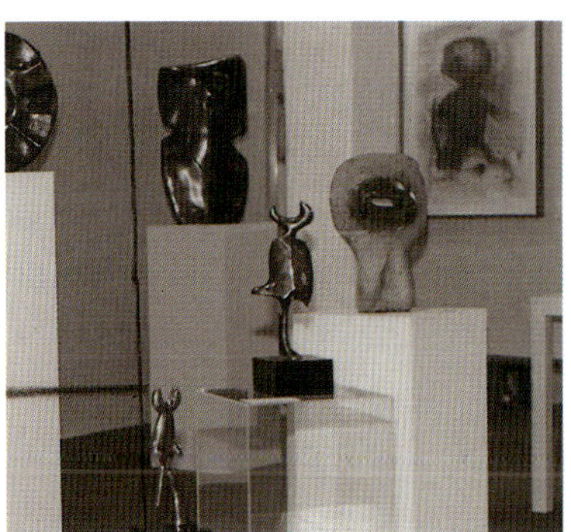

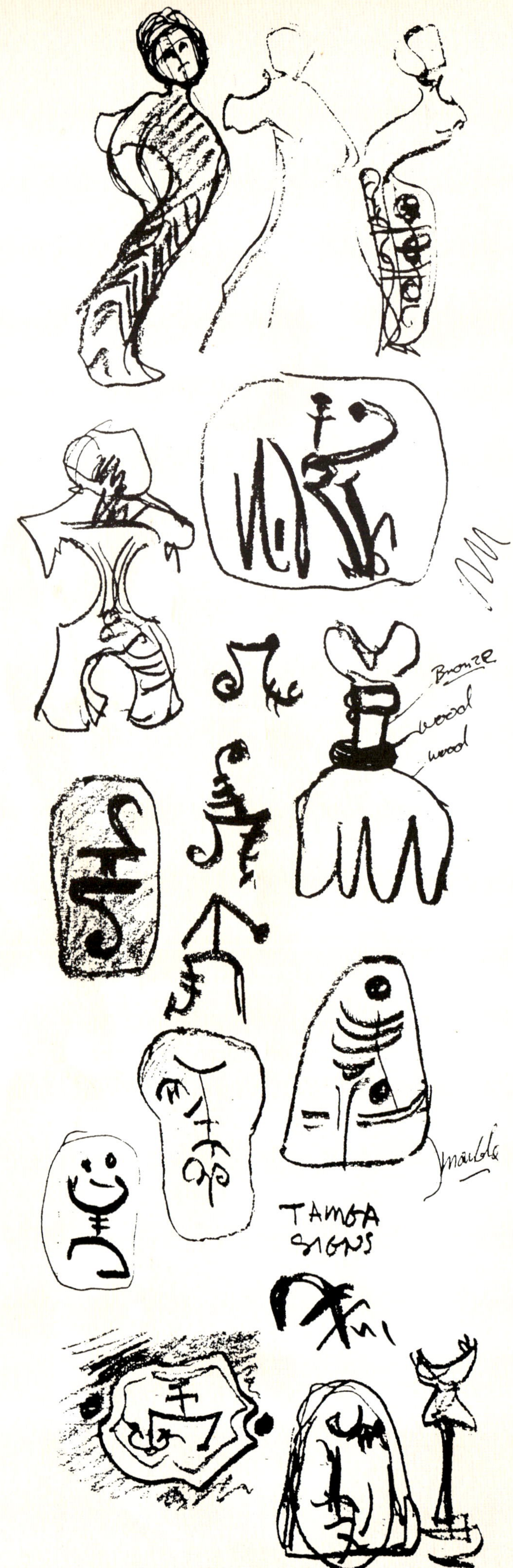

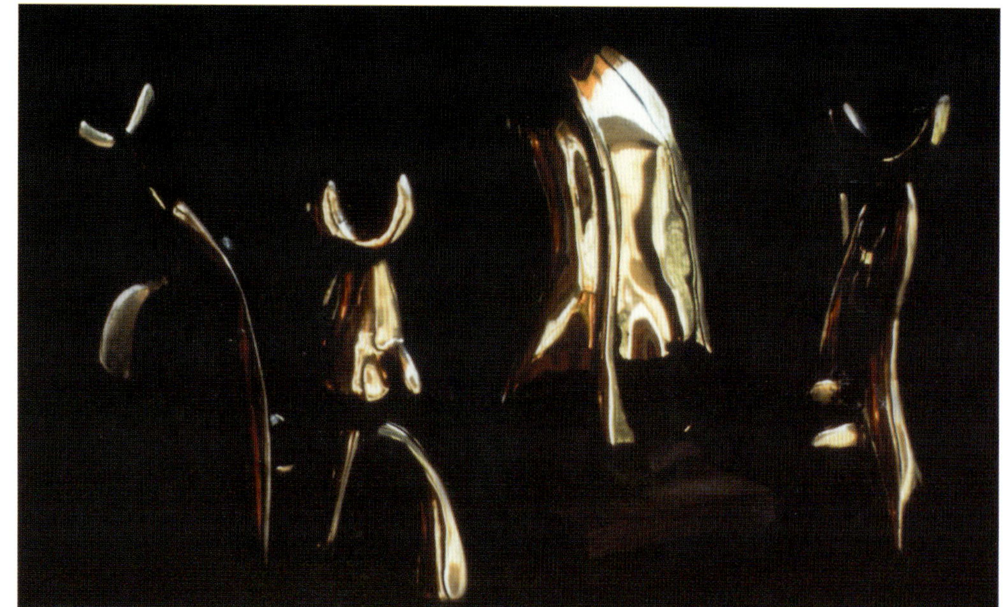

48

I feel that the styrofoam will work well for these strange creatures. 10 - 14" high is a good size. The key is to get used to the process and then work on the form. They have to be both happy and serious, complex and simple. A combination of dark patina and high polish. Should include a base with each. $250 ea. – especially if I can get a gallery enthused about them. Easy to ship and fun to do. Perhaps I can save enough money this way to continue with the more serious pieces.

Have made fifteen of the styrofoam pieces. Have to do at least 100 more. Many things are changing as I proceed. It's that old familiarity of materials that allows the process to be creative. Of the 100, I should get 15 - 20 gallery quality pieces.

The usual low has not hit this time. There is calm and excitement unlike other openings. I don't know why but I feel many pieces will sell. I have traded a drawing for a tuxedo I'll wear tonight. There is a classic ambiance this evening – perhaps that will help with the magic success of the myth. Tomorrow we go to New York. I have to look around and just take it all in. Have so many commissions ahead. And more exciting, the Ohio show. Have many wild and free ideas for it. Want to call it "Forms from the Stone Drums" – lyrical and childlike, dancing forms, animals . . .

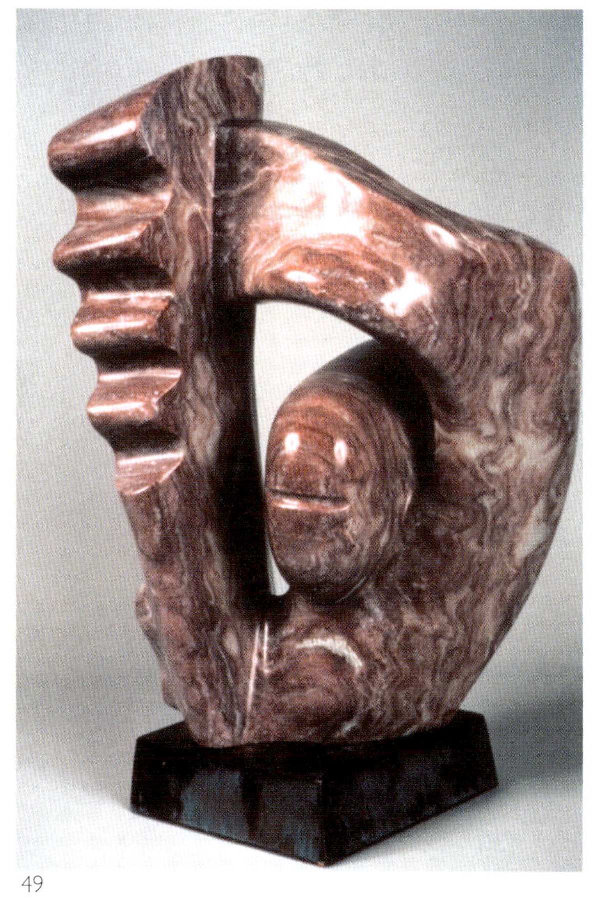

49

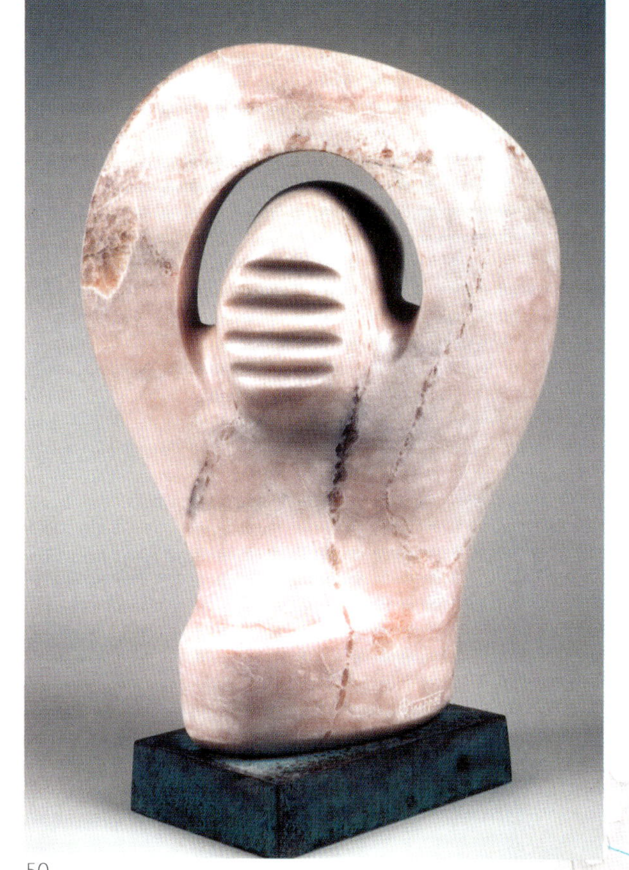

50

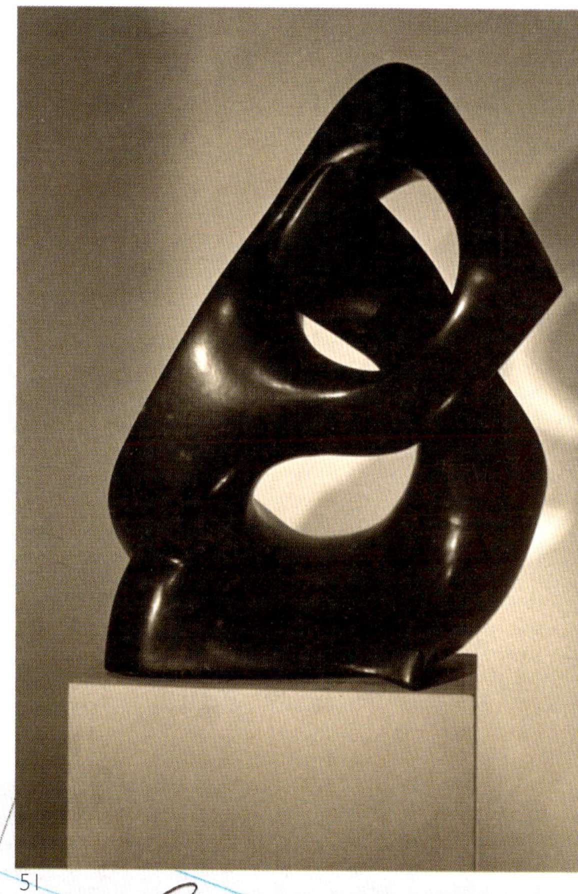

51

There is
something
powerful that
happens when
you pierce
a stone –
powerful both
artistically and
emotionally.

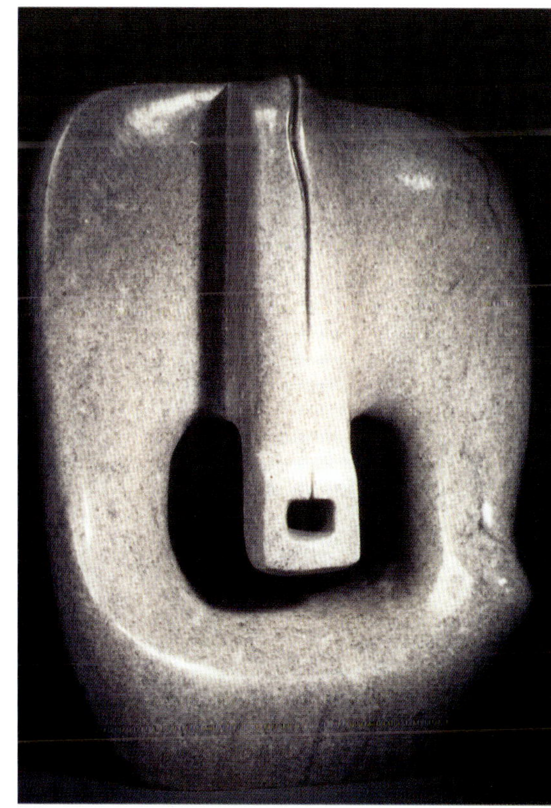

52

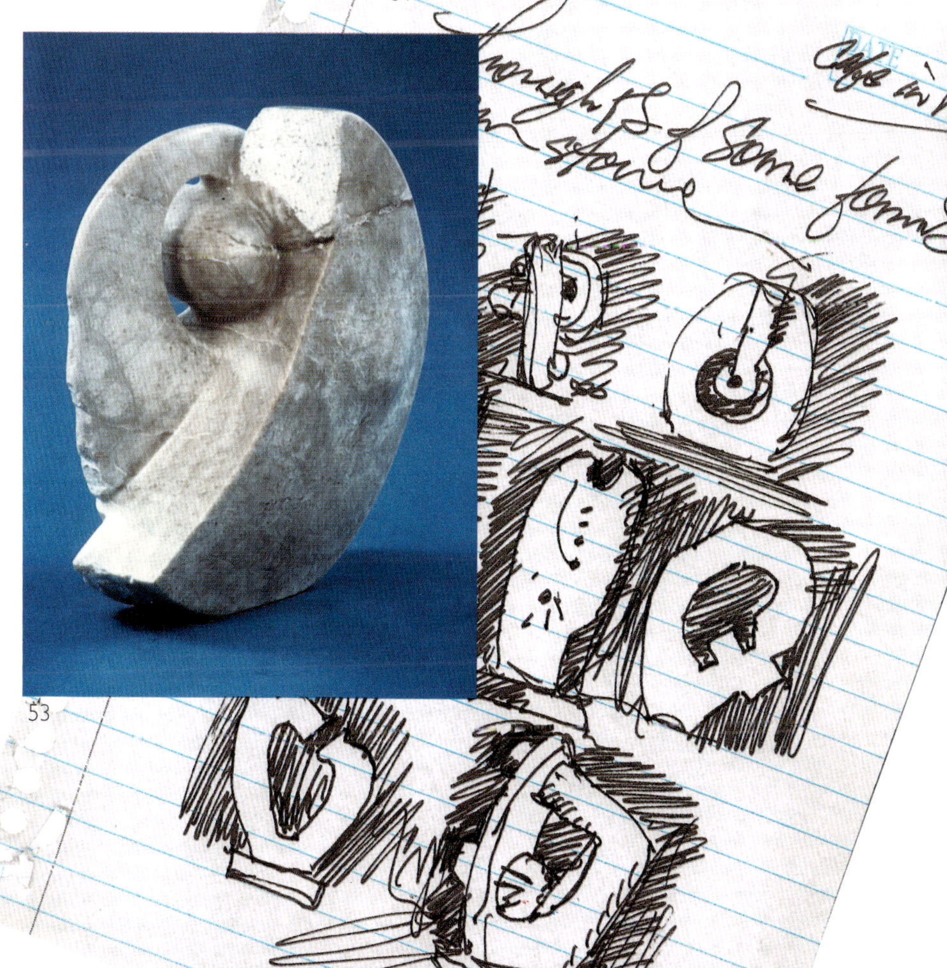

53

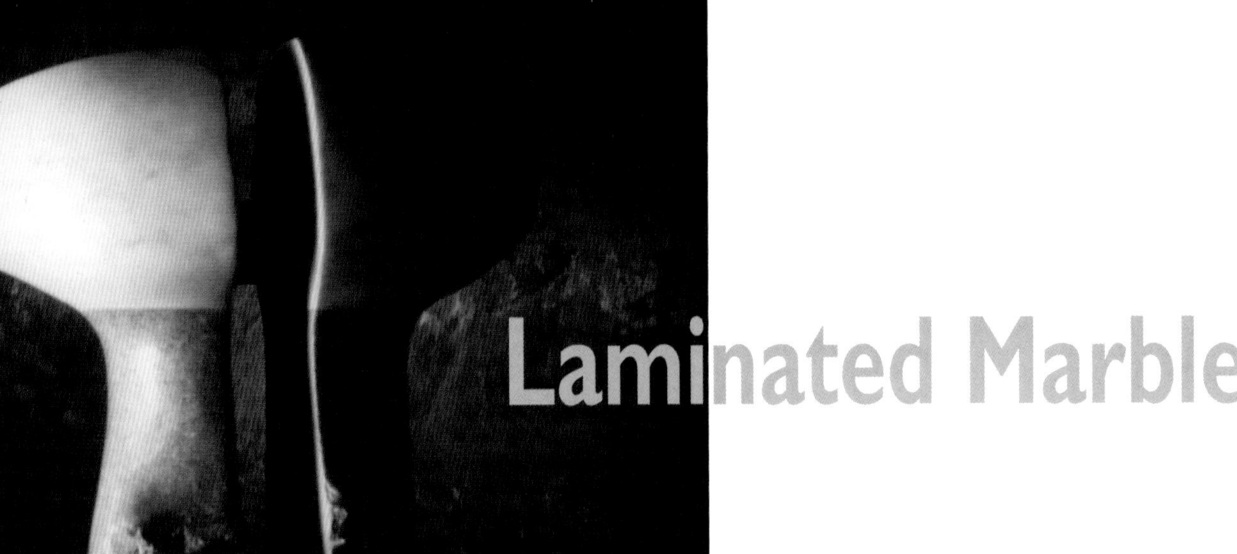

Laminated Marble

Space is a critical part of sculpture. If you agree that space exists and then break it apart by projecting into it, is that not a contradiction or a denial of the reality of space? How does one avoid the contradiction? Calder has tried with his moving wires. Picasso has tried with wire structures that one actually walks into – but they don't work. The moment you put anything into space you consume space and it no longer exists. Then again, there are Gabo's clear forms. They exist while giving the illusion of not consuming space. Perhaps that's the road to travel, but where does it lead? Perhaps it leads to 'nothingness' – just the mind imagining that something exists.

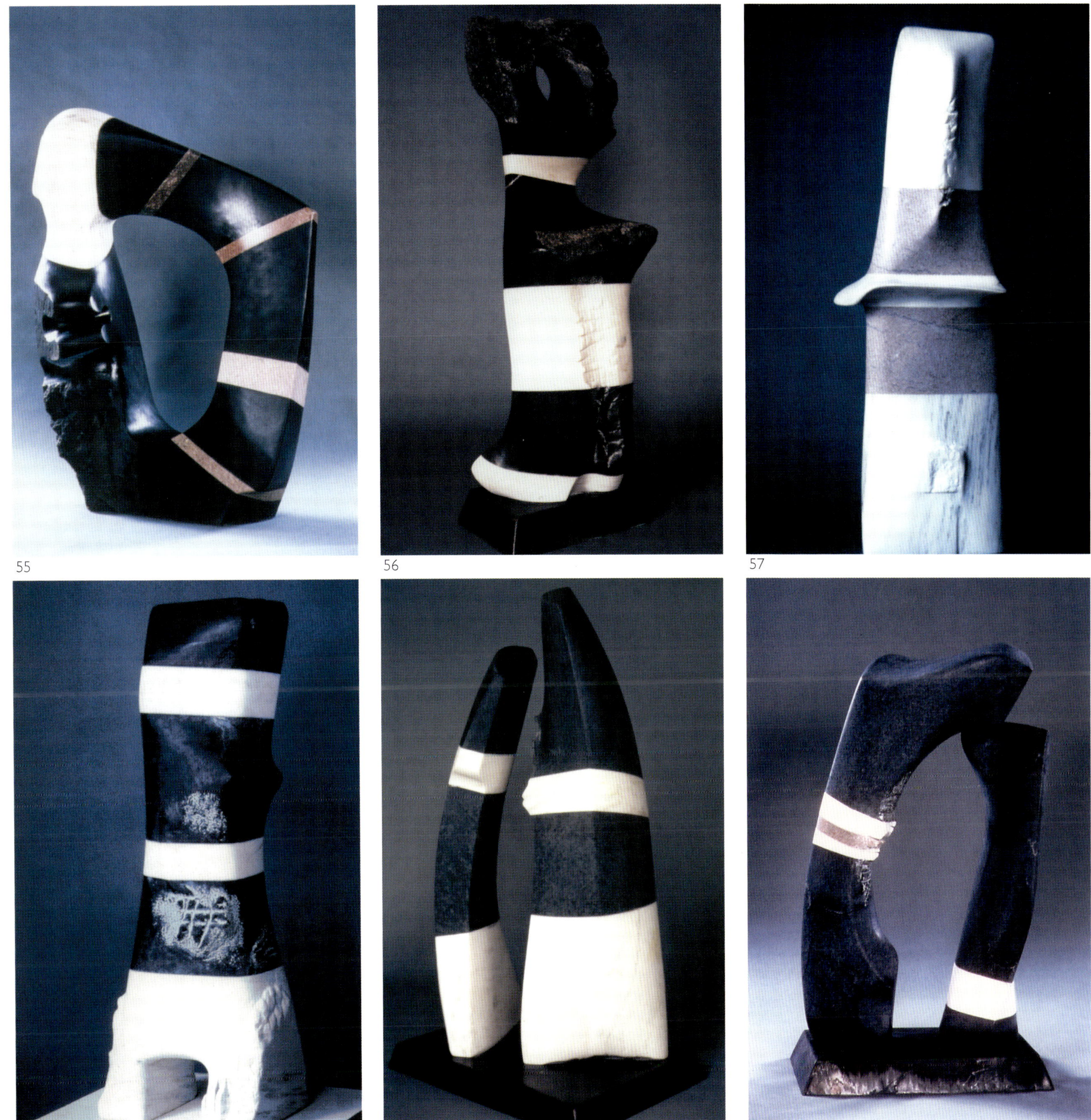

55

56

57

58

59

60

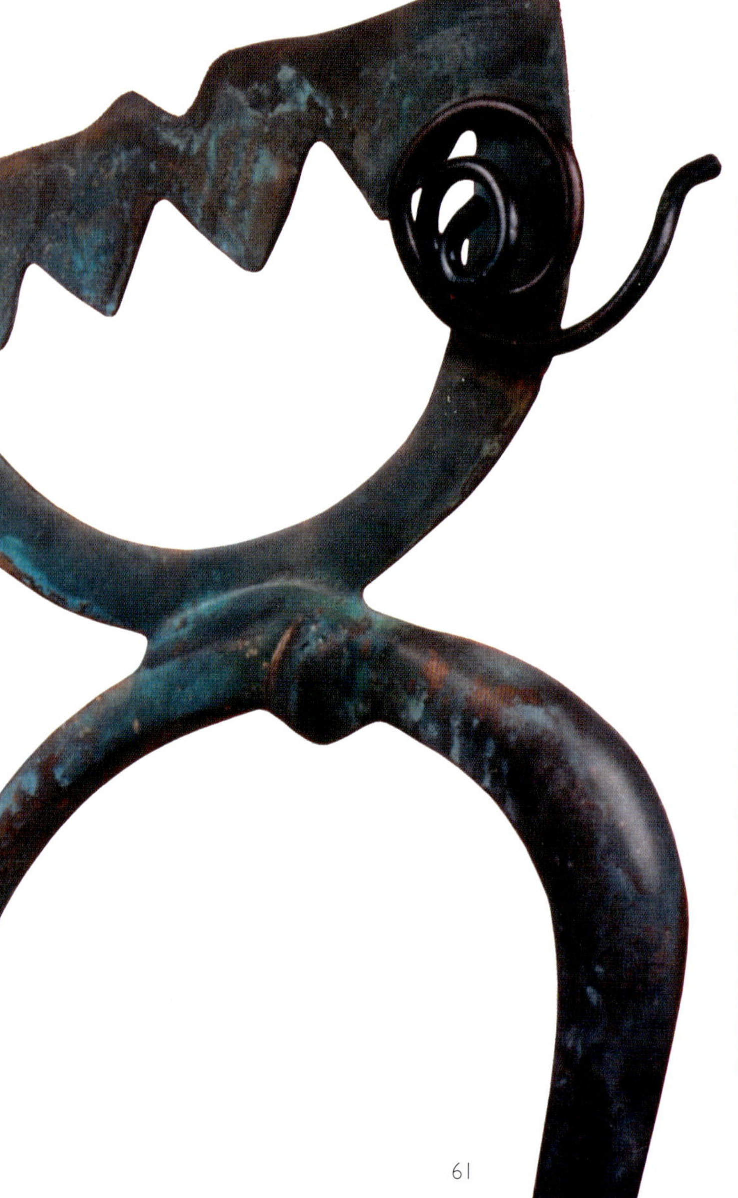

At Hotel Europa. Feel the show is unique. There is a calmness and a soft energy that pulses out of each work. The pressure of stones pushing against each other is quietly obvious – 'postures' that required careful thought – using subtle lines and uncompromising detail (but detail not overriding the importance of the form itself). Joe described the show as serene, a delicate word . . . As I pause and reflect, I feel the show as a whole is very serious. I have tried with a few of the forms to suggest light-heartedness even though that is next to impossible with the weightfulness of stone. The pieces, all of them good, will wear well with time. Each has enough excitement, each has some measure of magic and intrigue with a soft counterpoint.

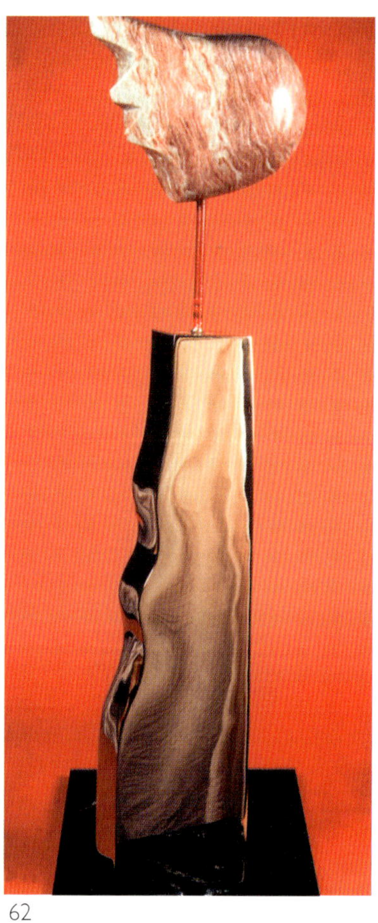

62

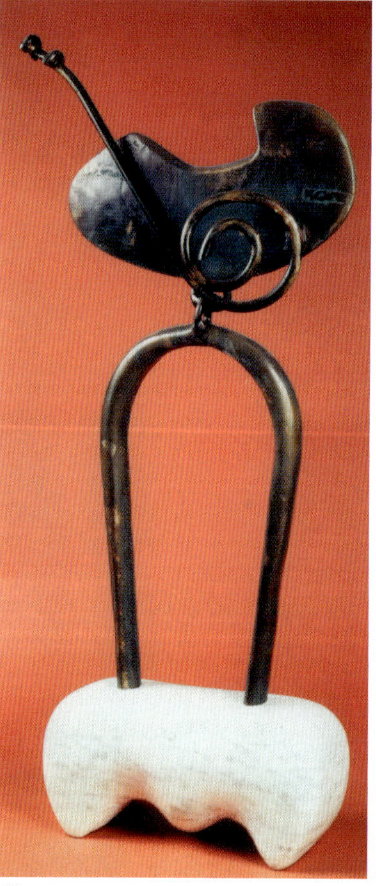

63

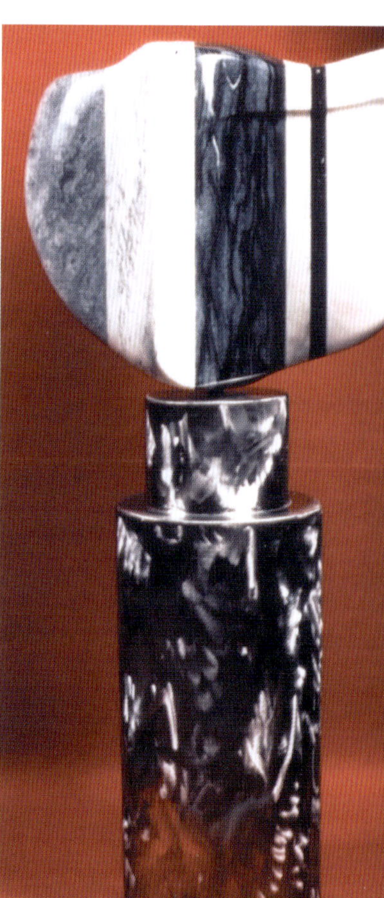

64

61

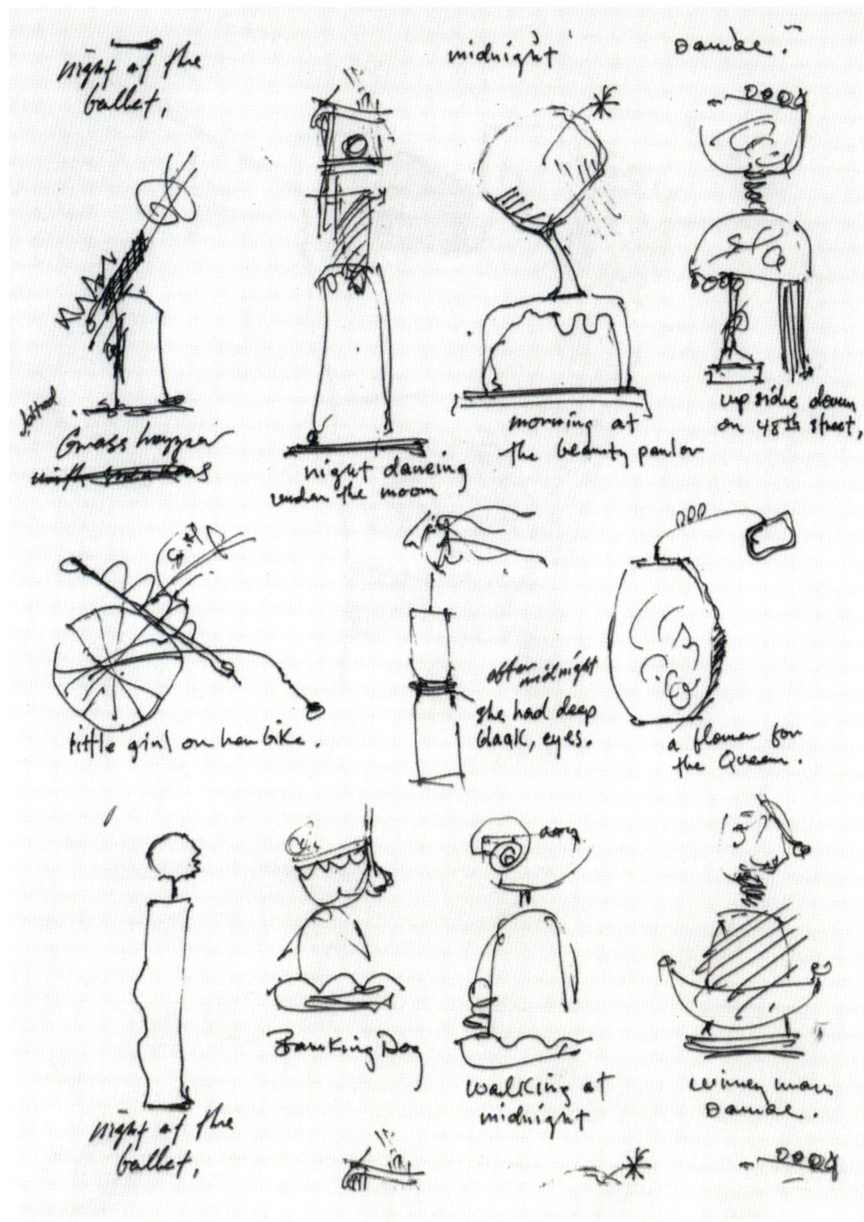

I must find and live truth
if I'm to express truth
through my sculpture...

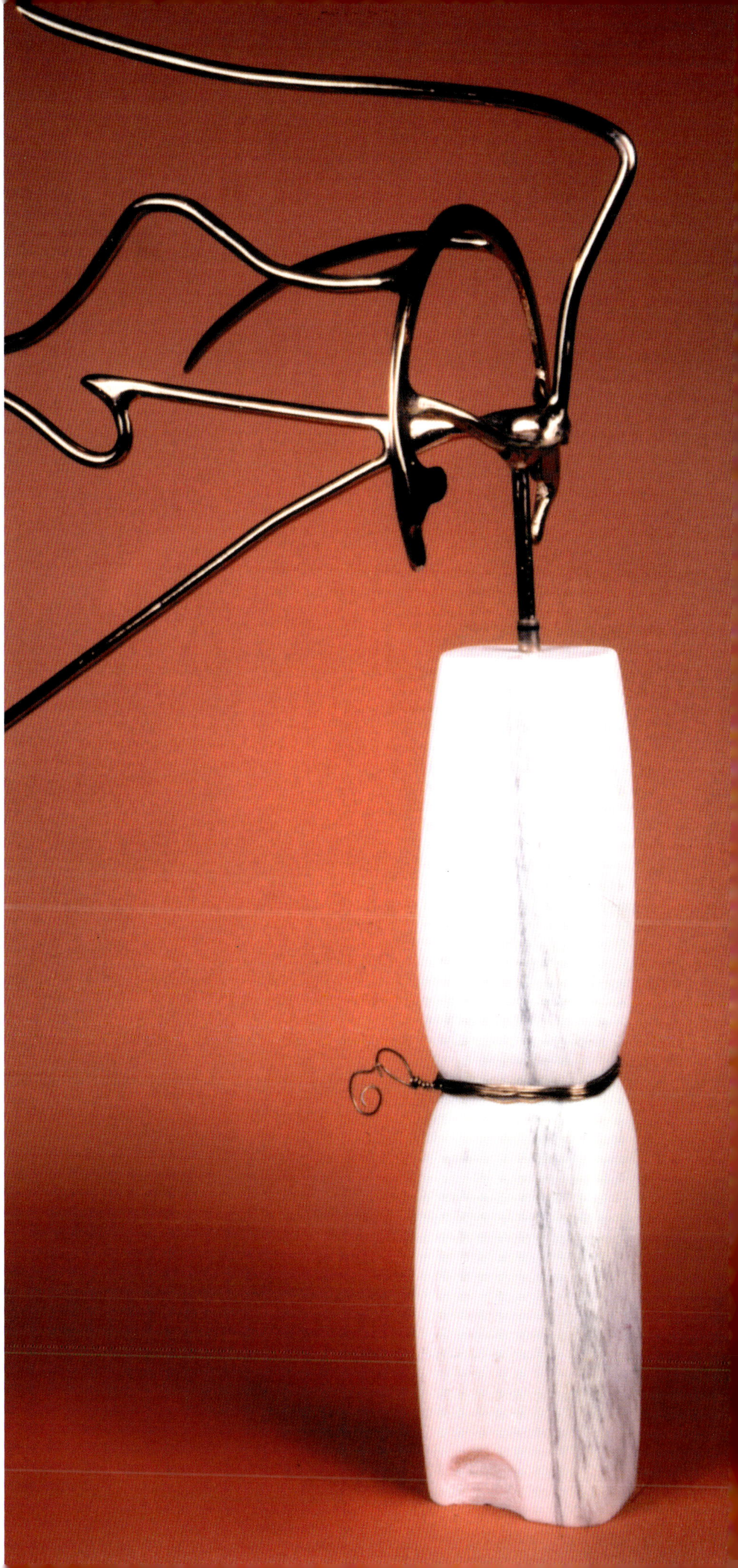

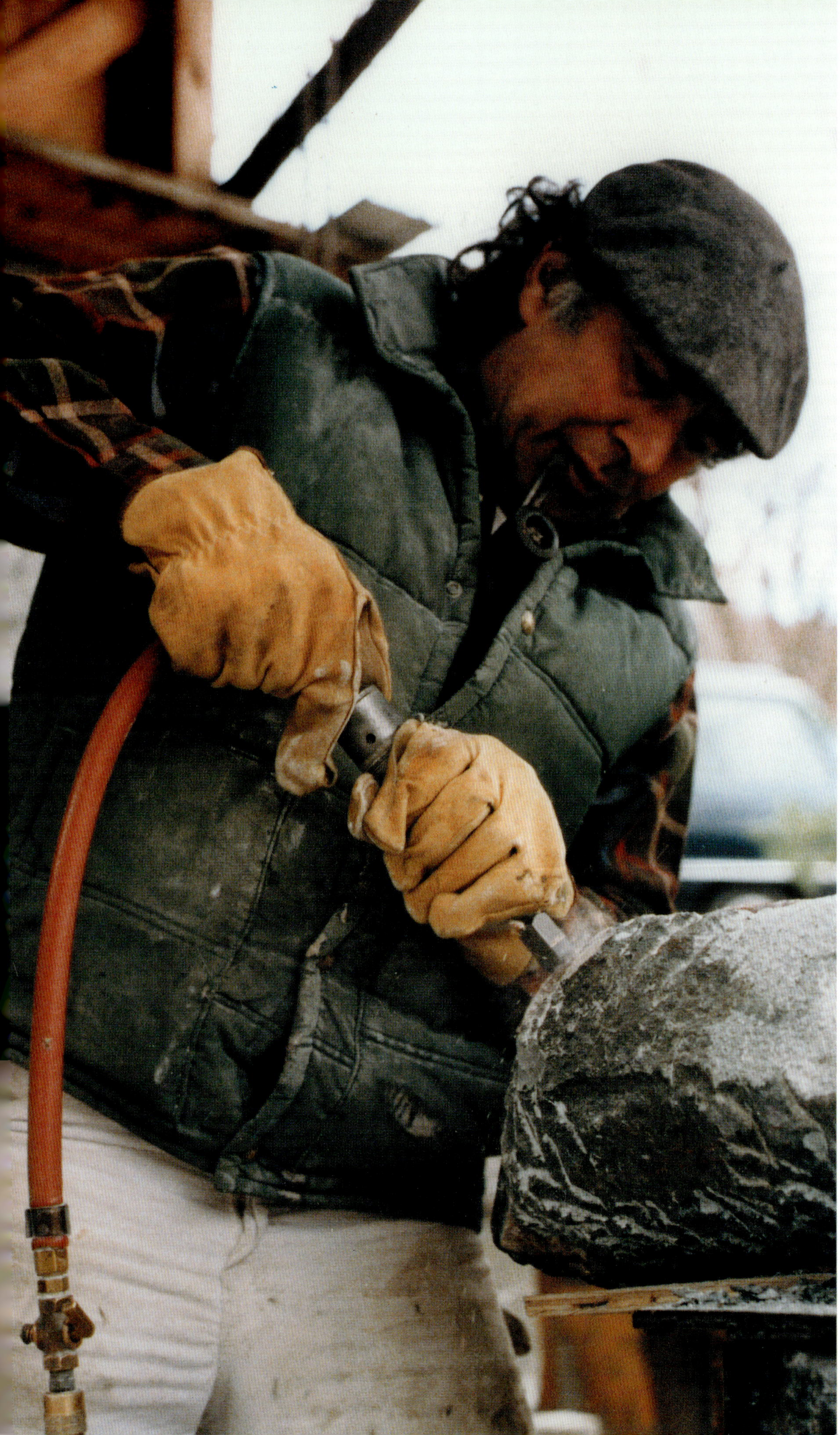

A good-music Sunday morning. Outside it is 15F and windy but bright. I keep having this feeling that Spring is about to happen.

Once again I have to say that life is wonderful. I guess if you are an artist and eat three meals a day and are warm you have beaten Art in this country. I have much, much more than that! In past years, no – but now I'm 'golden'.

Question: How do I get volume in a large piece and yet at the same time not have it appear too heavy?

A rainy Saturday morning. Can't do a thing but relax (ah?), listen to music and try to control my thoughts, try to be calm, try to maintain the illusion of sanity at least for the benefit of those around me. It is hard – almost impossible. I float between those two worlds once more. The eagle and the lion. I know I have written this before, but this time there is something down deep, deeper than ever before, that is saying 'go on, it doesn't matter anymore, let it all go this time'. What I am saying is that I want out. I don't want to be a part of all this. I no longer have that need to be remembered by some act or production. I no longer have that need to be around just in case something good happens. I have no need to grow old. The joys and experiences thus far have been enough for a life.

The person who has gained courage enough to question all things and accept the truth which results is then free to go beyond. If he is able, he can proceed with the issue of growth. Growth, above all else, has to be the most important issue.

To reach this level of thought, the person has to have decided which of two paths to take — to live, or to exist. To live is to grow, to wonder, to pursue all directions yet unknown to the self. To exist is to follow a pattern of life and flow mindlessly, as if serving a sentence. To choose to live requires courage and strength. To maintain the extra energy to ask better questions and pursue the answers, and learn to accept only those which are honest, regardless of how they relate to our perceived notions.

Truth survives. We tend to dismiss it when it doesn't fit or feel comfortable. This becomes confusing. To grow is to allow and meet truth regardless of the consequences. Growth of the self, once again, is the best pursuit we can give ourselves and in turn, give to others.

The word 'selfish' is a positive/negative word. In the positive sense it is important to be selfish — only then can we judiciously determine our needs without guilt. We choose an event, a person, silence, madness, etc, that will promote growth. This is being selective — and the end result is a better awareness of self.

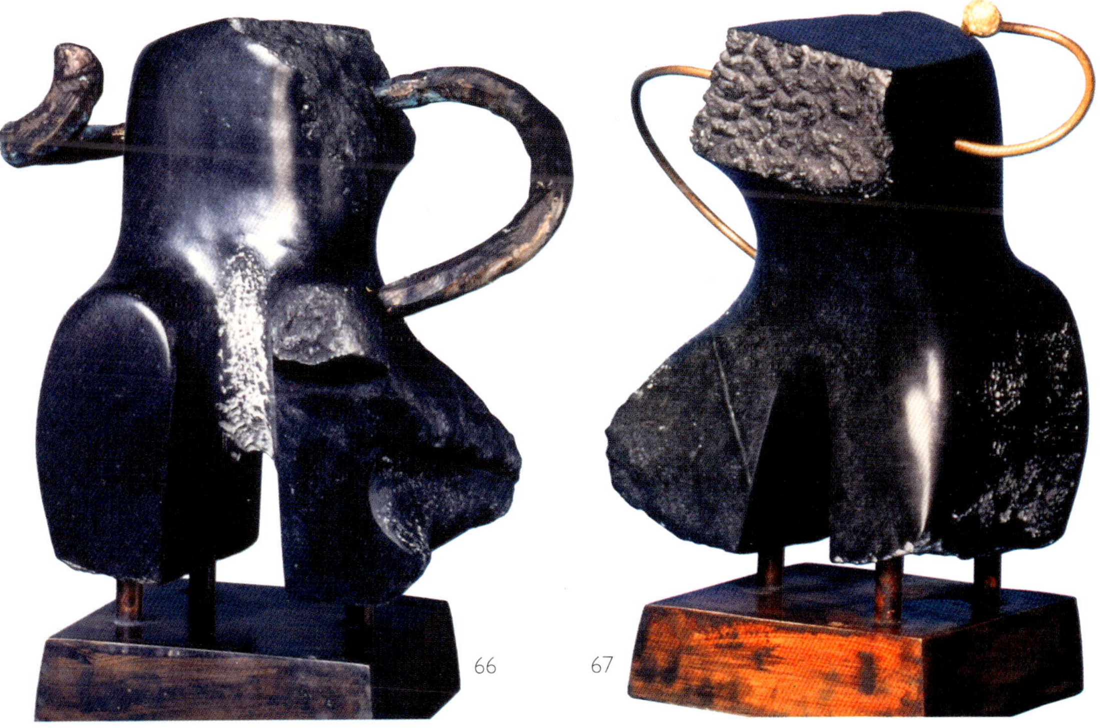

66   67

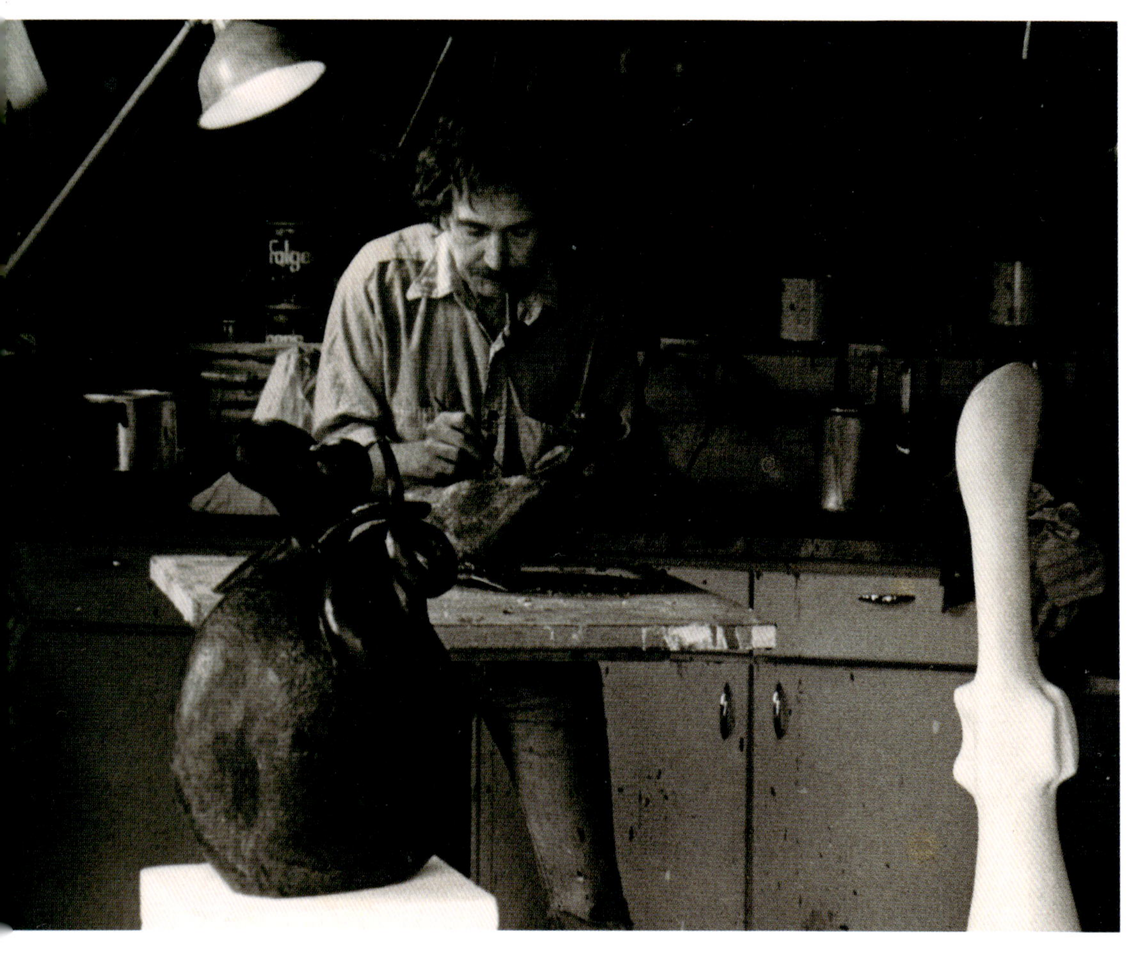

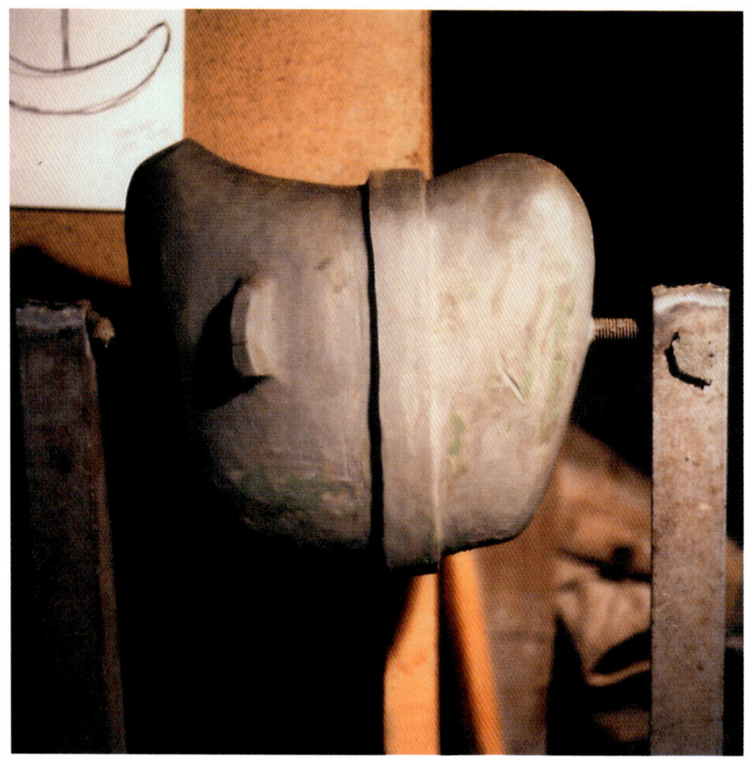

68

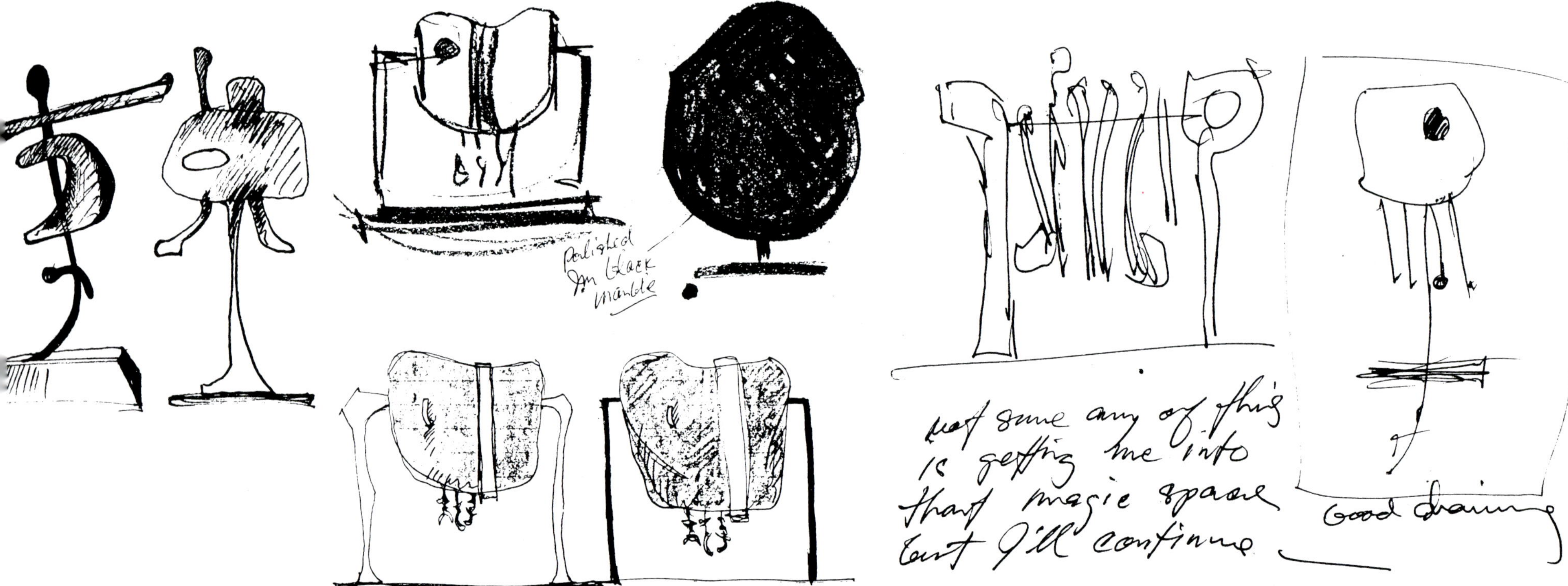

Polished in black marble
not sure any of this is getting me into that magic space but I'll continue
Good drawing

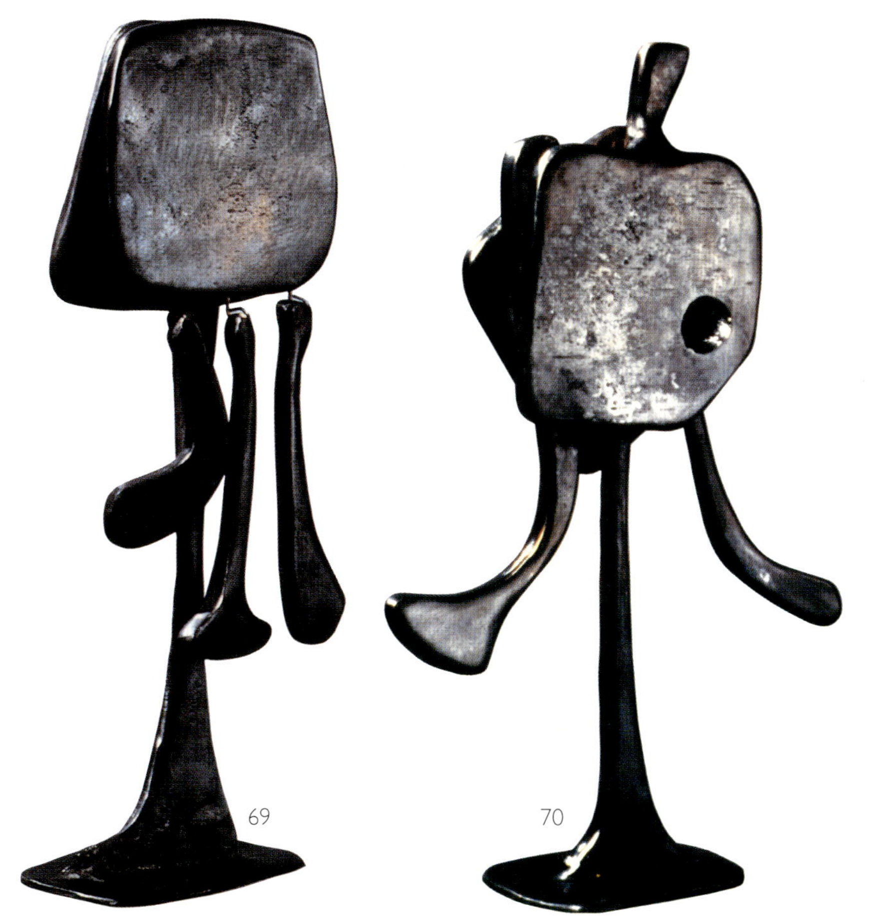

69

70

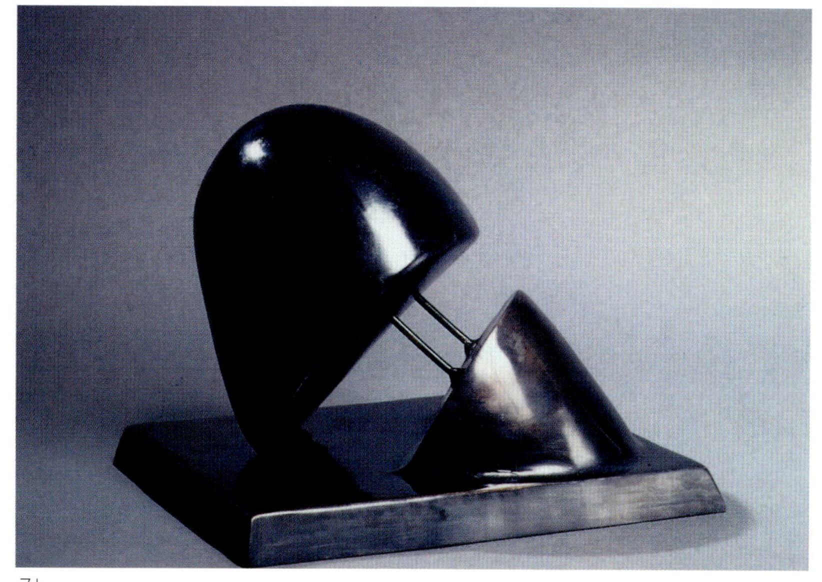

71

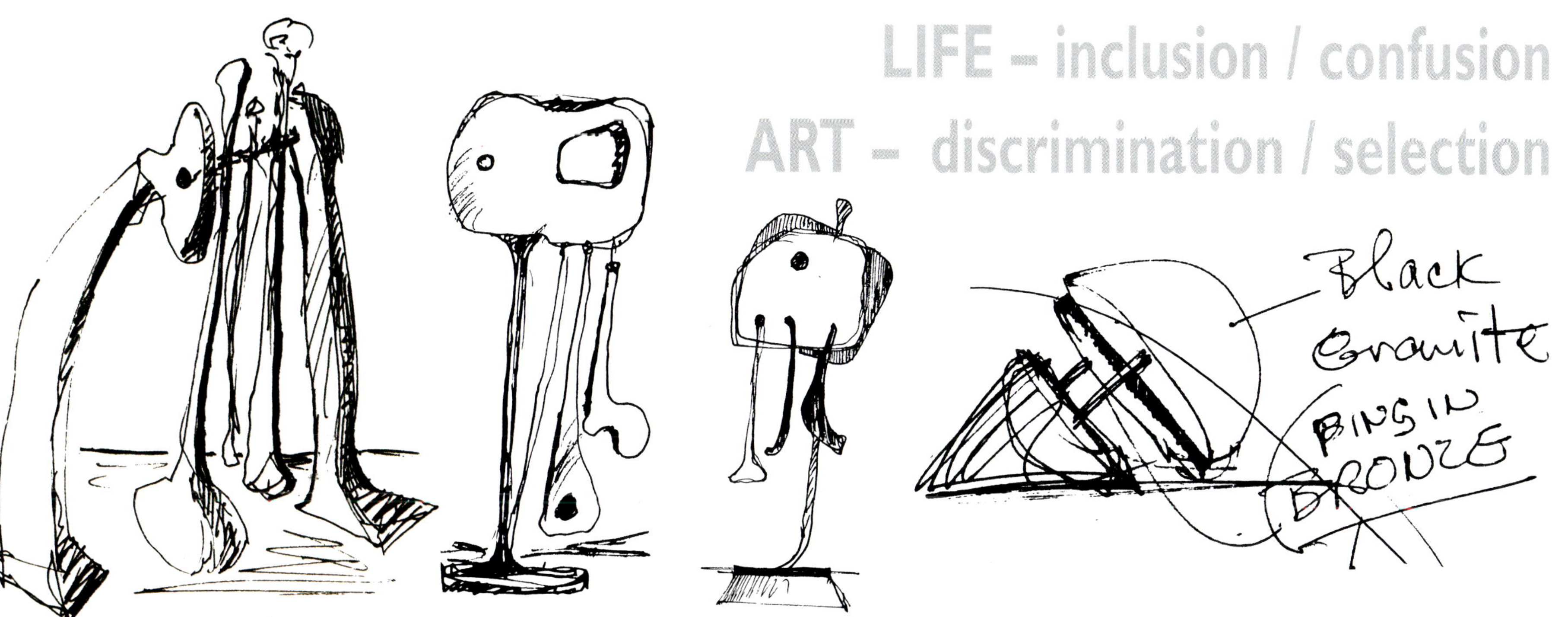

LIFE – inclusion / confusion
ART – discrimination / selection

Inlaid bronze into the marble block – a first for me. I'm not sure what possessed me to do this, but it felt good . . . and while the piece isn't the best it could be, I don't remember ever seeing anything like it, so perhaps it is truly an original idea!

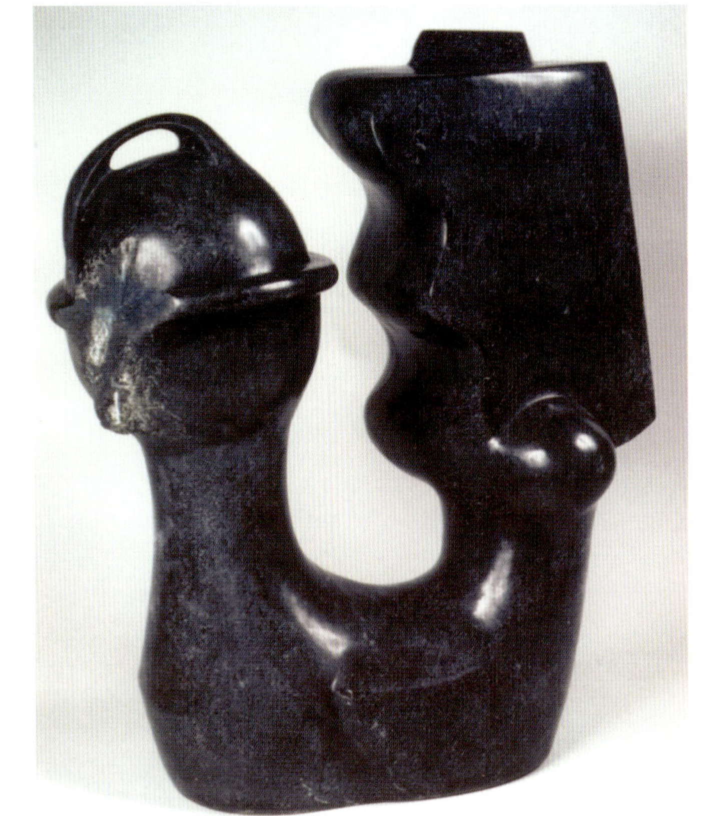

72

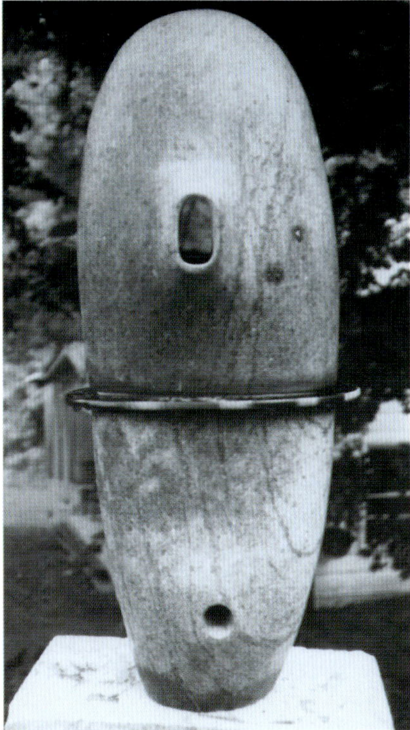

73

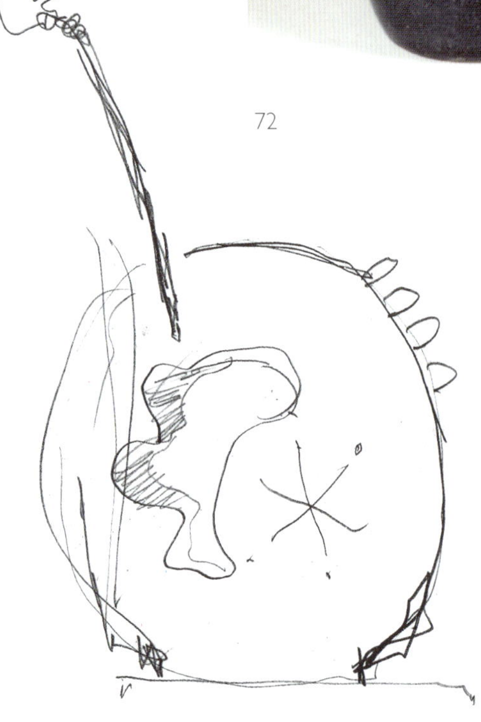

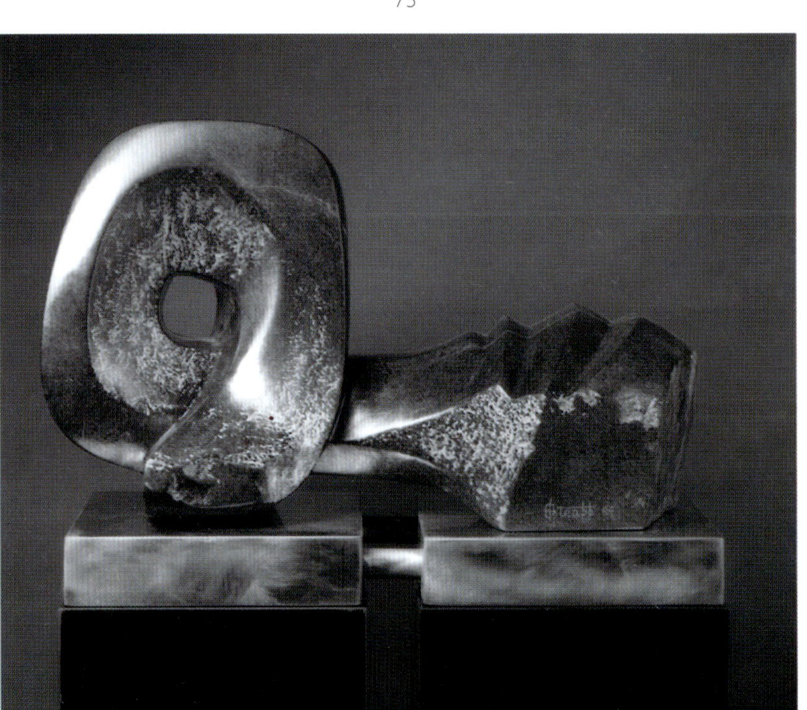

74

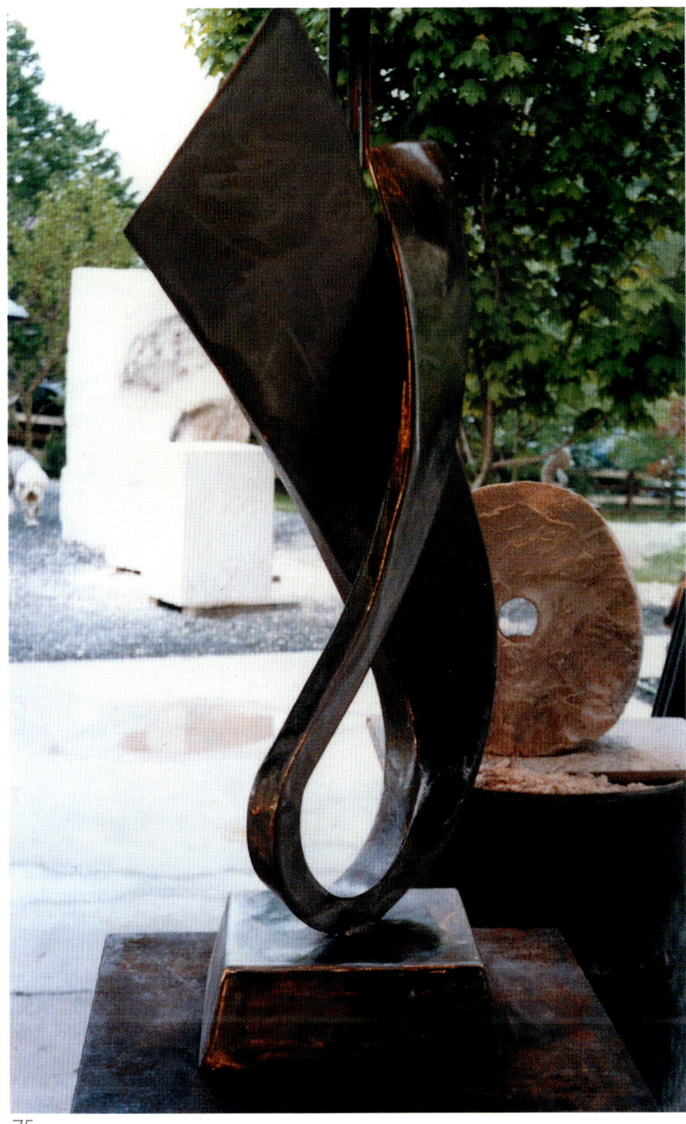

The fight for simplicity is so complex …

…I have the feeling that this is the real turning point. Have been doing so many drawings, it's impossible to record them here. At least two a day, and today I did two reliefs. The reliefs are concerned with the two people in man. Good/Evil. Flesh/Spirit. Lion/Eagle, etc. Will continue with this theme until it ends. On the way to the library now for more books on primitive man's art and ice-age sculpture. Need to have better quality paper to continue this series on. Also need a new journal without lined paper.

…and so it goes, the delicate balance of man. Alone vs. together. The joy of sharing vs. internal awareness and self. The pain of aloneness vs. the joy of giving and being with someone — of receiving and doing and having done for you. The inability of controlling the loss of energy vs. the energy of another force.

It's the thought
process — Have
to change the habits
get rid of safe
thoughts

How?

Go deep inside the self
trust the genes
and take the simplicity from
the East. work!

Ritual is essential – the anticipation of ritual, actually.

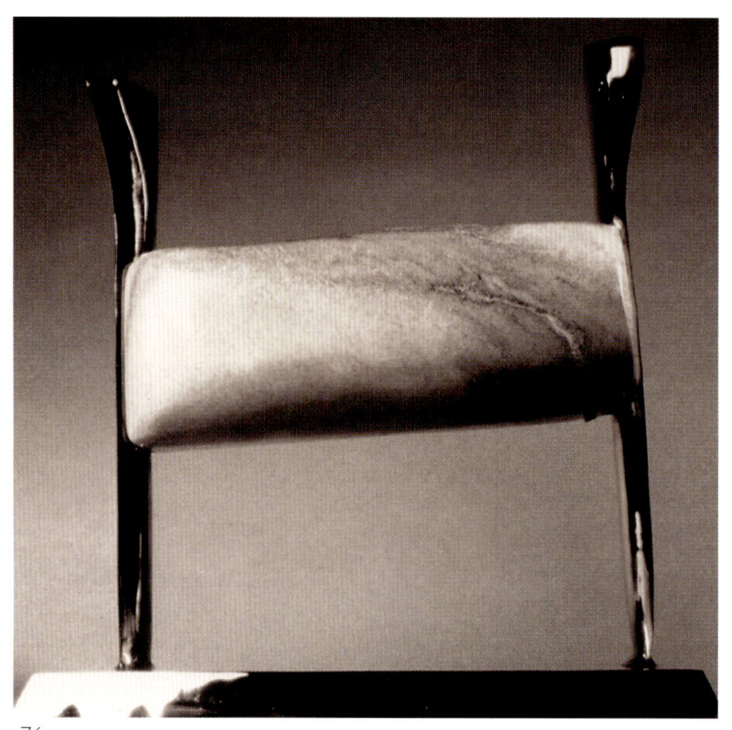

76

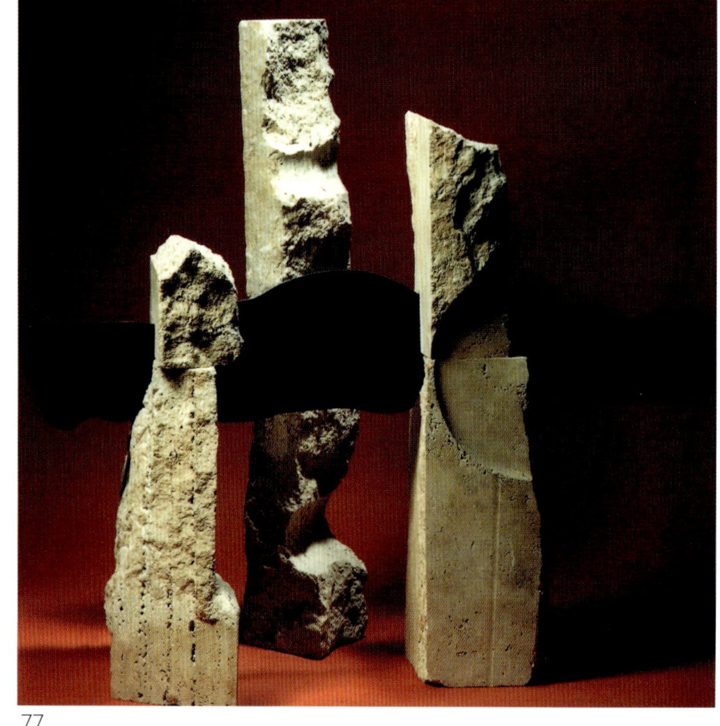

77

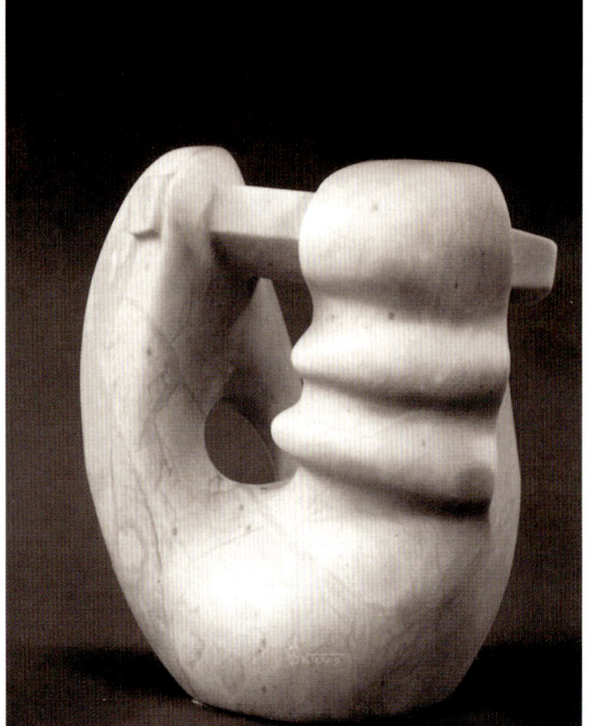

78

I know death, therefore I know life. Klee said that too. On his grave are the words "I can not be grasped in this world, for I am as much at home with the dead as with those yet born – a little nearer to the heart of creation than is normal, but still too far away."

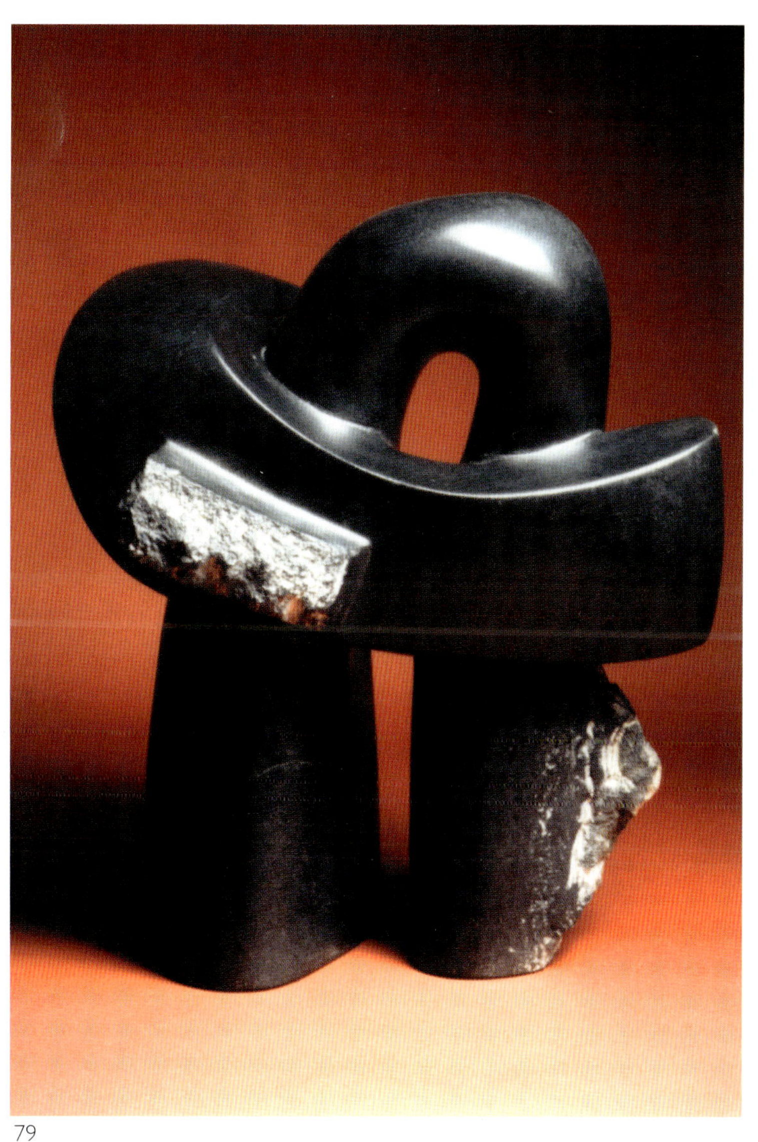

And then,

just as the earth's juices

were about to produce spring,

you arrived making birdsongs apparent,

sunrises and sunsets intoxicating,

moon bright as day, grass greener,

skies once more cloudless.

You transformed the 'hill' into a

Greek island as it had once been.

Who are you anyway?

What magic do you

carry in your long body?

How dare you inflict conflict

into my world. You see,

I had just convinced myself that the

'hill' was just a hill and that

Winter would come.

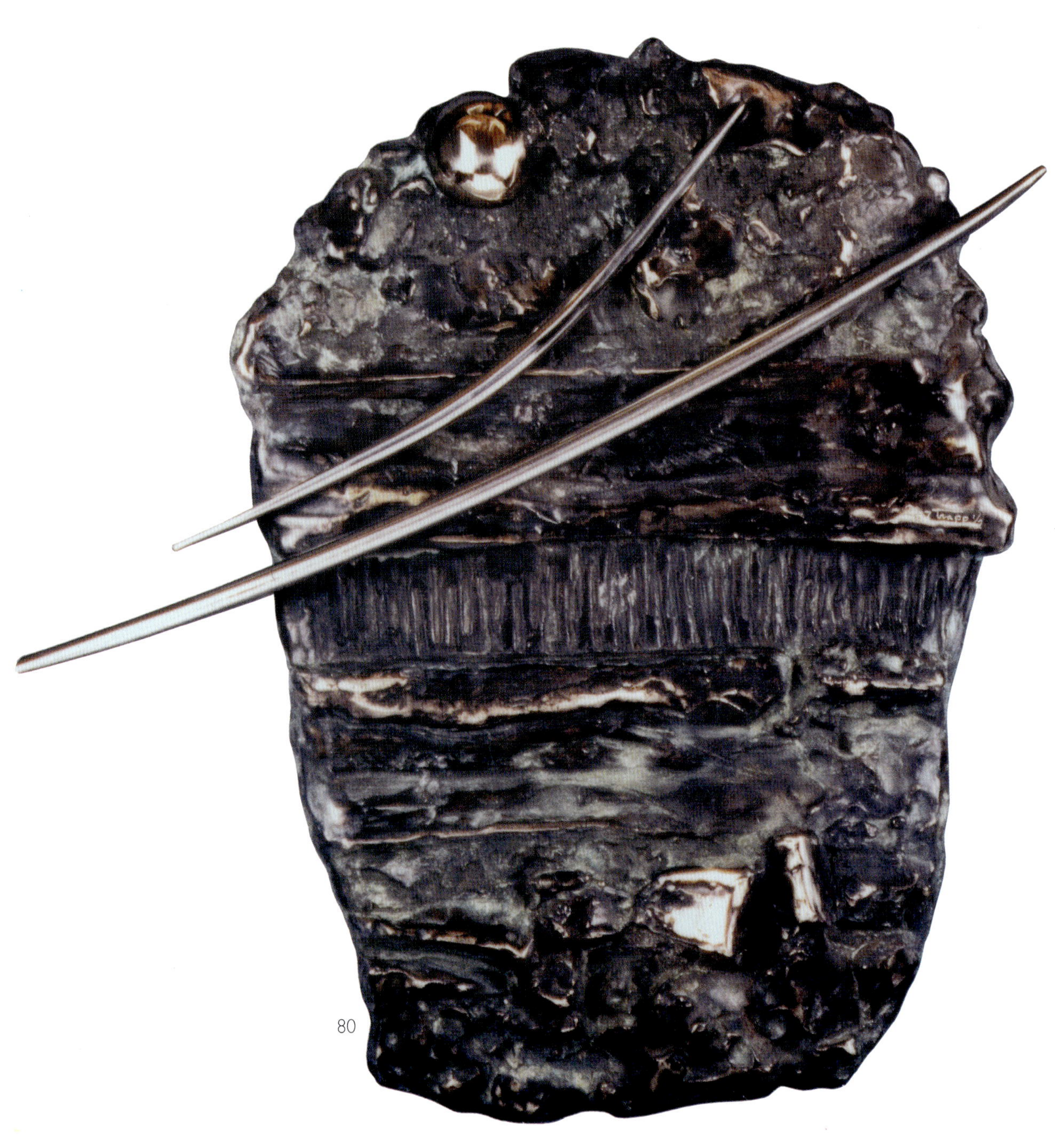

80

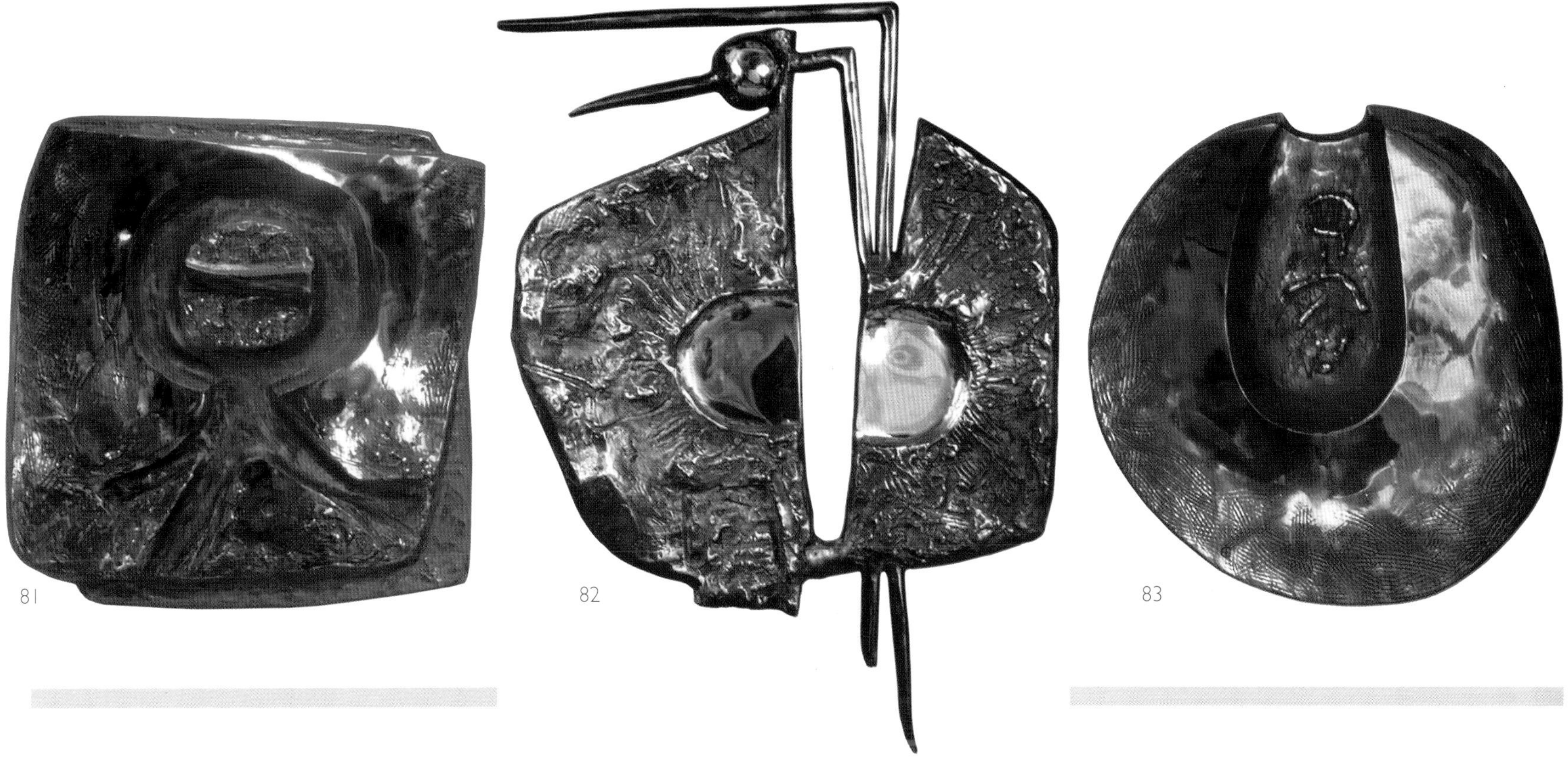

81

82

83

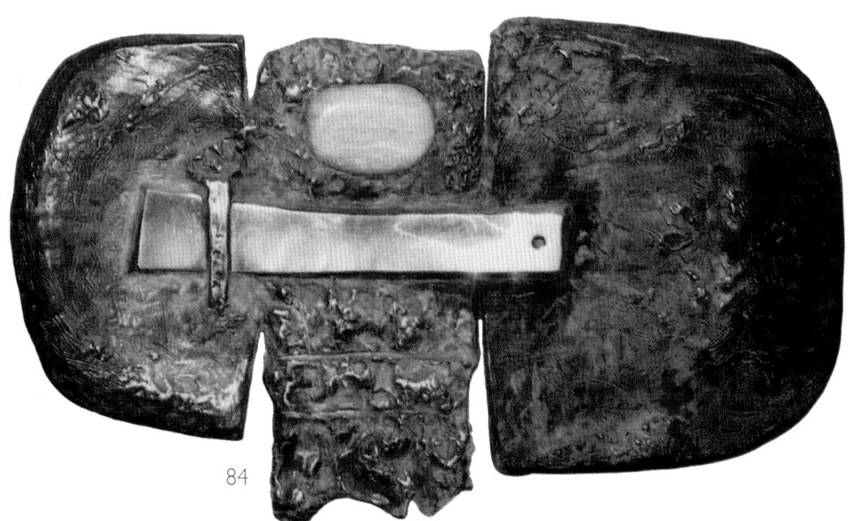

84

I must find and live truth if I'm to sculpt and express truth through my sculpture. Life is a gift. Man must live it. One interpretation of this is to control your environment so that you can live naturally and as you see fit – it requires one to become completely selfish, to think of and consider only the salvation of the self – no one else should matter. That's how I must be. That is the only way I will be able to sculpt the truth of man as I see it. Free to walk as I choose, a yes, a no, as long as I choose.

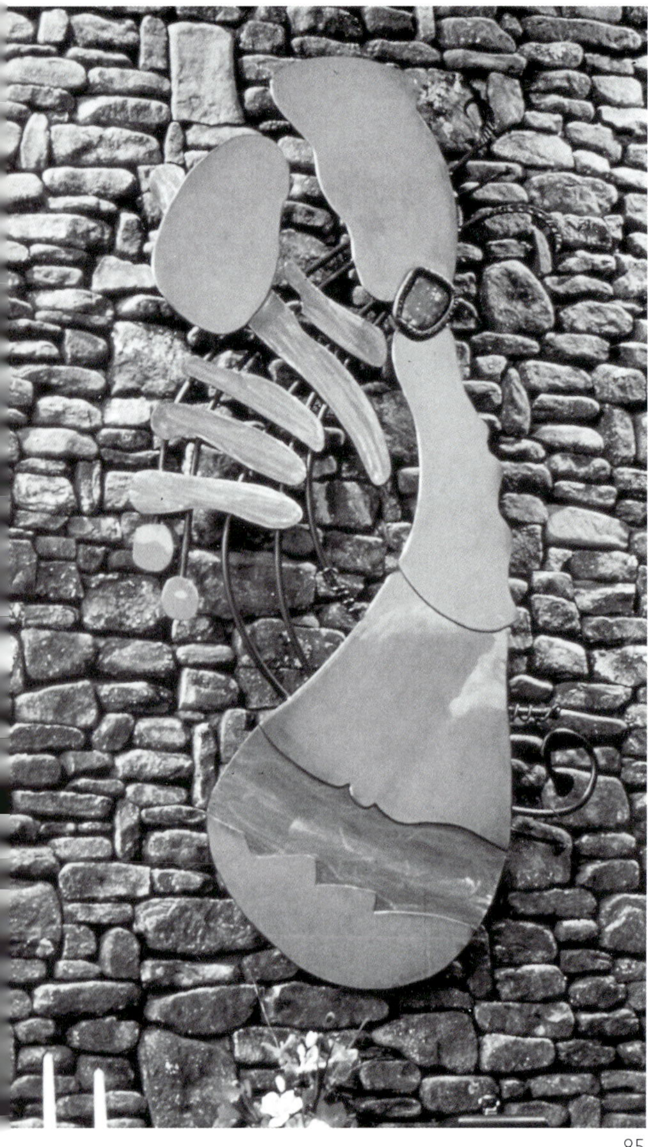

85

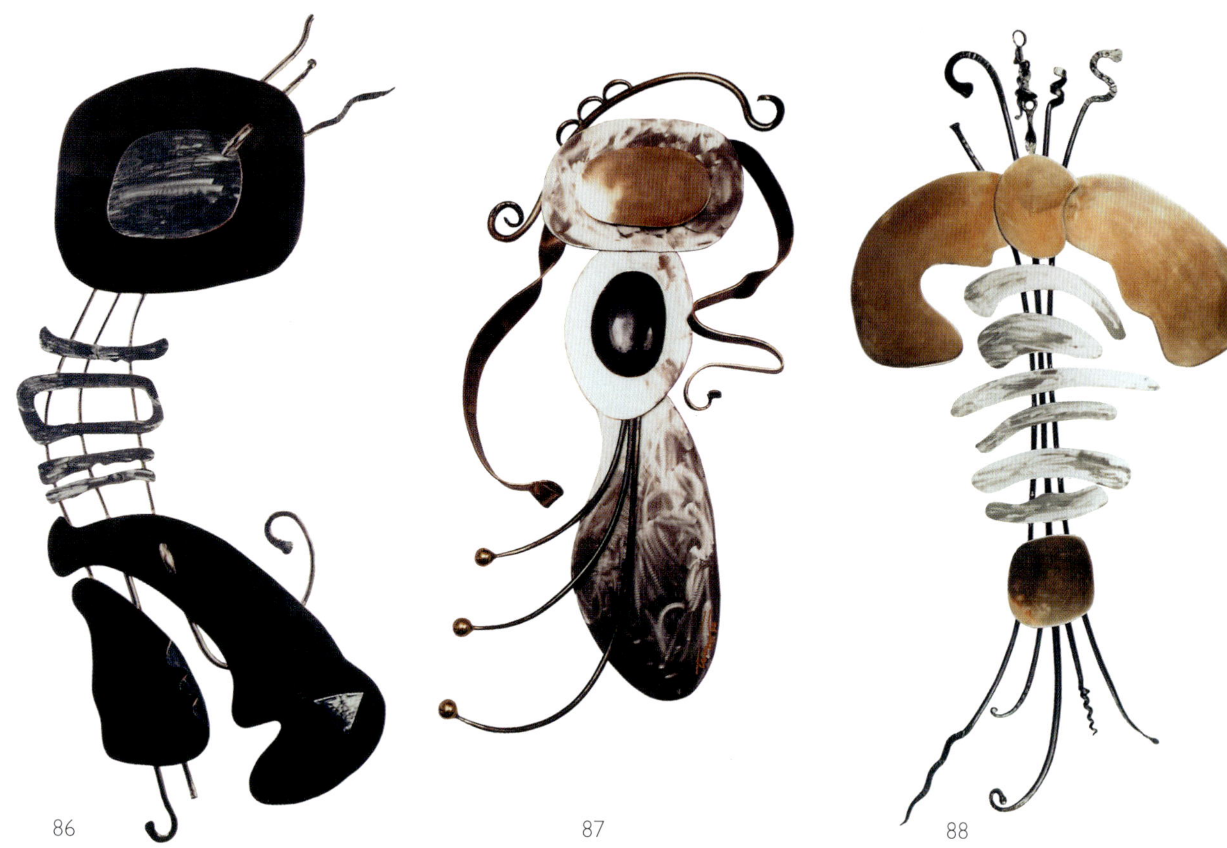

86   87   88

That old thing I've felt about life applies to my

world of art: We never know what we really want,

but by pursuing everything of any interest, we

discover that which we don't want or need or

require – then we are free, and grow.

What a crazy thing … the lady who commissioned the first of these jewel-like wall pieces was so lovely and sweet, I gave her a broach in the same design … it's become a habit now … the giving of small broaches … where do I go from here? – I can't become a jeweler!

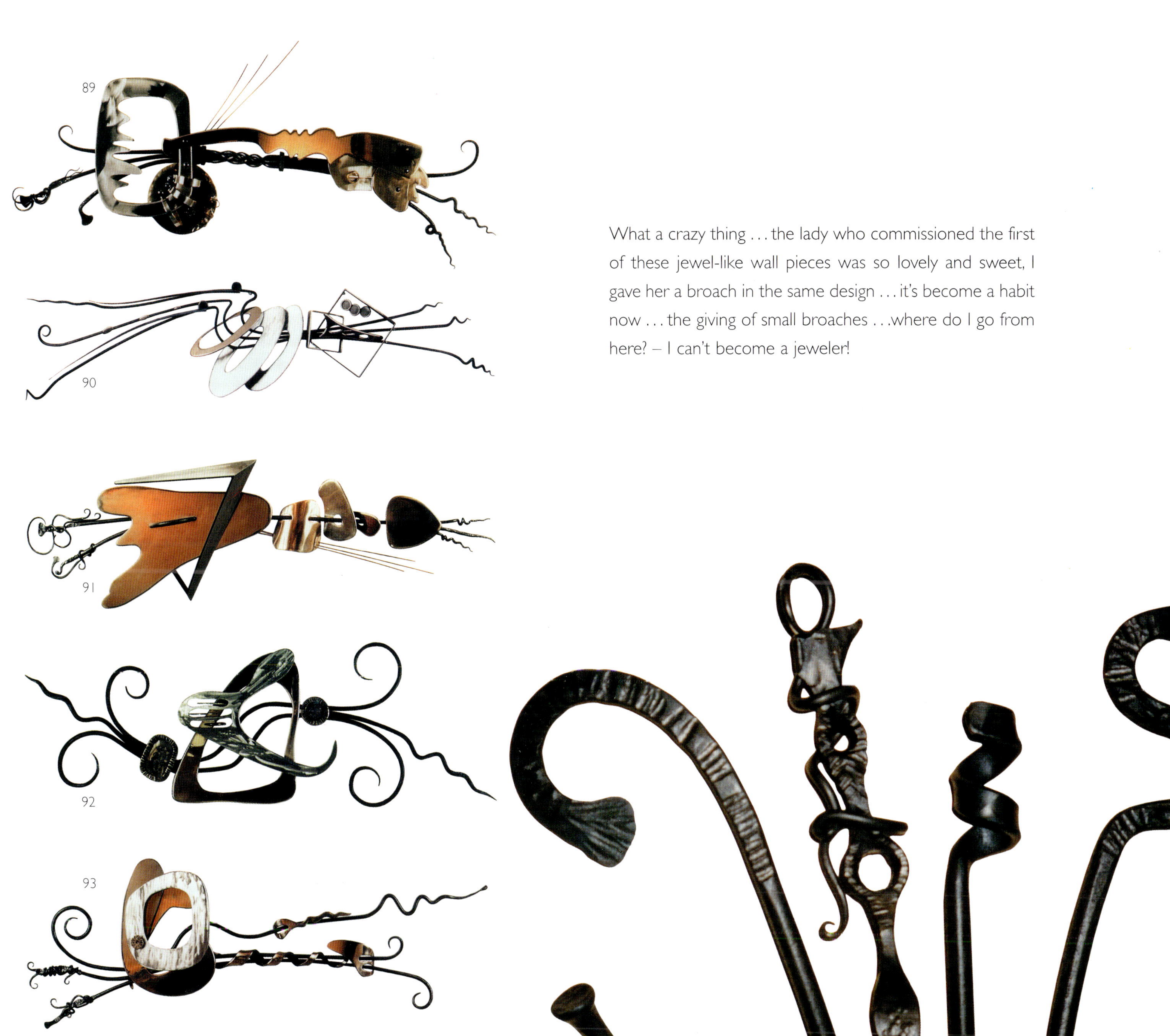

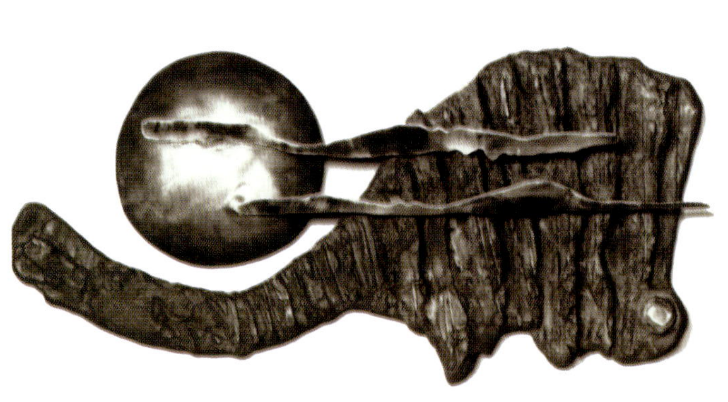

94

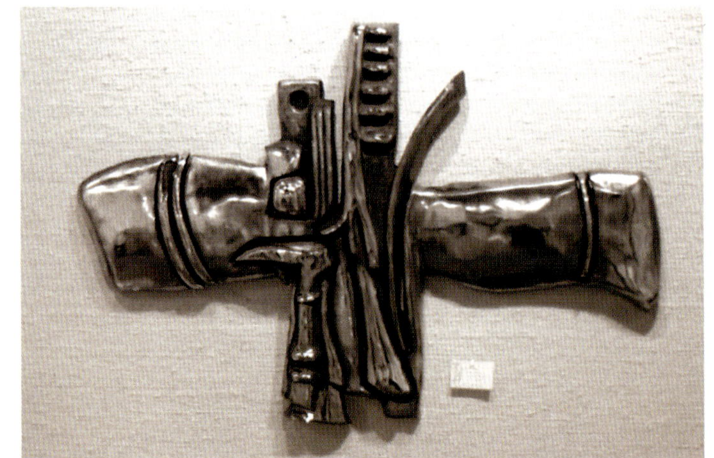

95

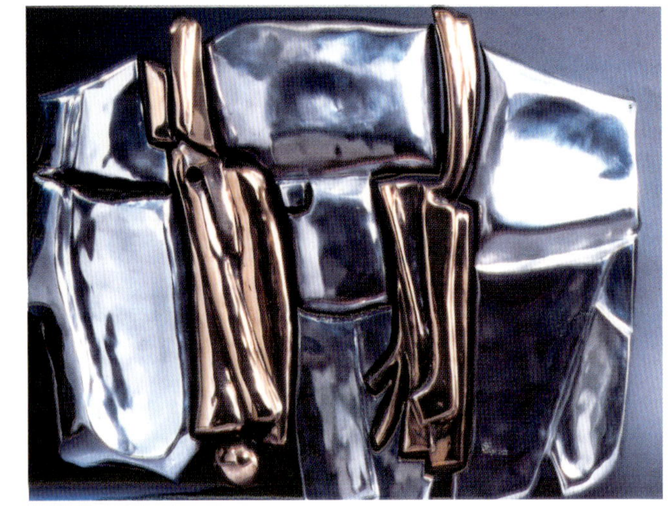

96

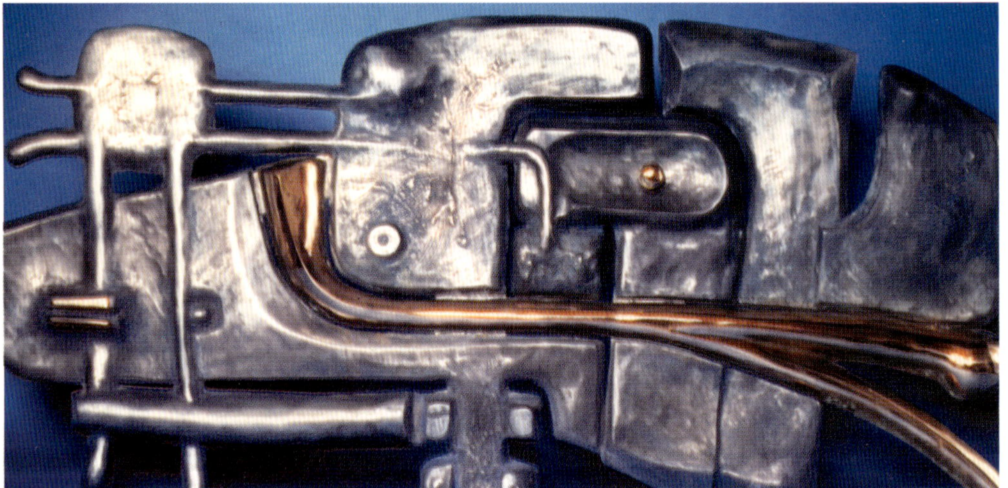

97

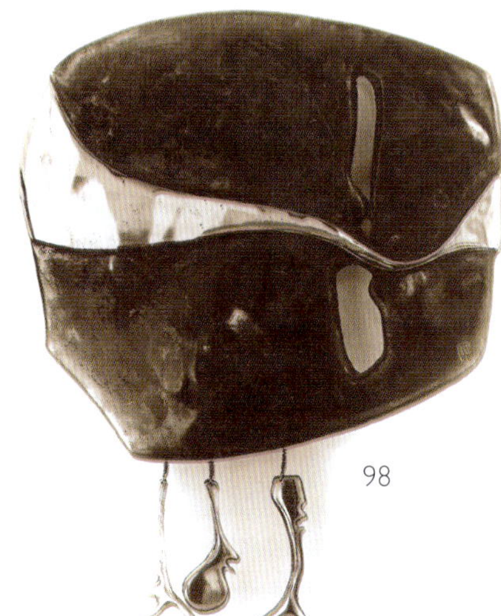

98

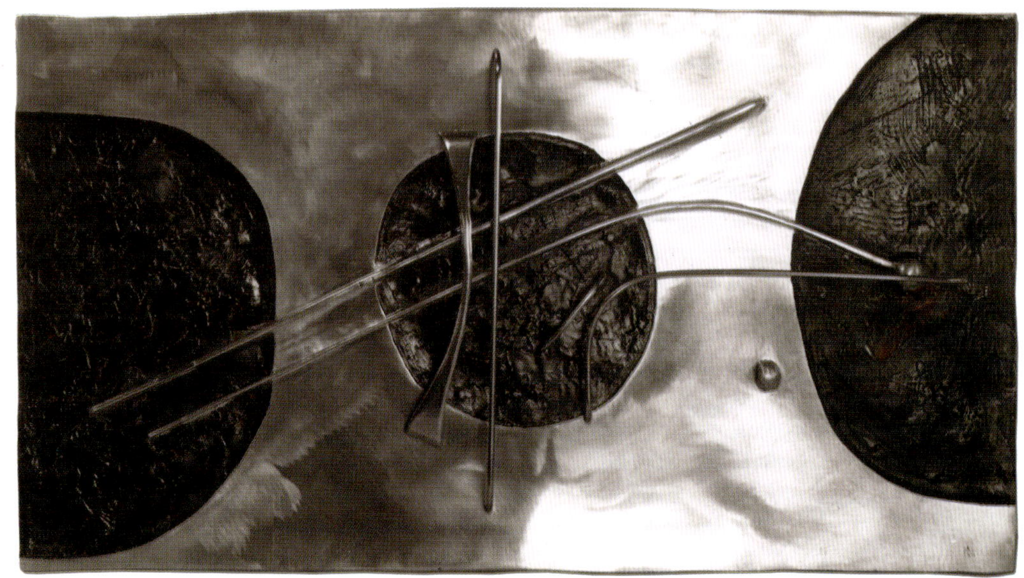

99

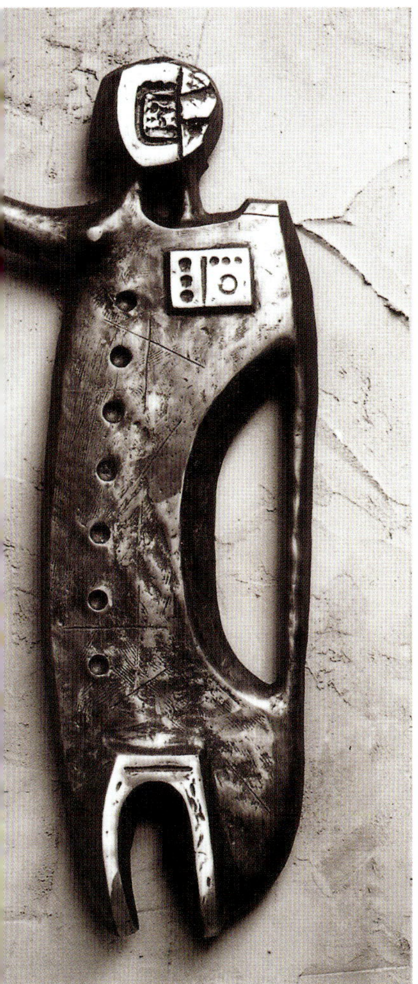 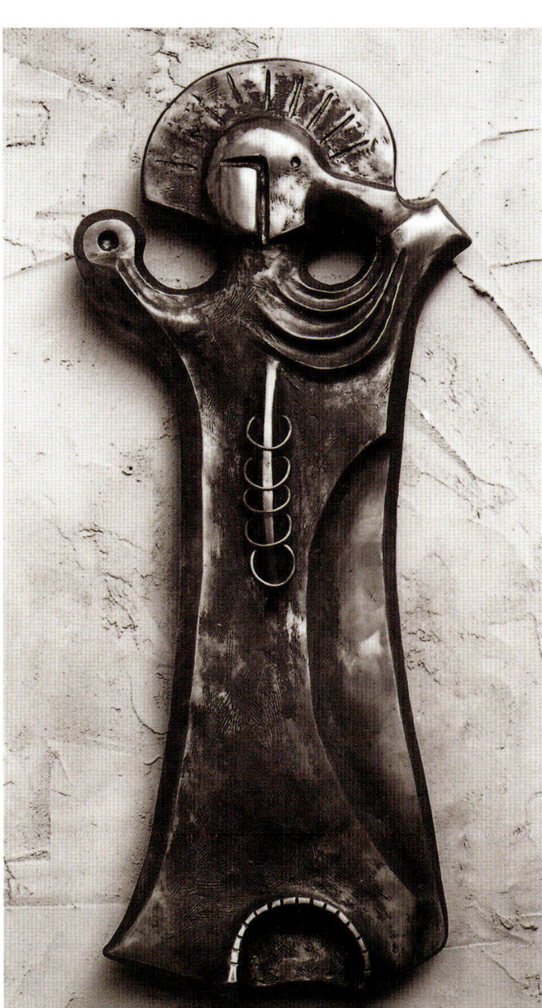 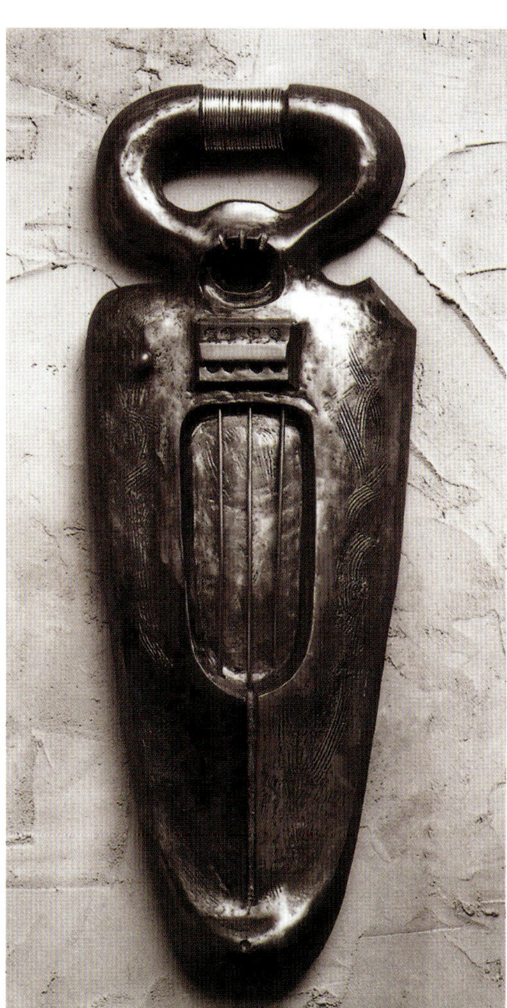 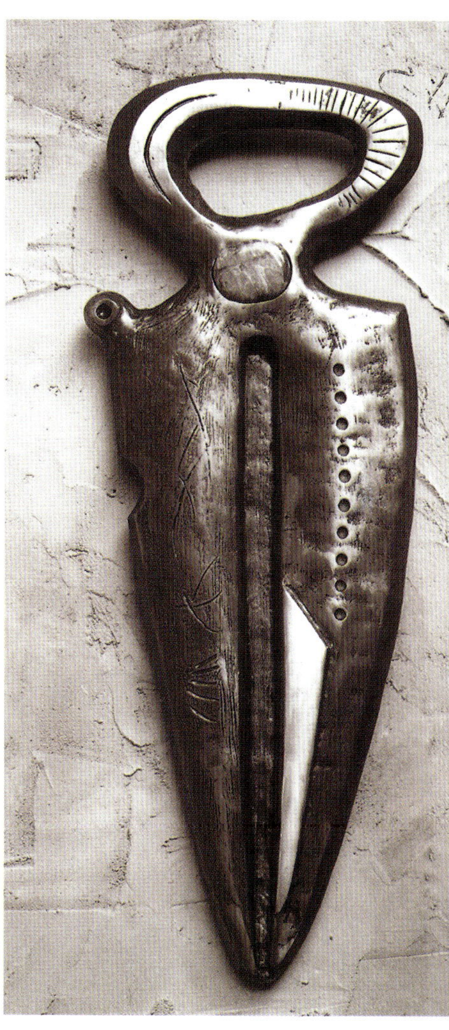

I keep going between 'form' and 'figure' – the two extremes – flesh and the spirit …

It seems that I'm working in two forms again. This has to be OK. I have to be free to invent, to respond to the idea and emotion of it all.

Each form takes me a bit closer to that new level of development. A long ladder to climb – the rungs are close together – the progress very slow, almost non-motion.

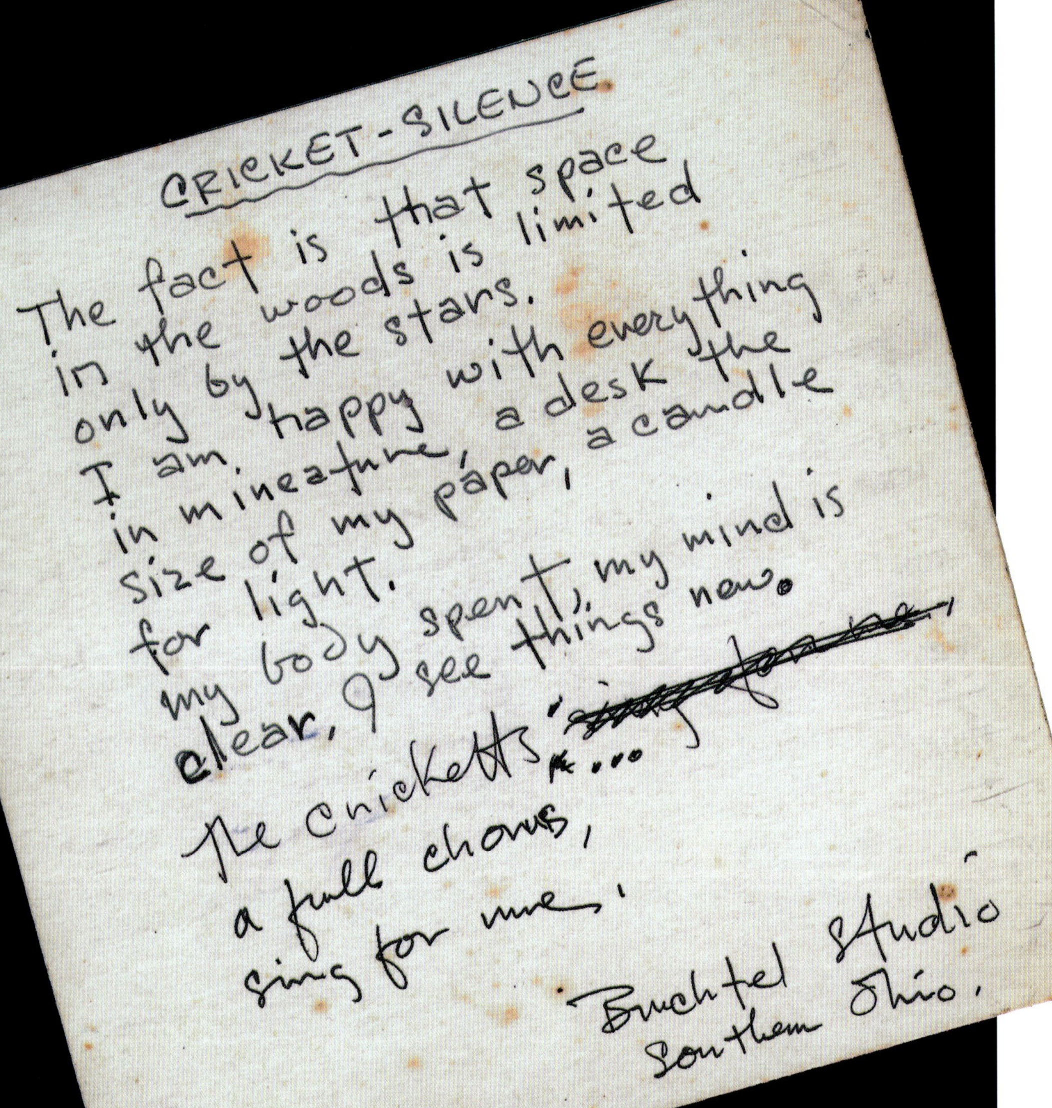

Just finished book on Klee. What a beautiful spirit. Am understanding his work a little better now, but still far away from 'knowing' it.

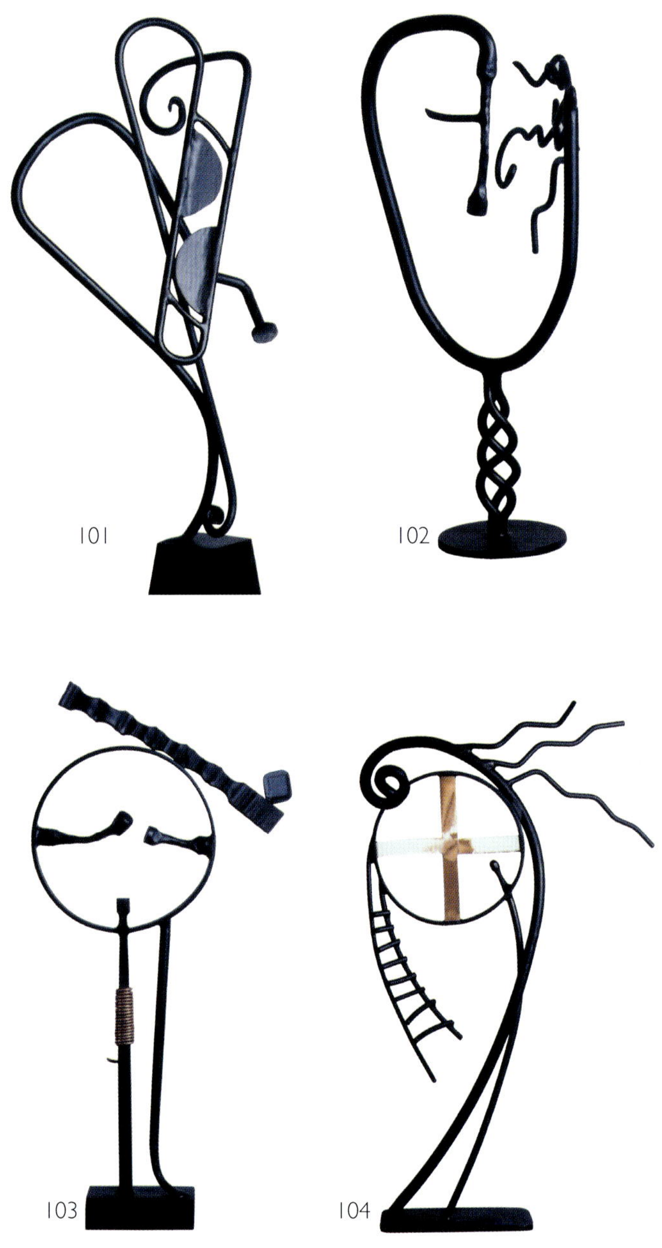

101

102

103

104

The eccentricities are what determine the quality of life . . .

Sometimes an idea has to be done to think it through. The end result either works or is trashed (unless someone buys it before I have a chance to destroy it).

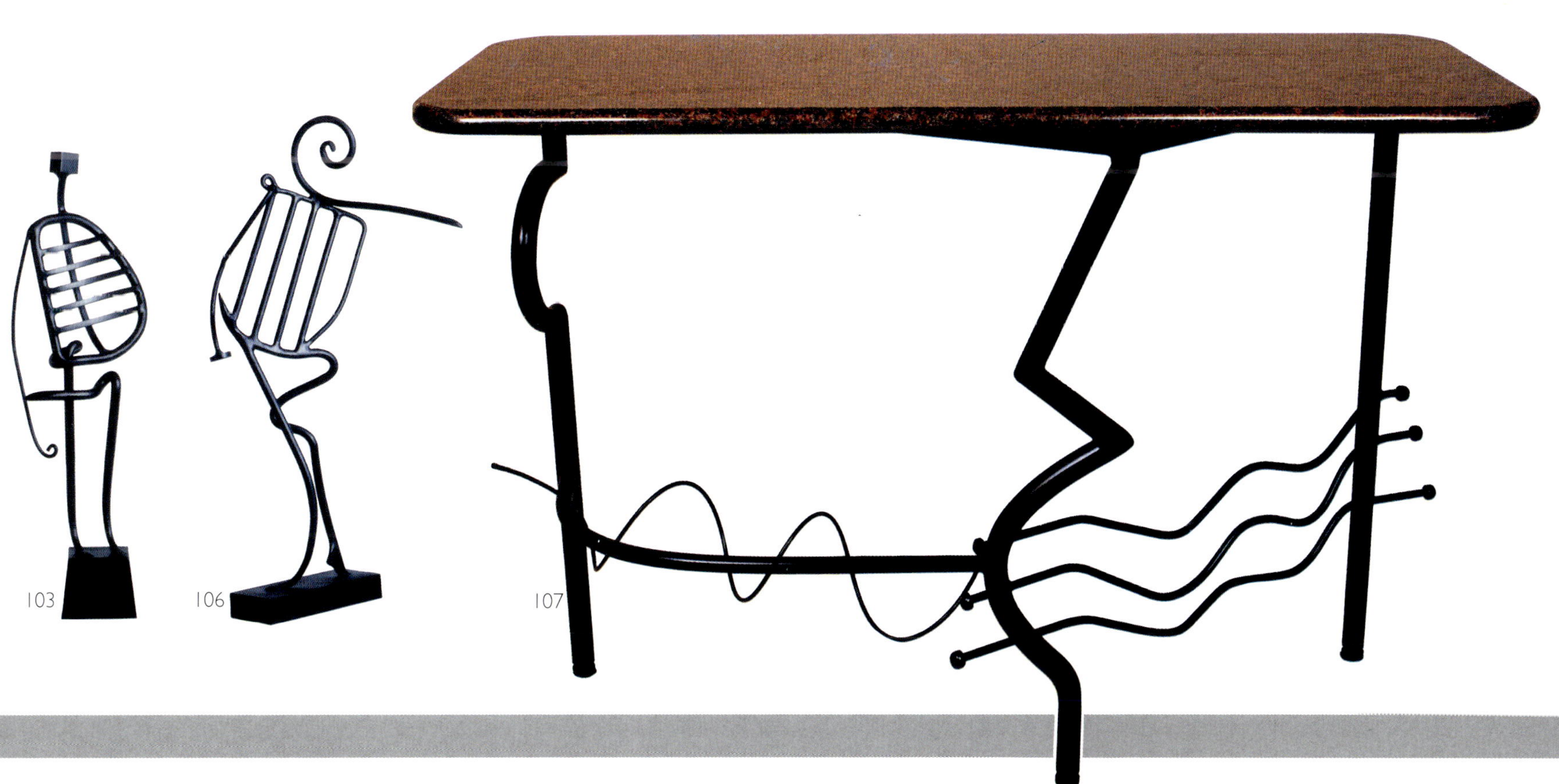

103

106

107

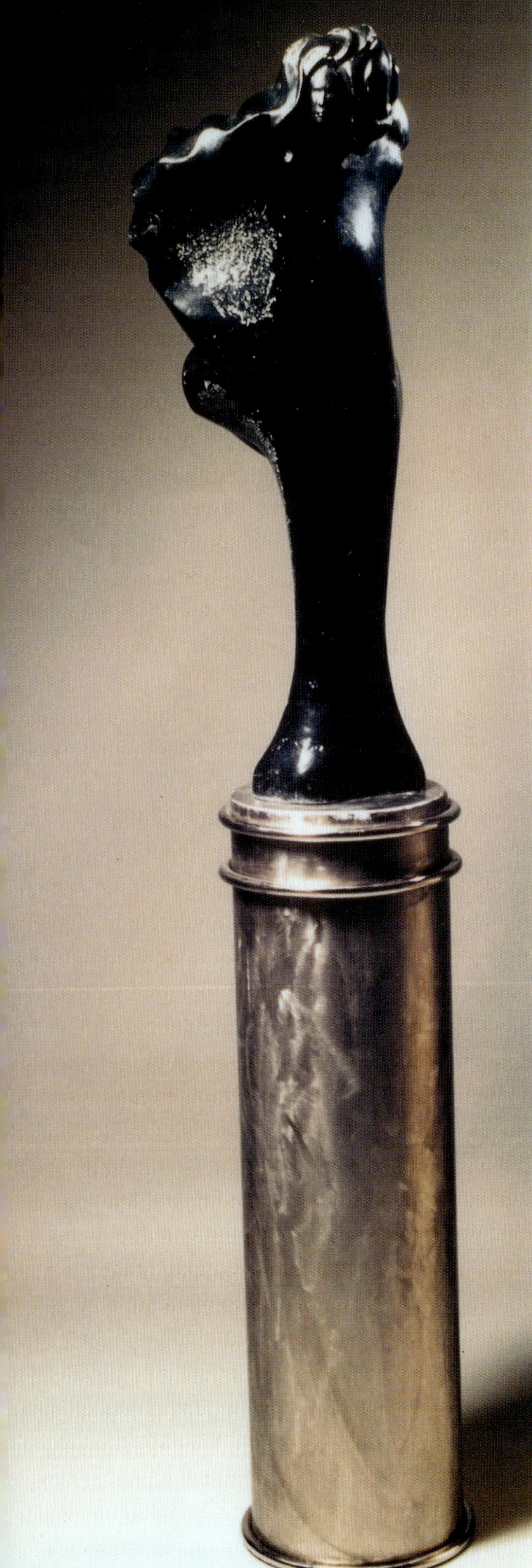

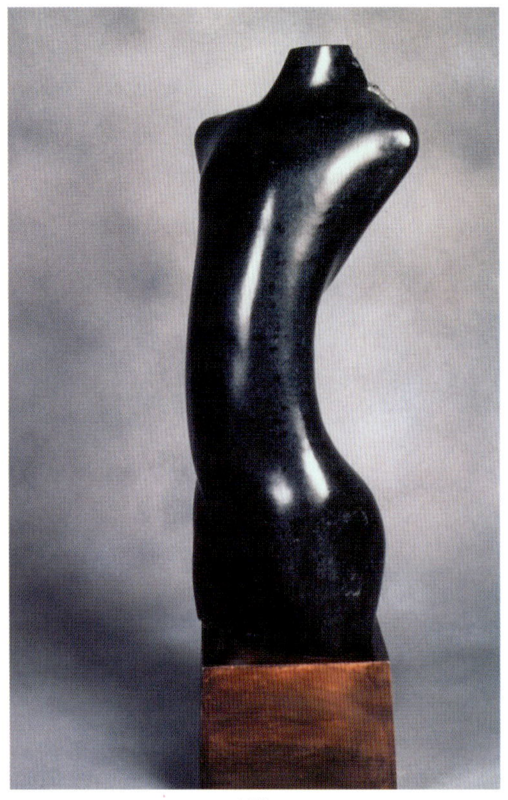

112

Artistic growth – refining of the sense of truthfulness.

Again, a conflict about truth. What is good sculpture? The most recent piece I've done was inspired by a rock formation. The transformation is mine. The resulting form is unlike any other I have ever seen – but is it really mine?

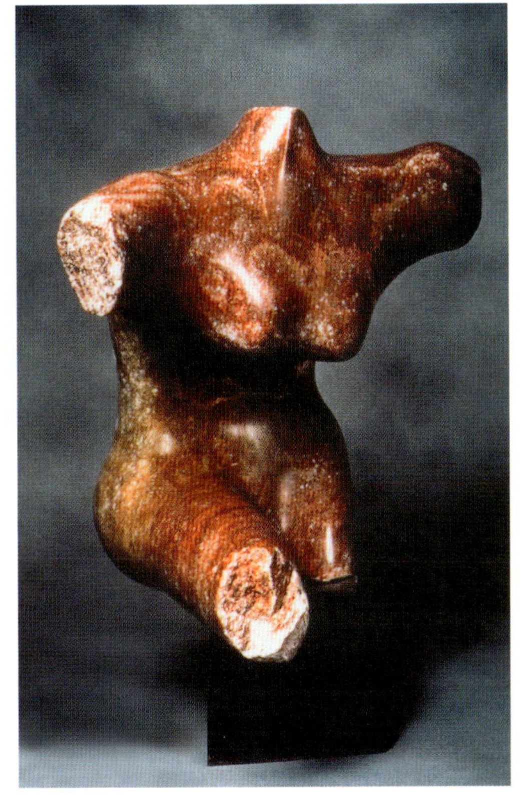

113

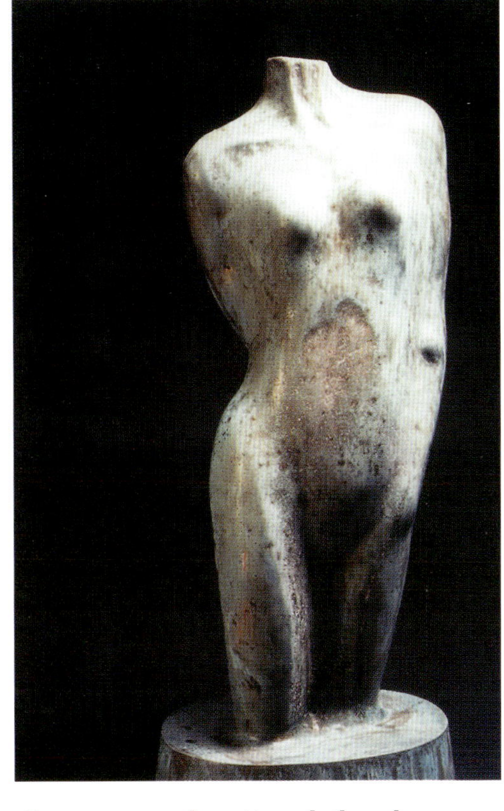

Some people attend the dance...

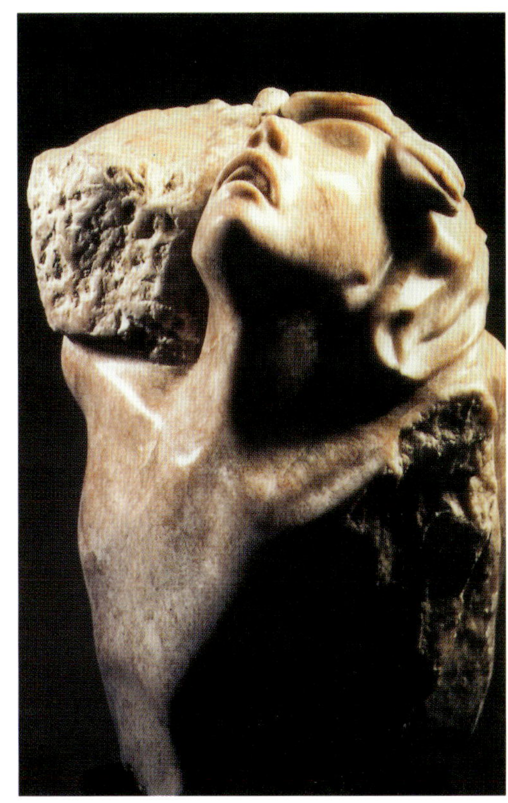

115

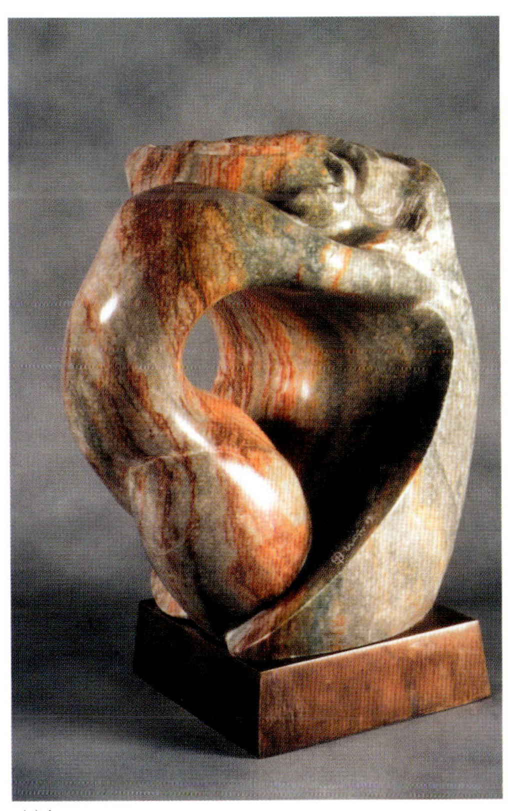

116

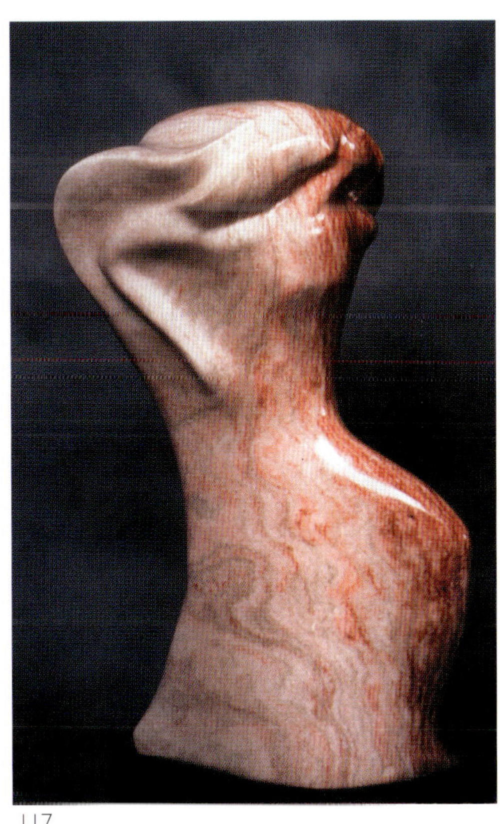

117

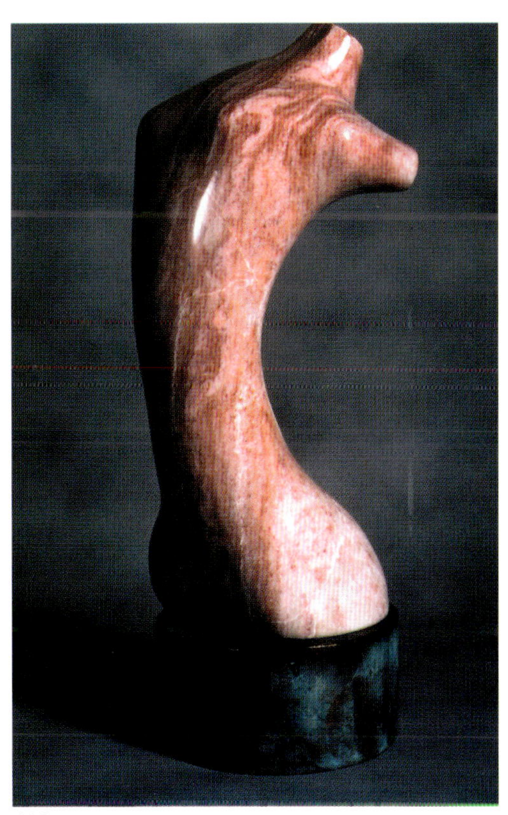

118

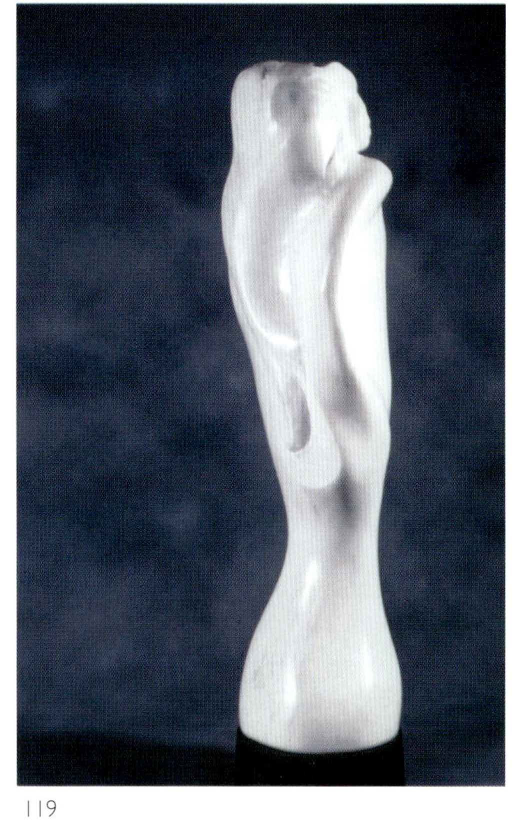

119

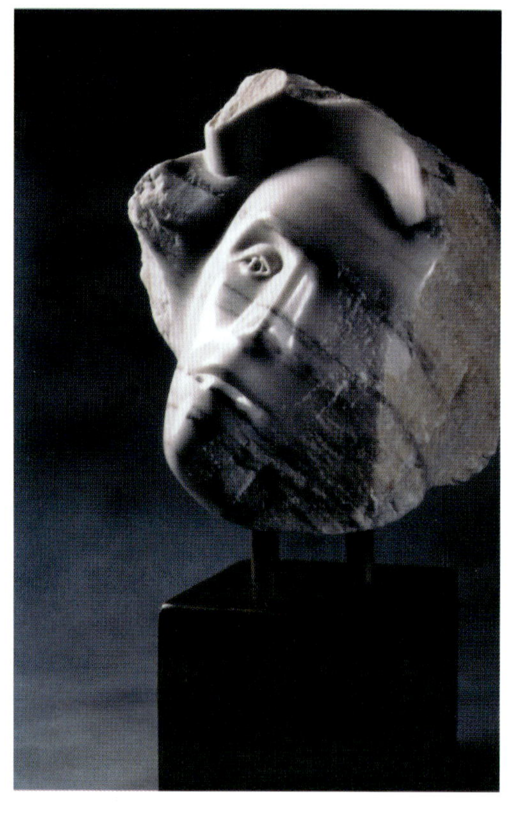

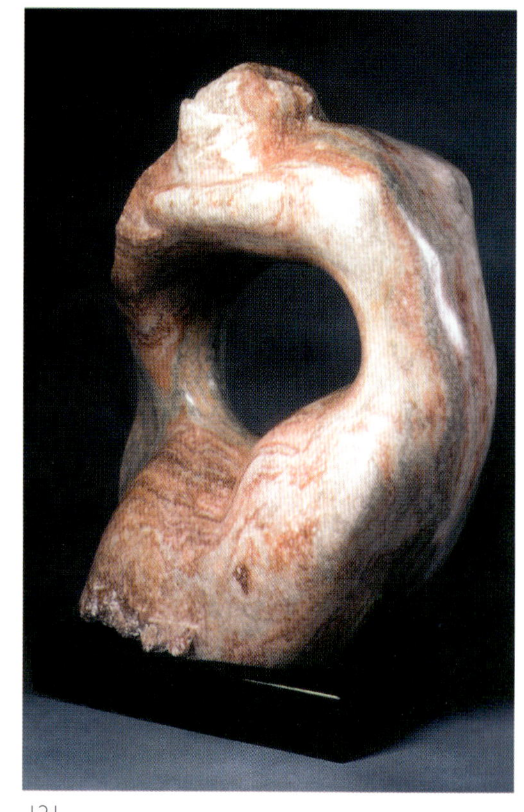

121

...some even dance...

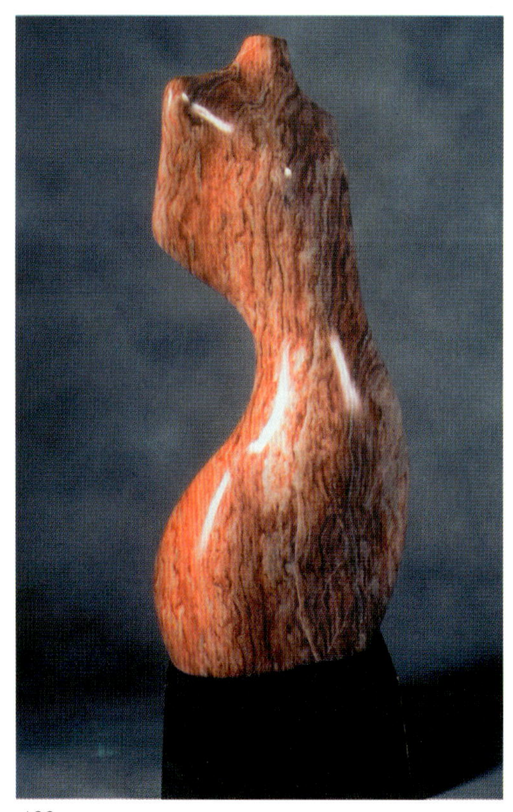

122

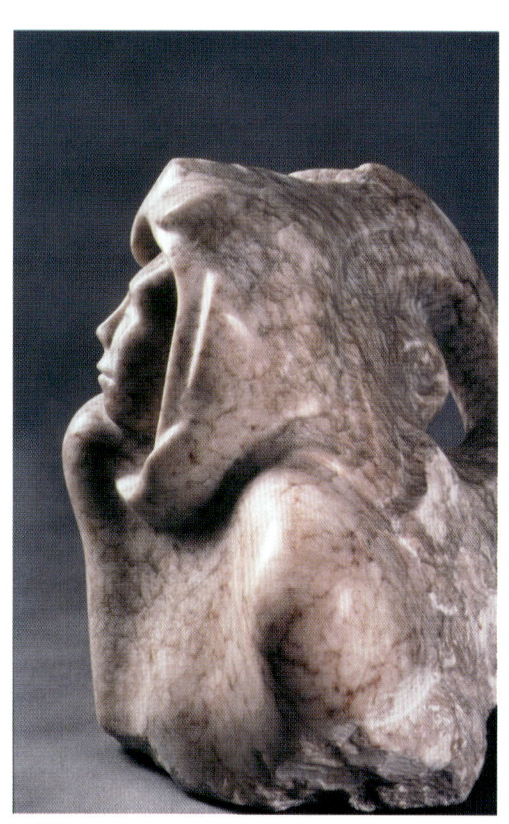

123

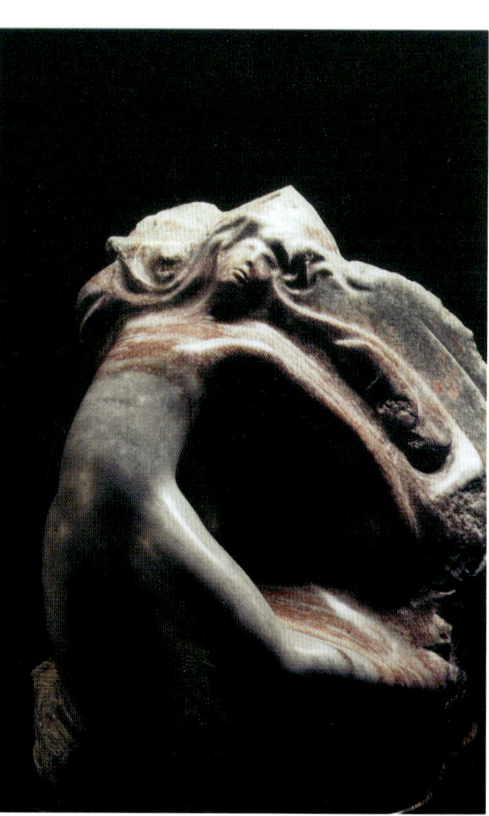

124

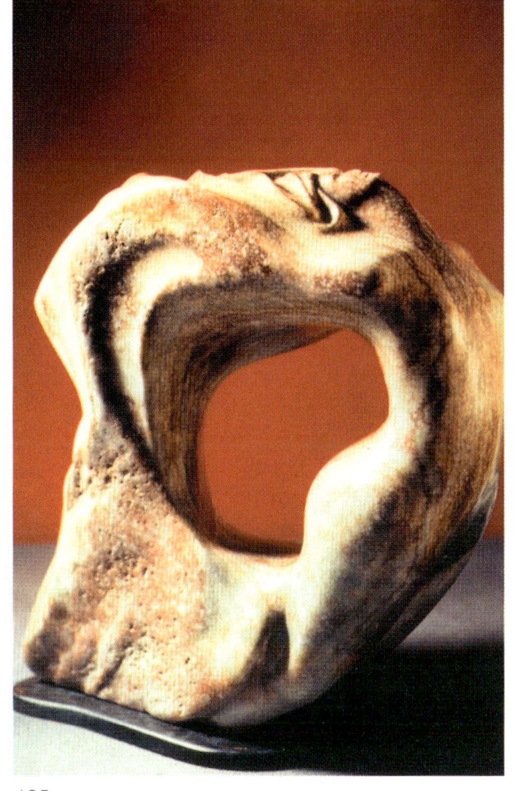

125

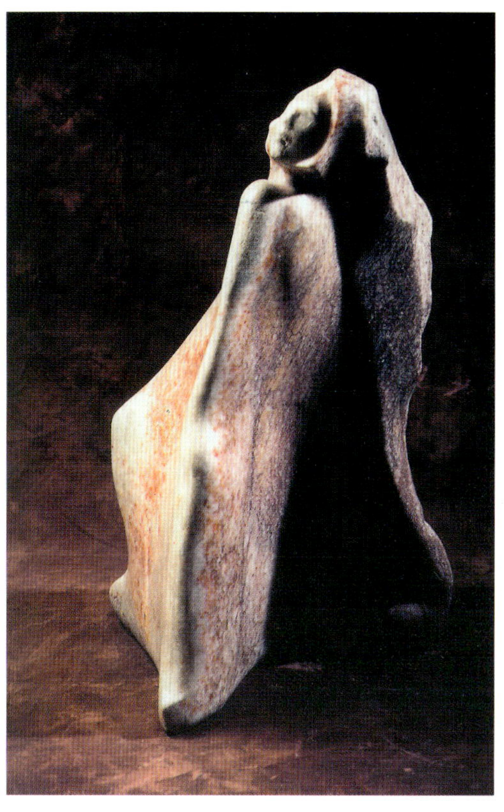

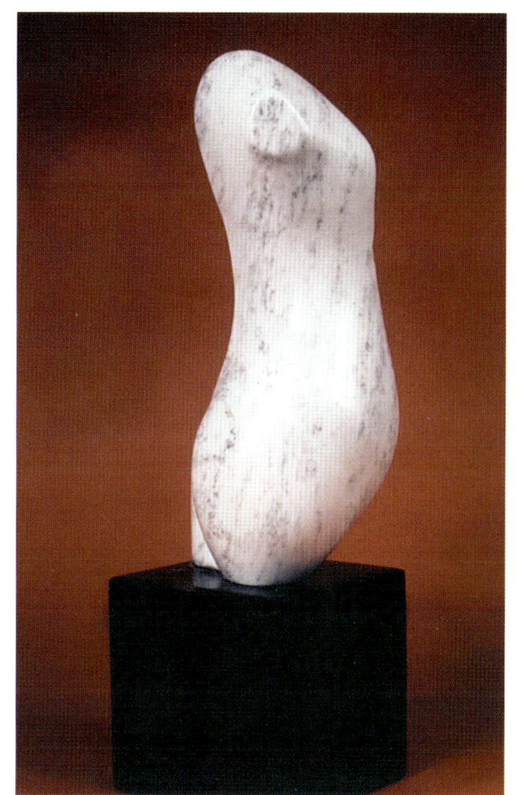

127

...and then there is the dance itself.

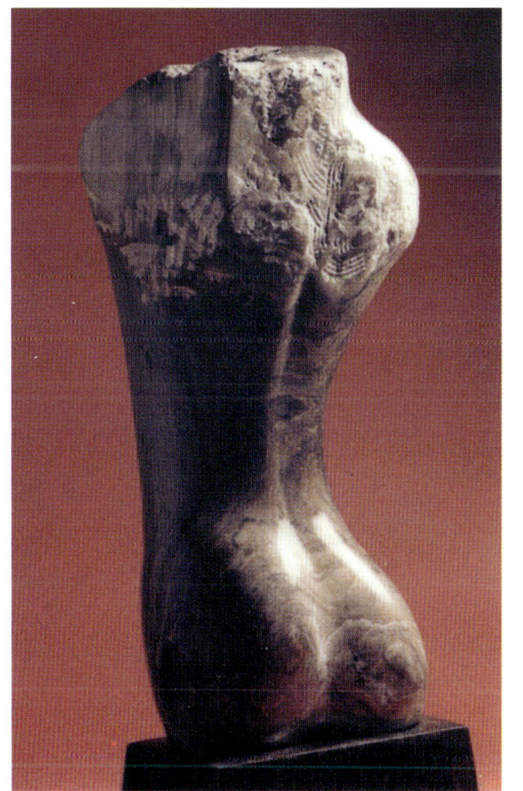

128

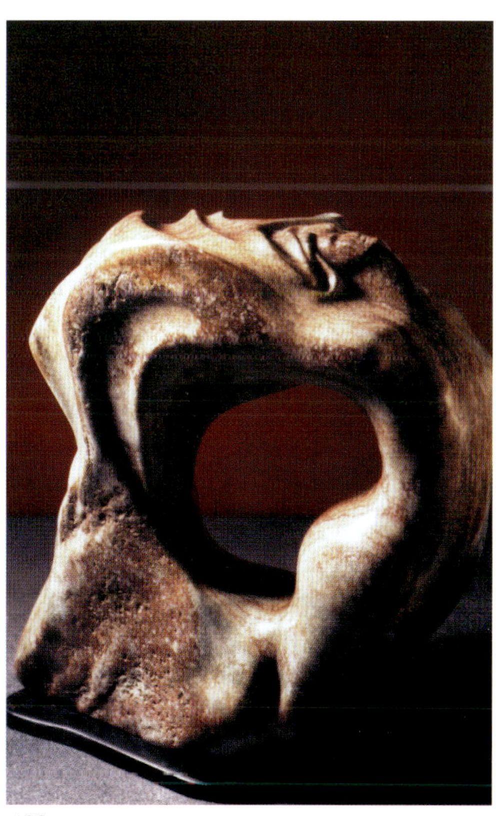

129

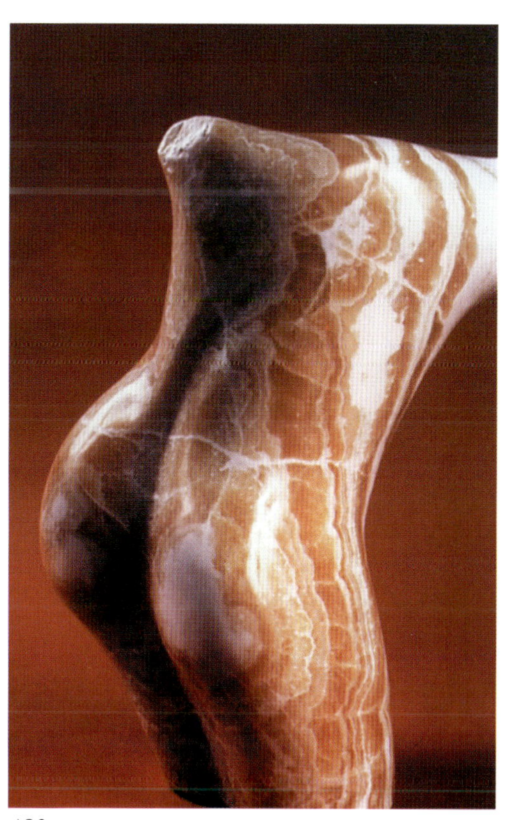

130

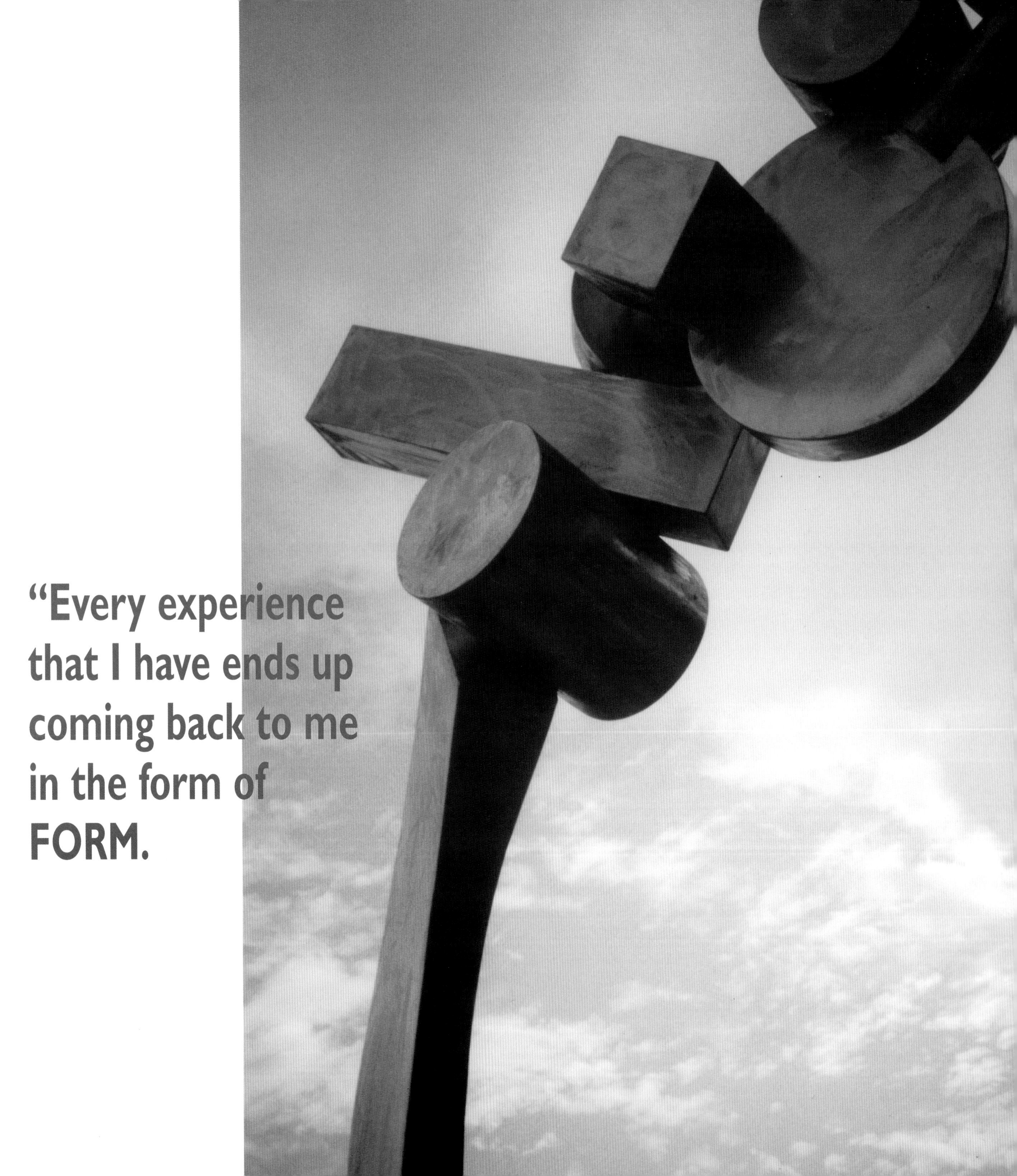
"Every experience
that I have ends up
coming back to me
in the form of
FORM.

Bronze, Stainless Steel, Aluminum . . .

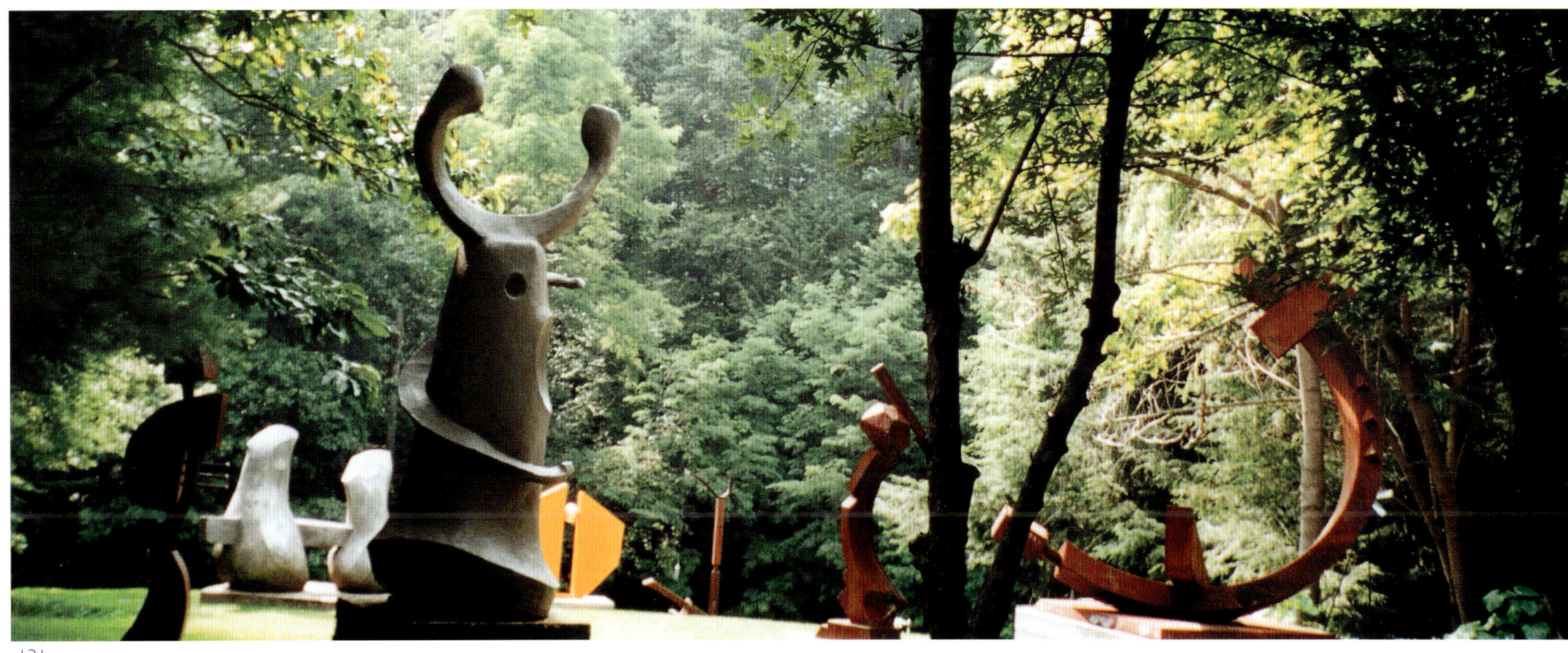

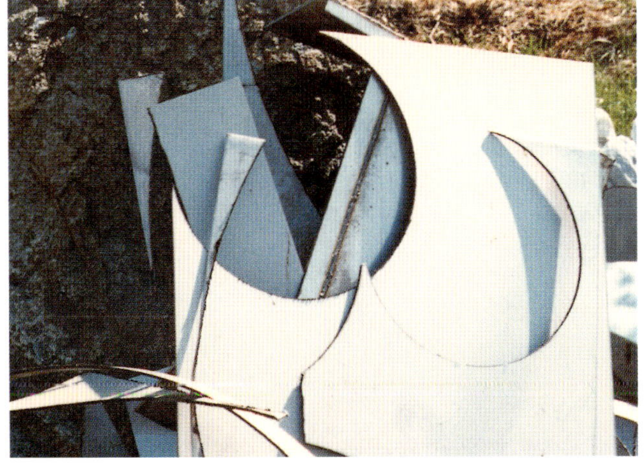

I do it (art) most of the time because I have something inside that asks to be let out. Each piece is an attempted escape for that hidden monster. I must live. That's why I make art.

Presently going through dictionary for words that recall images to my mind. Will begin to draw them one by one. (The year Klee died he did 2000 paintings.) I have done 397 sculptures in 8 years. Fuck!

Ran into a fellow sculptor today who had run out of money and just STOPPED.
How can he consider himself an artist? It is inconceivable to me that he couldn't
find a scrap of paper and a stub of pencil . . . who knows what the future holds in
its yet unseen open arms.

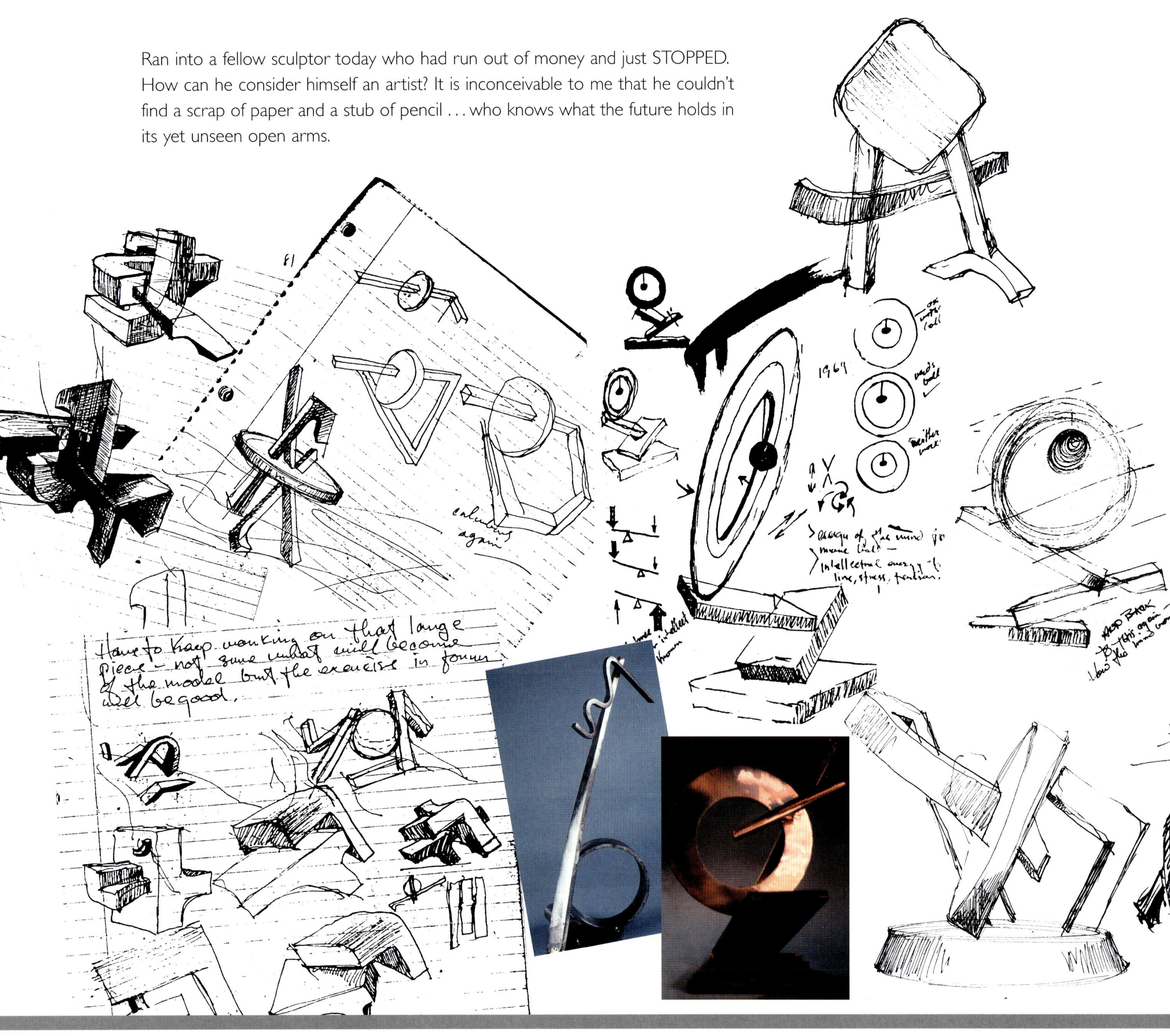

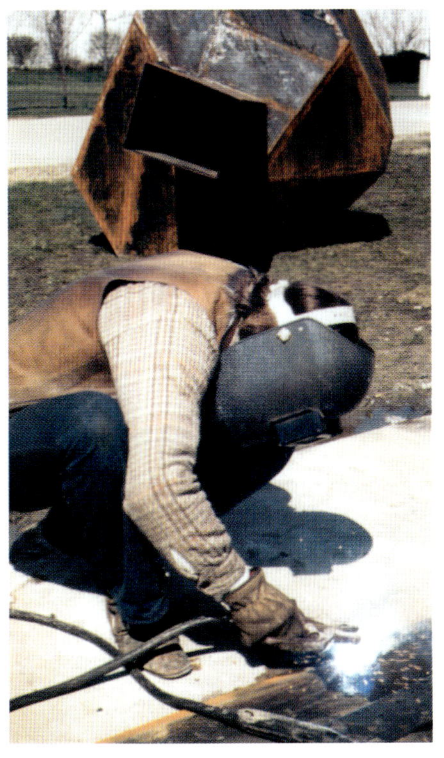

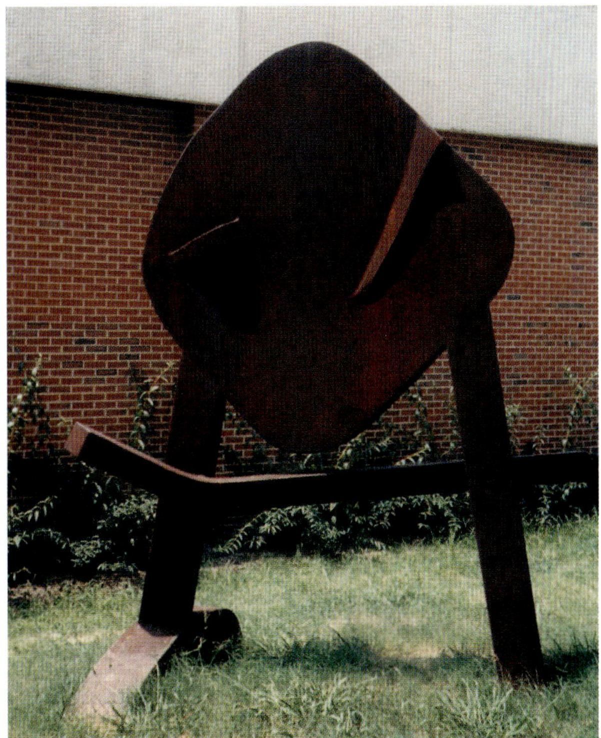

132

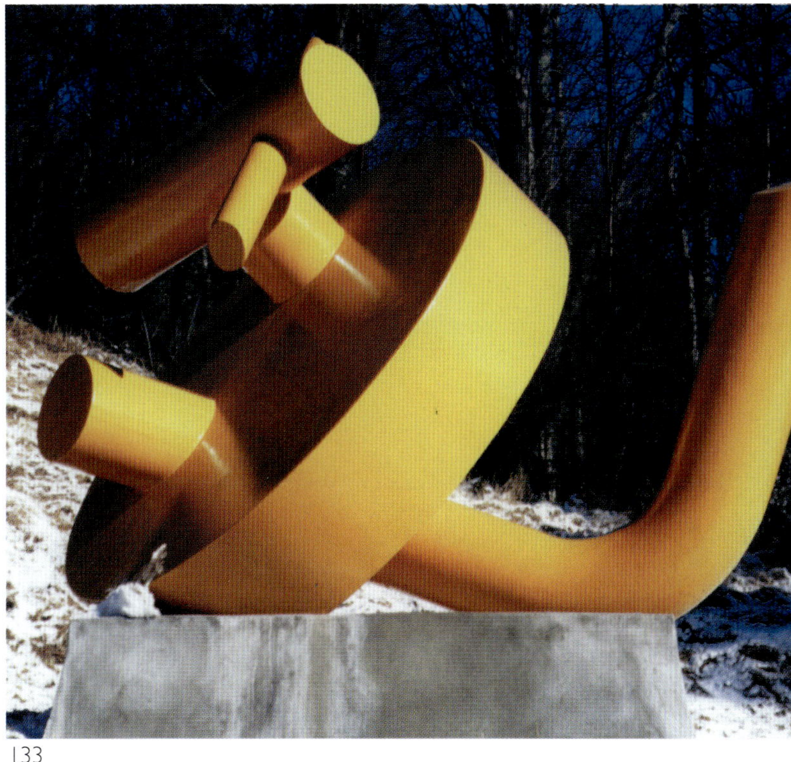

133

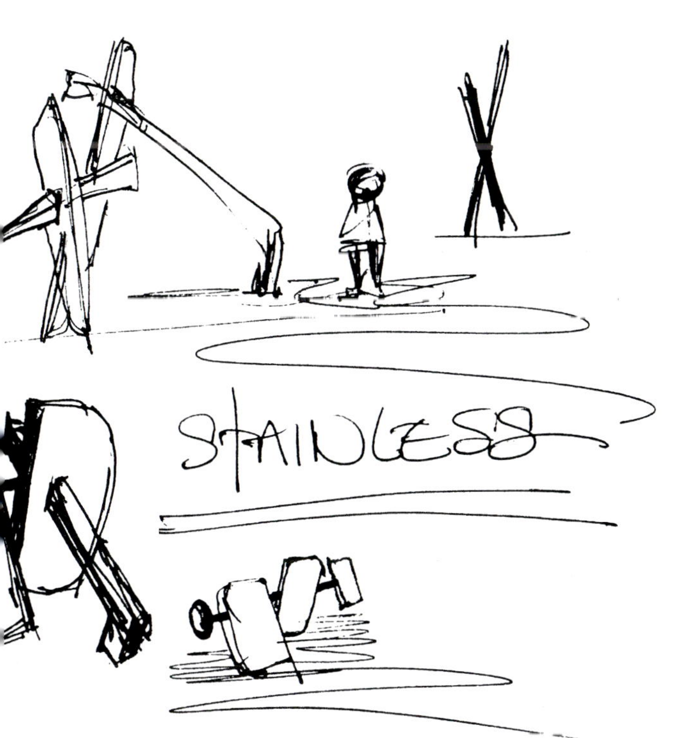

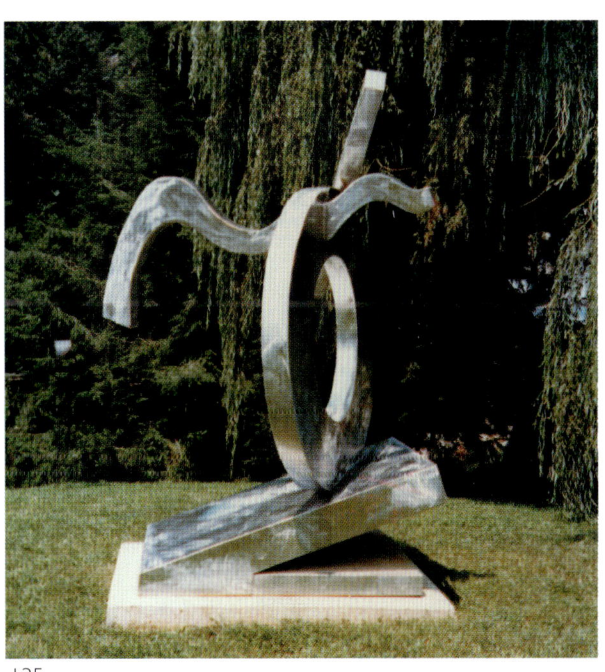

135

To be an artist one must stand naked in the world. He must put the daggers down. There can be no walls between him and humanity because he requires of humanity intake.

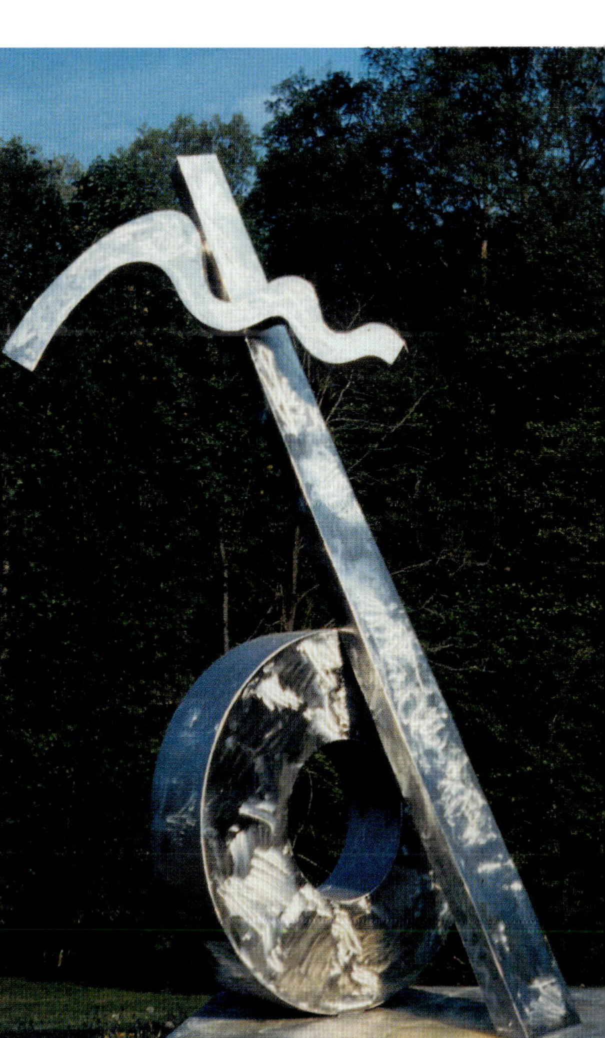

134

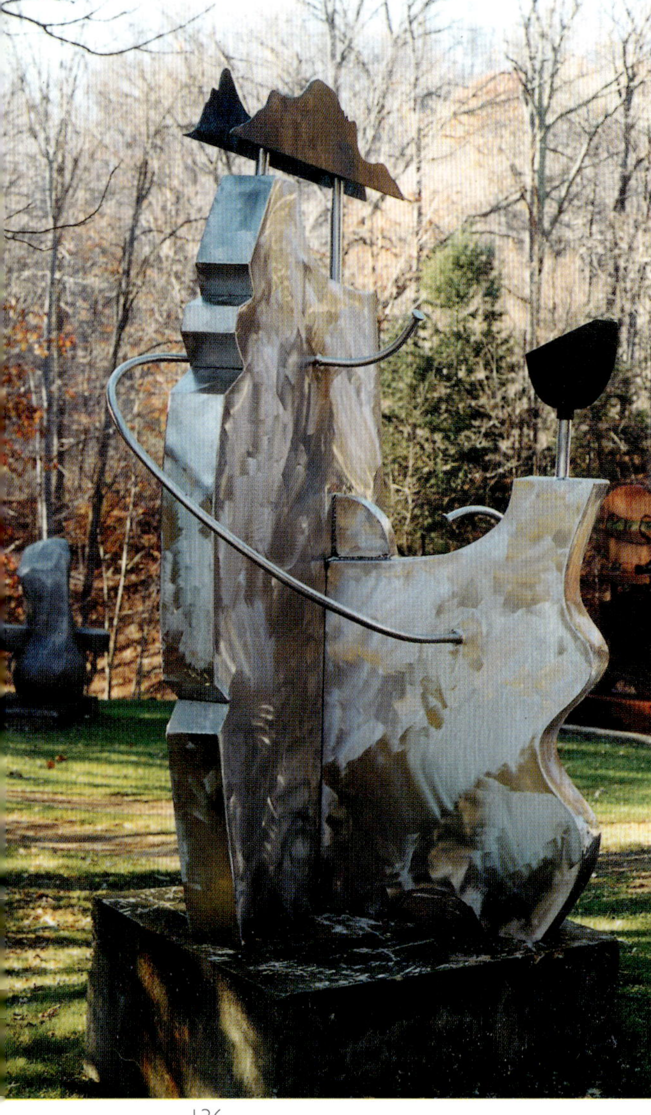

136

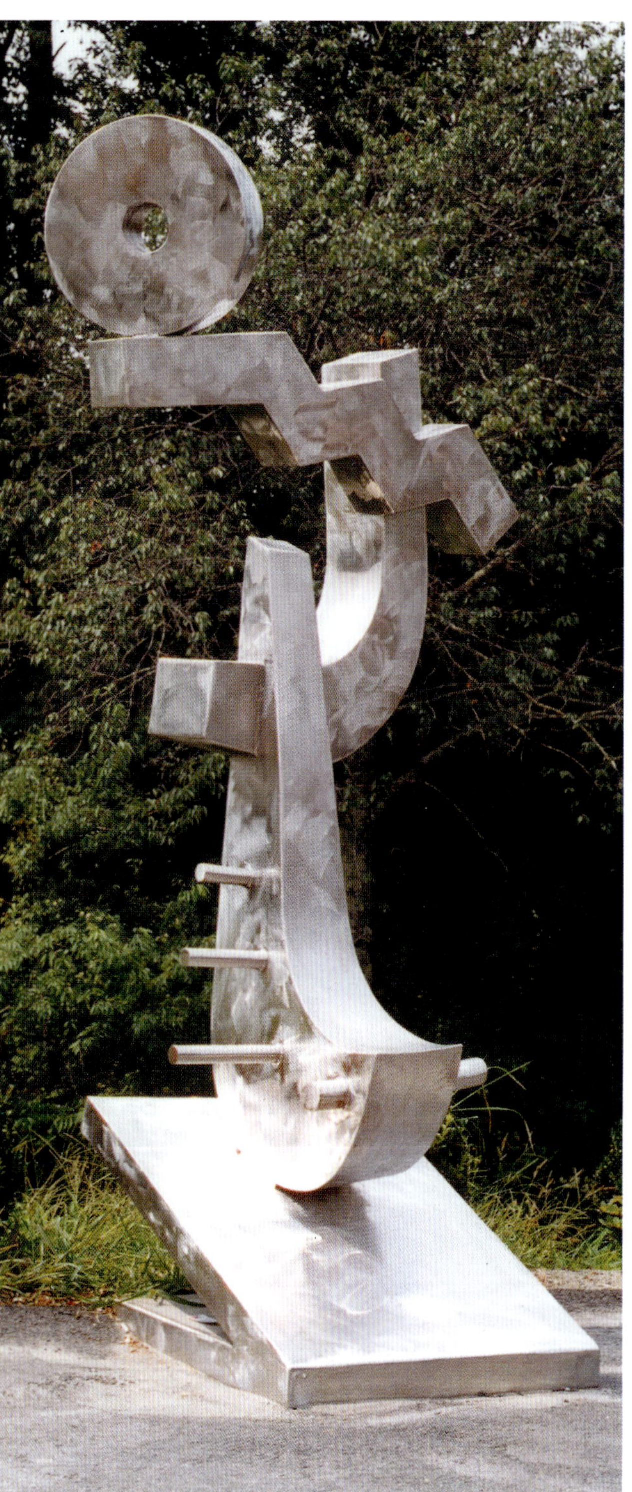

137

138

Heard an all-Schubert piano recital that was great! Many images passed through me as the music continued. One form will become a sculpture – many images are making contact with my conscious. They are coming together and becoming solid form.

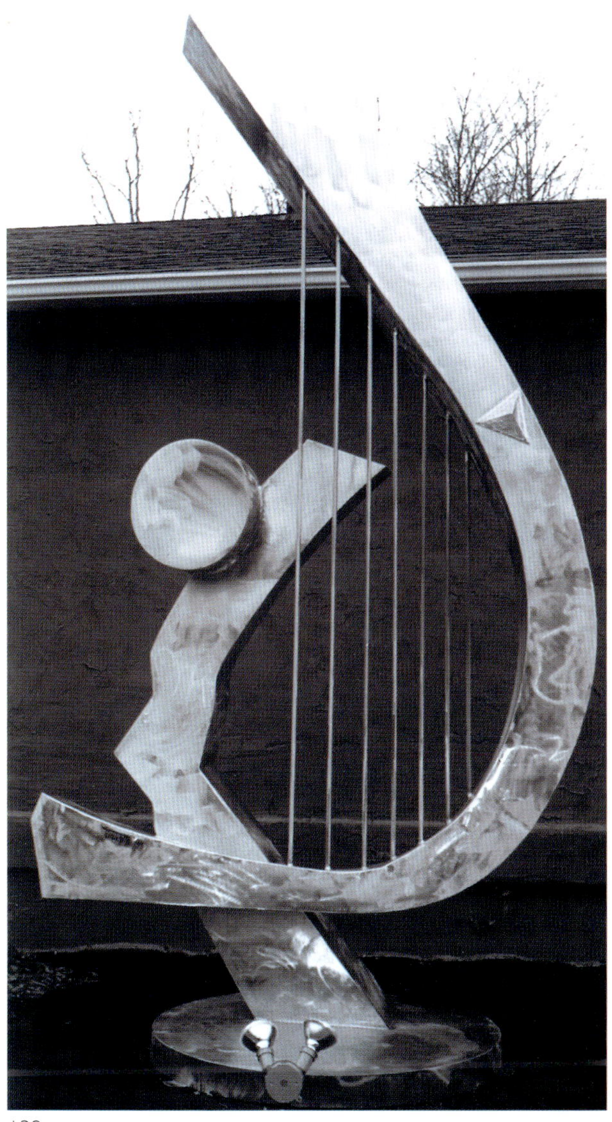

139

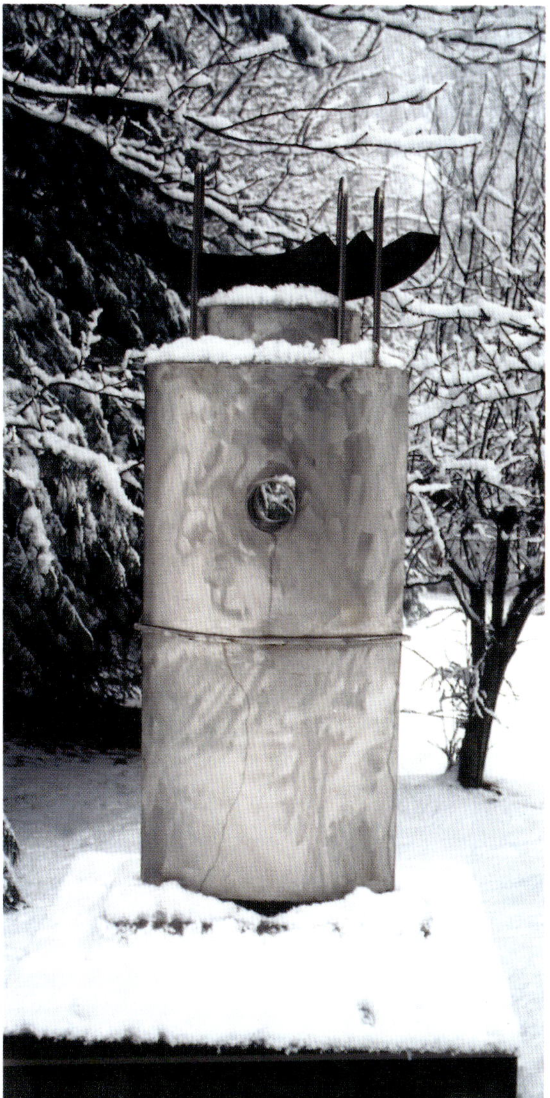

140

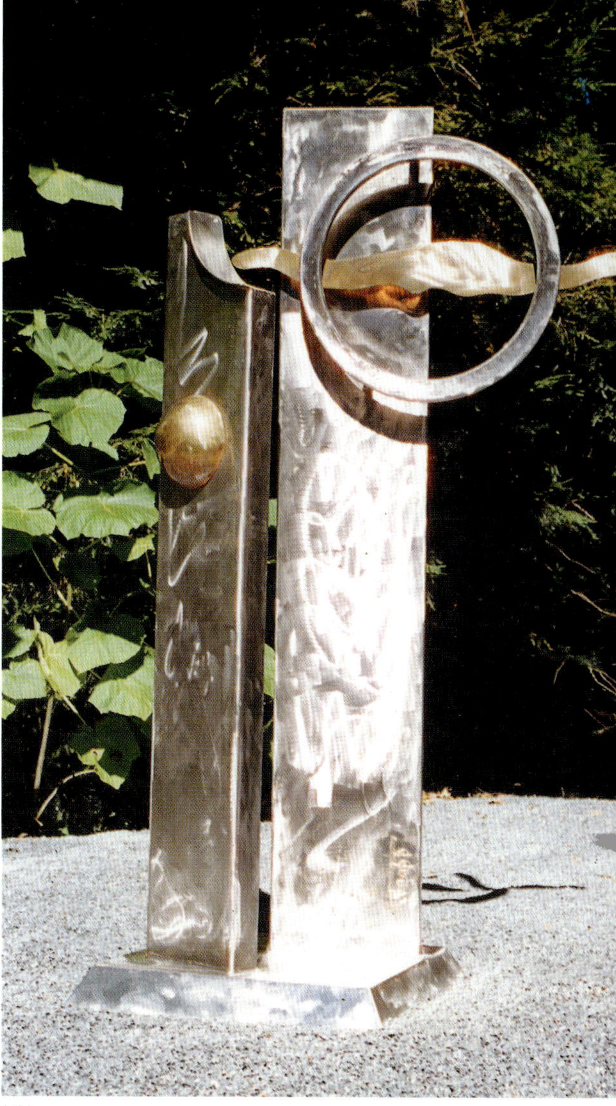

141

I'm not very calm and not happy. For 10 days now, things have not gone well. Have had trouble with the wax forms from the plaster, but managed to work that out. The biggest problem is everything that has happened at the school. I have tried to do the sand resin over and over and over (no tools to work with). Each piece (and there are five of them) has failed. The resin is old and not bonding with the sand. Also, the environment there is depressing me. Everything is dirty and abused. No space is mine and no tools are mine. I have to check everything out and sign for it. I can't work in both places. That is the reality. So I will have to build the foundry here and do my own casting of small bronzes. That is a reality. The second shock came yesterday when I went to Greensboro with the three bronzes. They are going to cost $500 each – much more than I had expected. Funds are getting low. I've heard nothing firm from any source (galleries or commissions). That excitement that I have maintained for so many weeks is now dwindling and I'm back into that old syndrome of wanting to work, but no money. Is this the way it's going to be forever? Soon I'll have to work 'out' again for money – and the creativity will have ended once more. Damn. I'm down. What can I do to maintain it? Who can I ask for help?

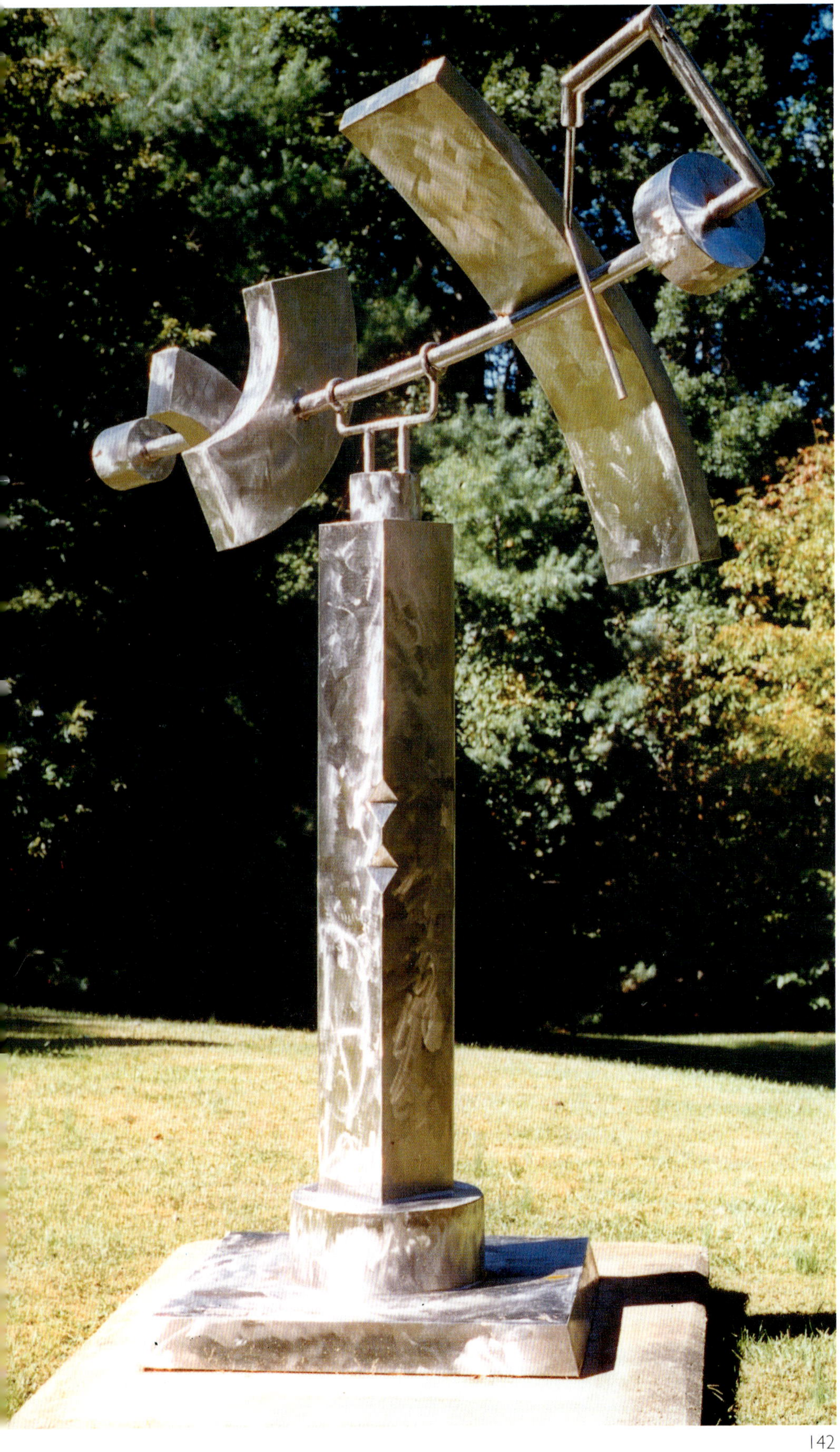

142

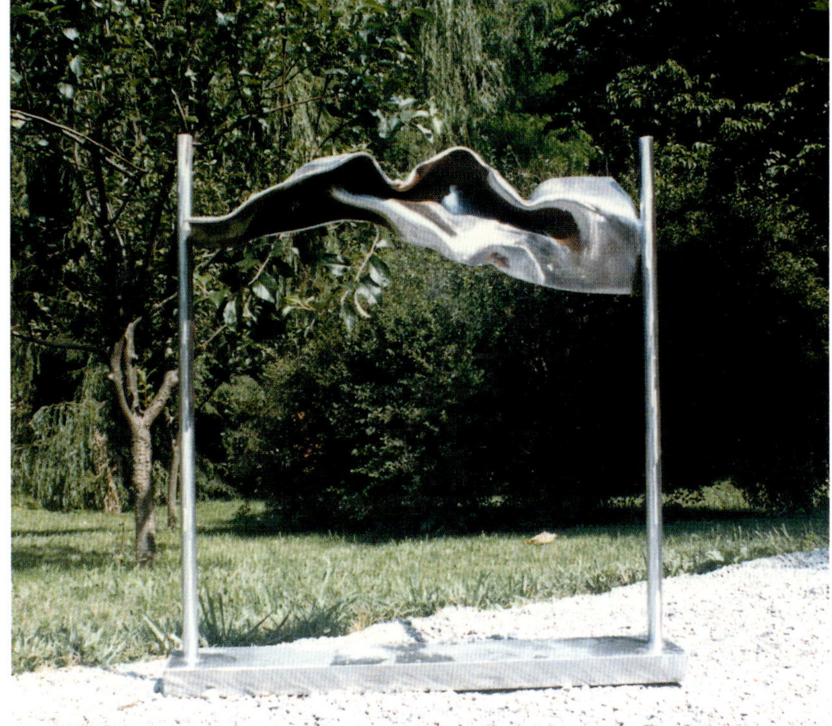

143

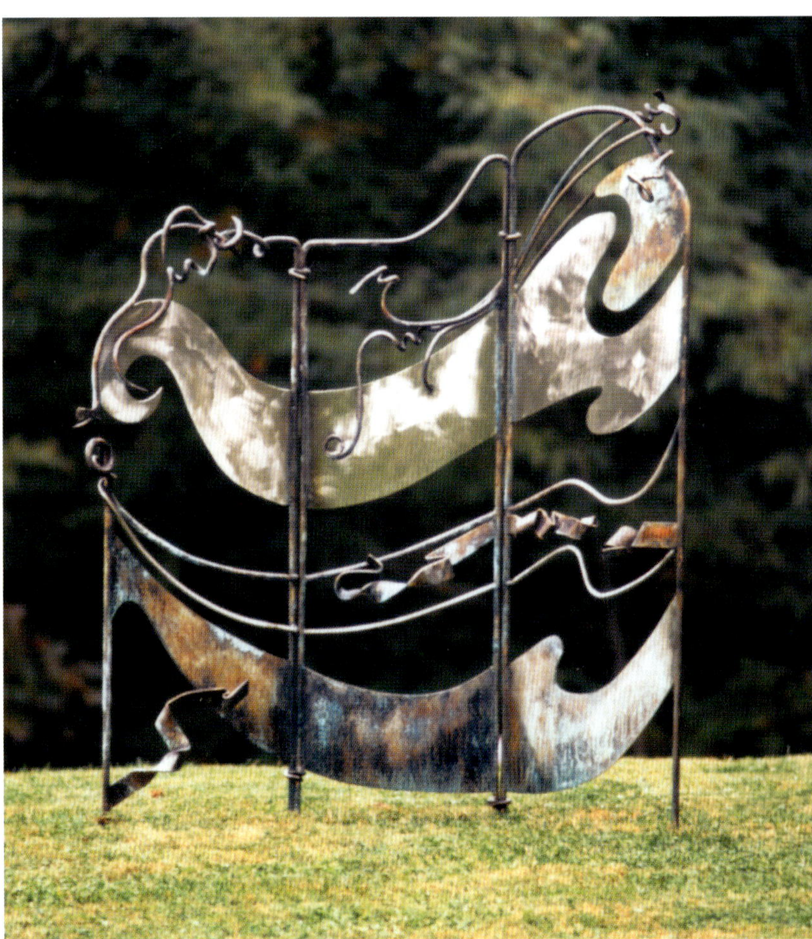

144

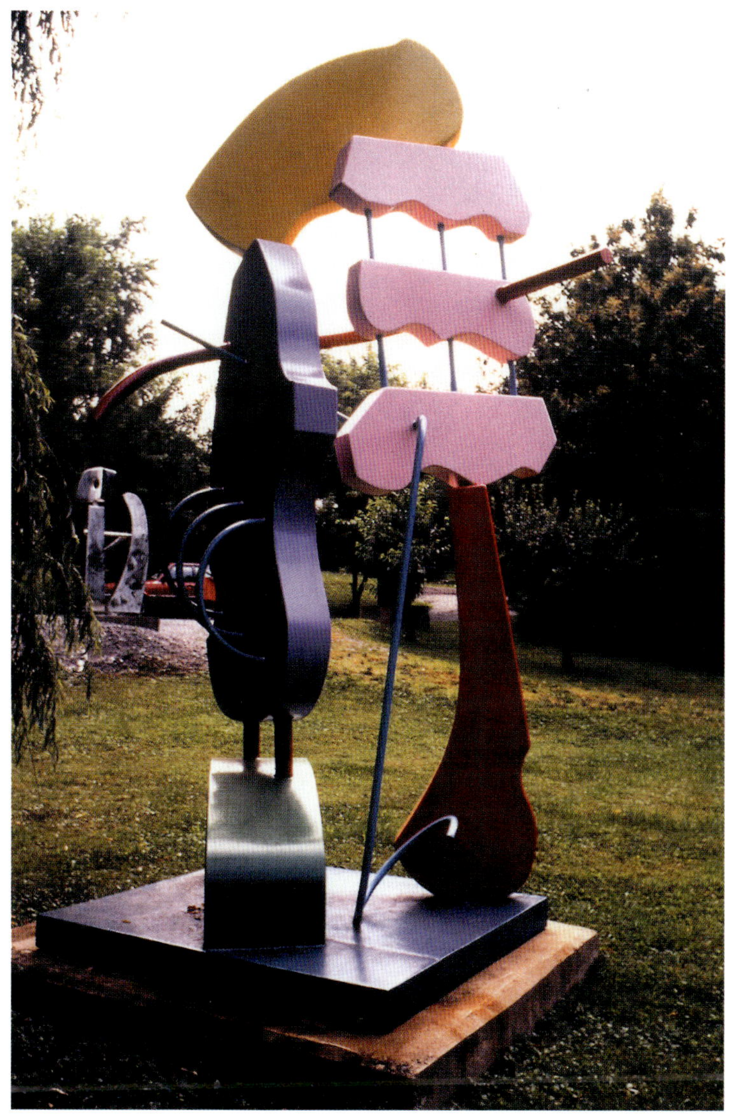

145

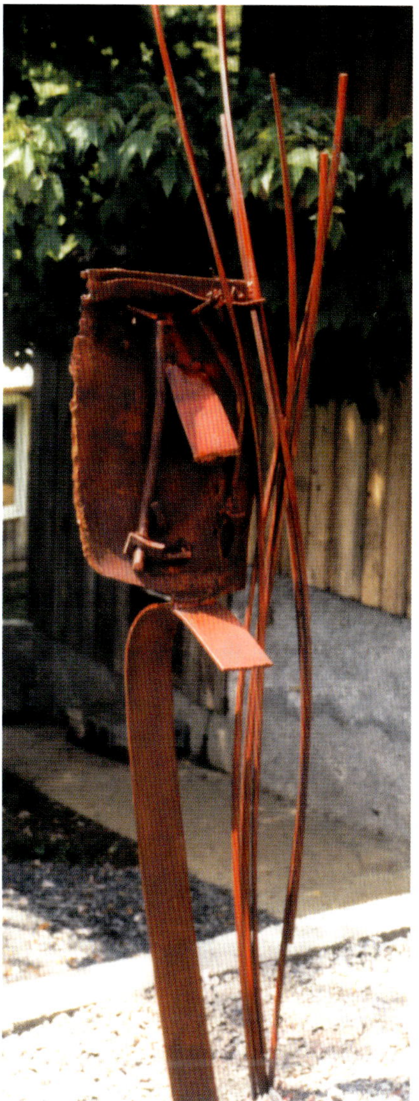

146

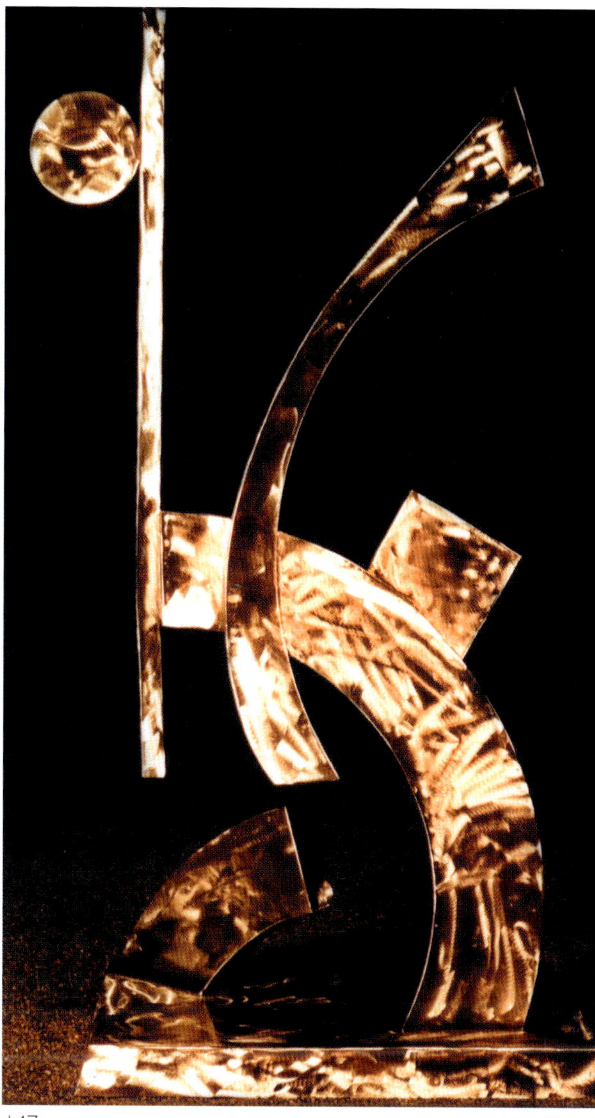

147

Now six years here in North Carolina. Life has been as I always thought it should be but never was. And on this soft rainy summer evening I go in and out of strange places. At times, when I'm as tired as I am now, I feel I'm almost ready to die. Then I remind myself of those dark days in Buchtel when I made the conscious choice to live. I now need no more, it's all Ok. I will be Ok. I do however need to write more about the many positive events that are the NOW. I need to go back to predictions for man on this planet, and in great detail for those who may read my journals. An ultimate is to predict the future.

The eve of Christmas eve. Have cleaned out the last scrap from the studio – the old pieces of sculpture that I have dragged about from studio to studio, and now have, at last, sold for scrap steel (60¢/100lbs.) At one time they were my life. A symbol of my belief in what? Art. Or did they represent my rebellion? My fight? Yes, they were all of that. I needed them to remind me and all that were around me that I was an artist, that I was different, that I dreamt different dreams, thought thoughts much unlike theirs – that in fact, all of me was different from them. And, as a bonus, the pieces were a symbol of hope for artists that made the decision to join the fight for man's only hope - ART.

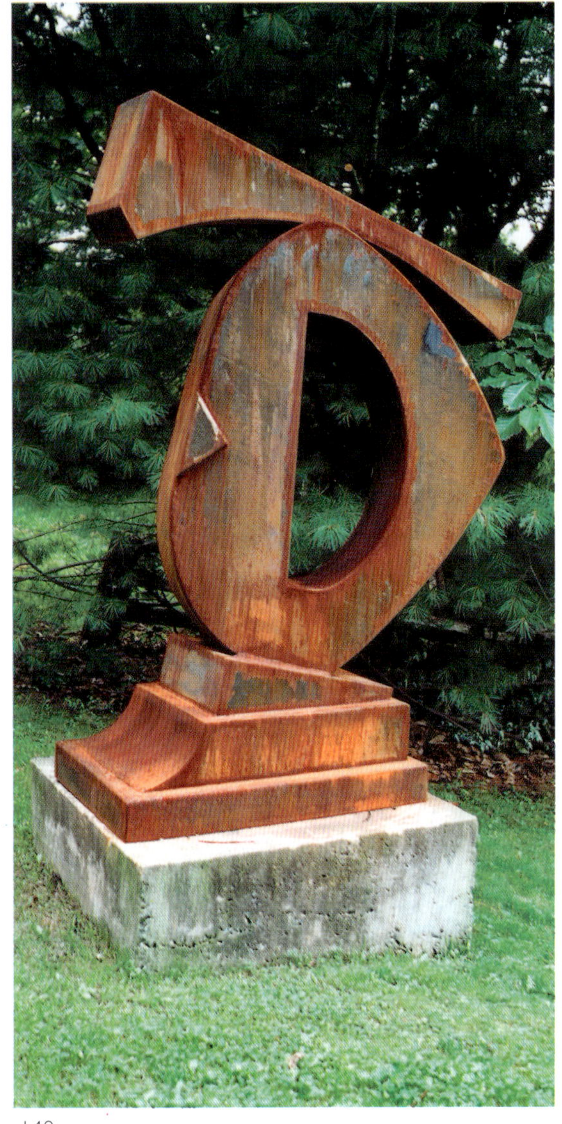

148

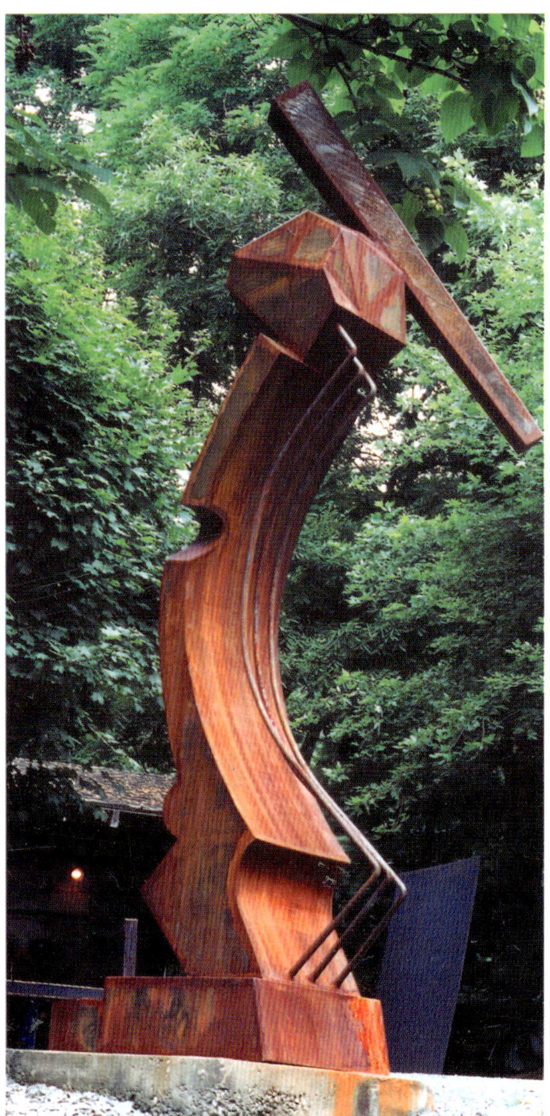

149

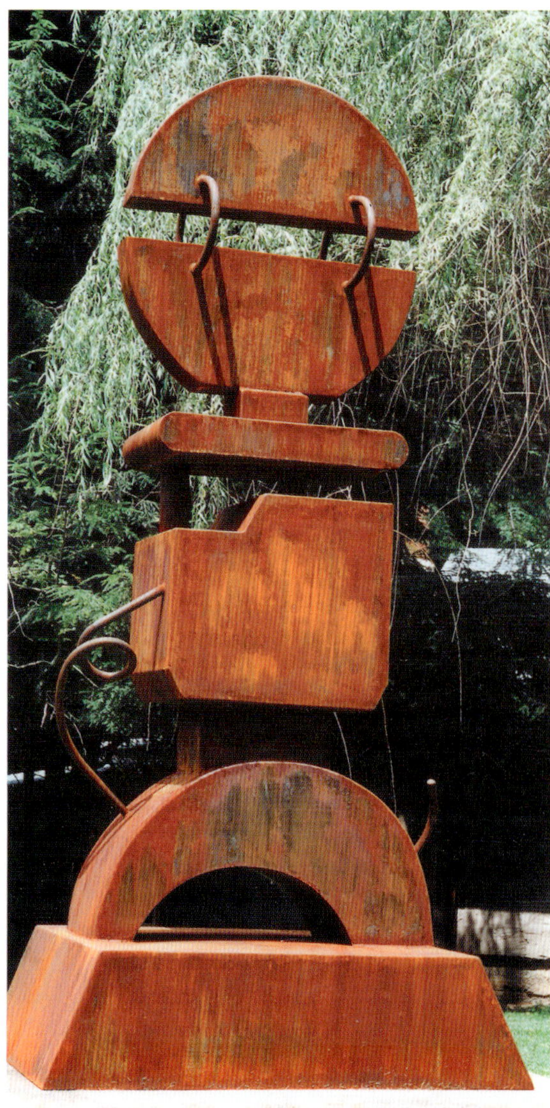

150

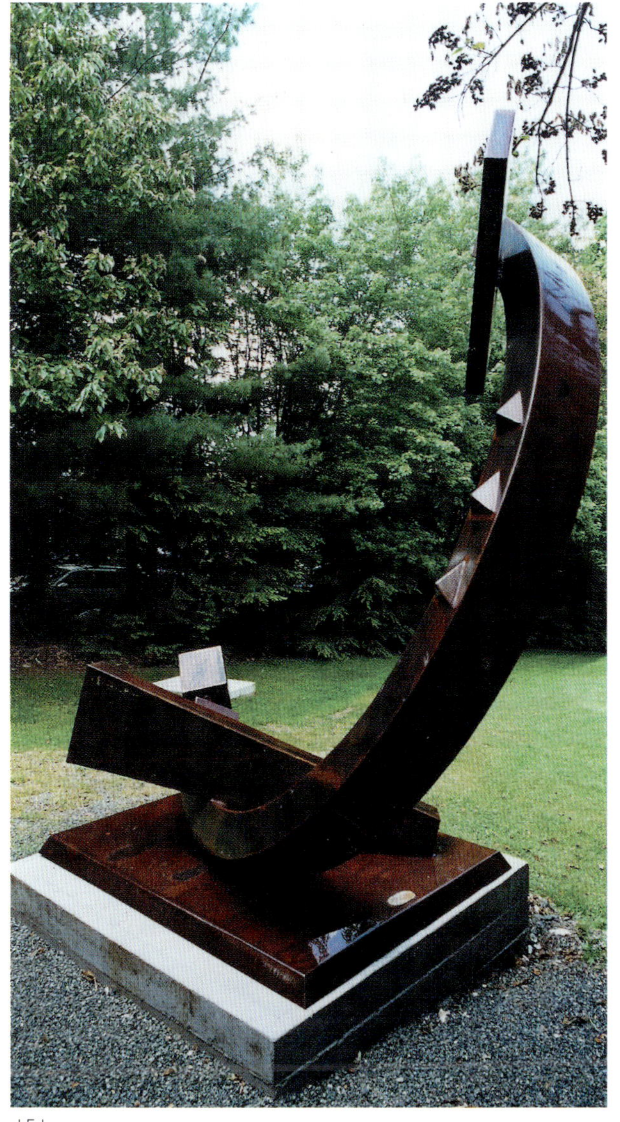

151

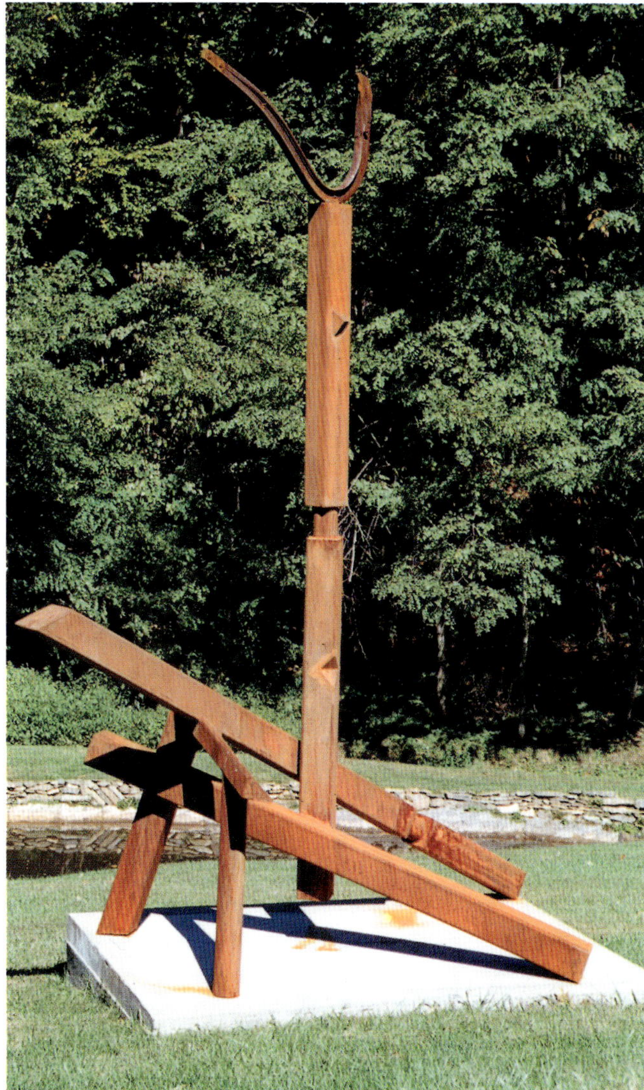

152

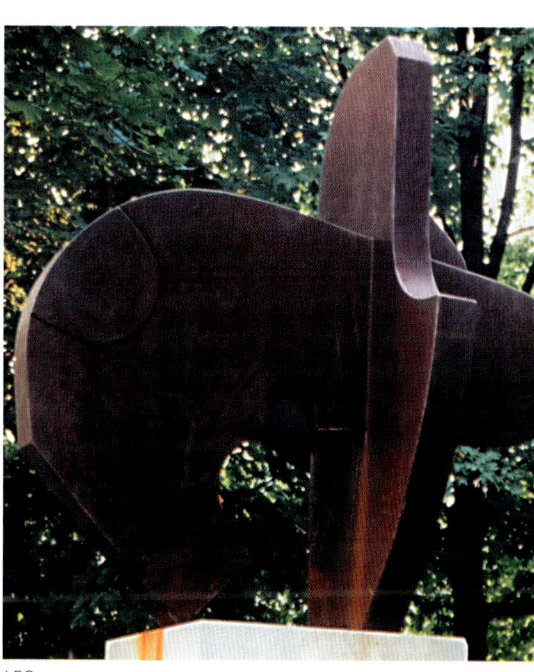

153

A concern for the future must essentially be the first thought.

Thought: In art (sculpture and architecture) the creator must go beyond the element of time. He must surpass human emotions and the effect that people and their personalities have on the created piece. Time continues. The time/use factor exists. That is the only reality. Everything changes as a result of this – everything else is created reality. It all happens as a result of time just 'being'. The inevitability of change results from time happening/passing. The effect of this passing time should be considered in every created piece. A concern for the future must then essentially be the first thought.

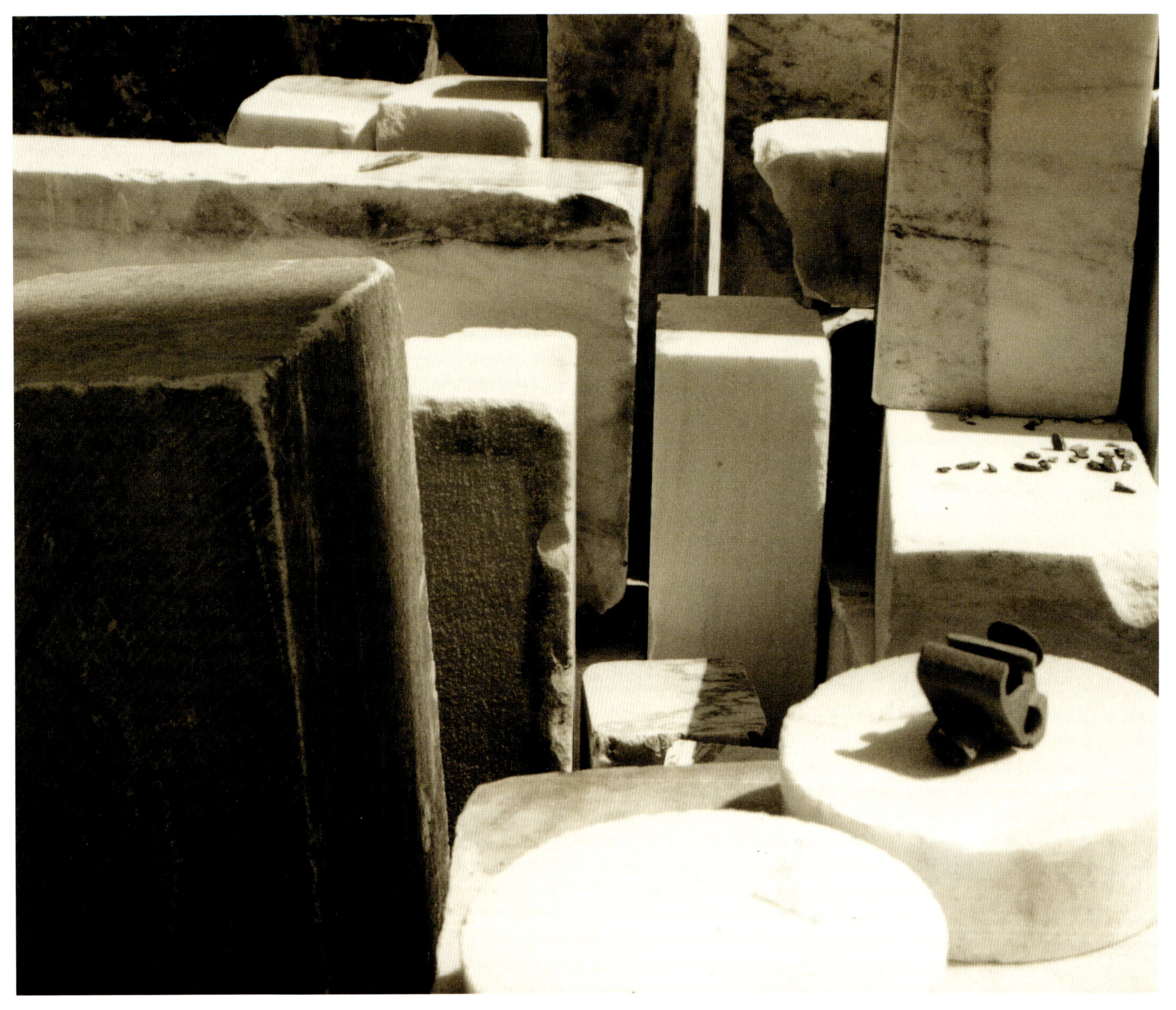

I must do whatever I must do
to maintain the celebration potential of each day.

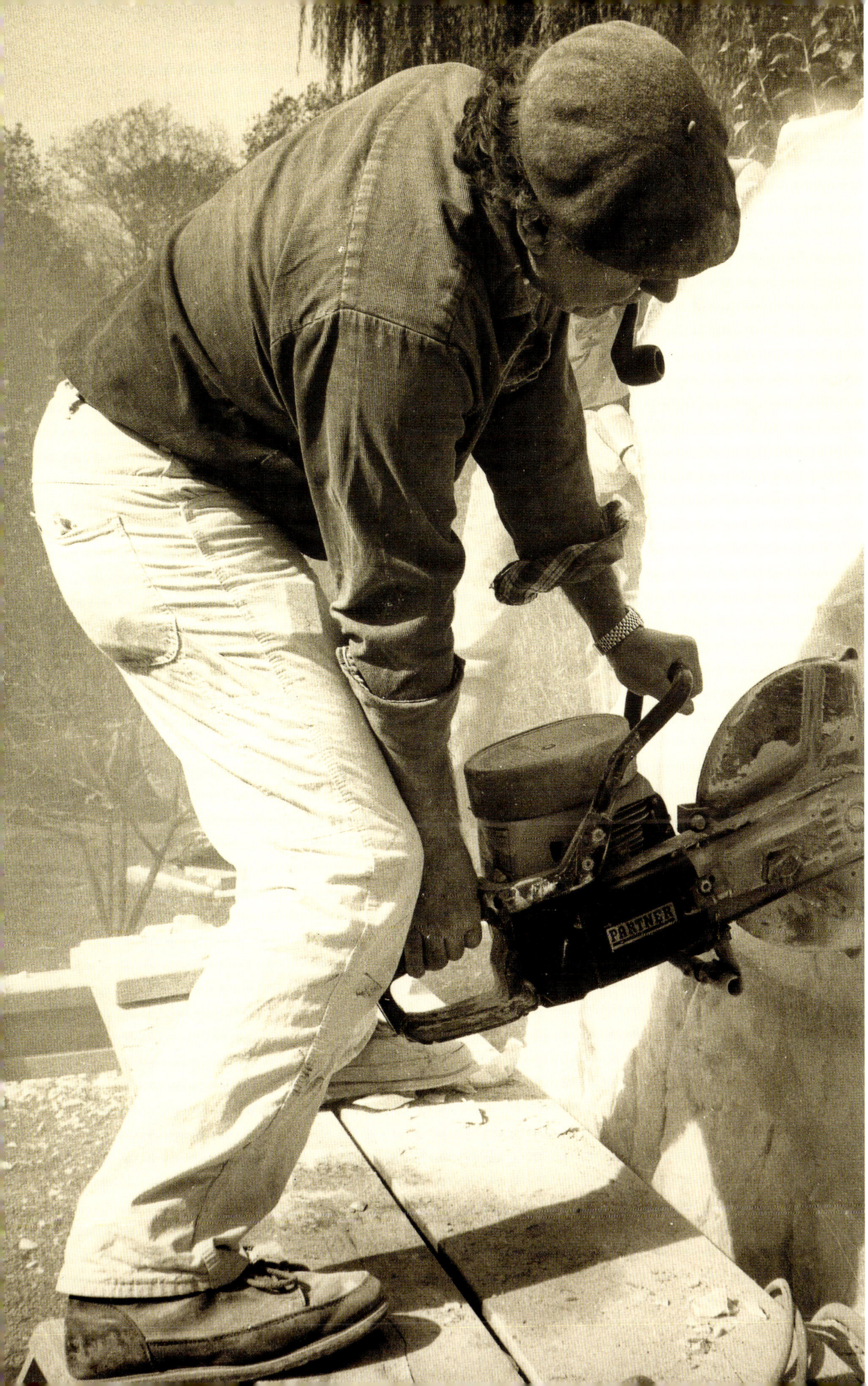

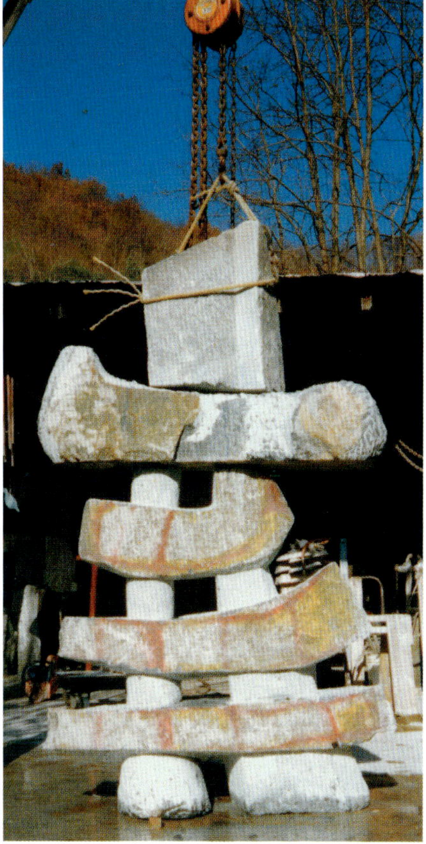

154

I must move in all directions, and be surrounded with the idiots of the world. The court jesters must dance. And the sunrise must once again be very special. And the full moon must light the earth at midnight and force me to scream. But the hot sun of noon will shine once more, and I will sweat under its inhuman heat, groan and swim in the earth's ponds and streams …for the magic will once again be broken.

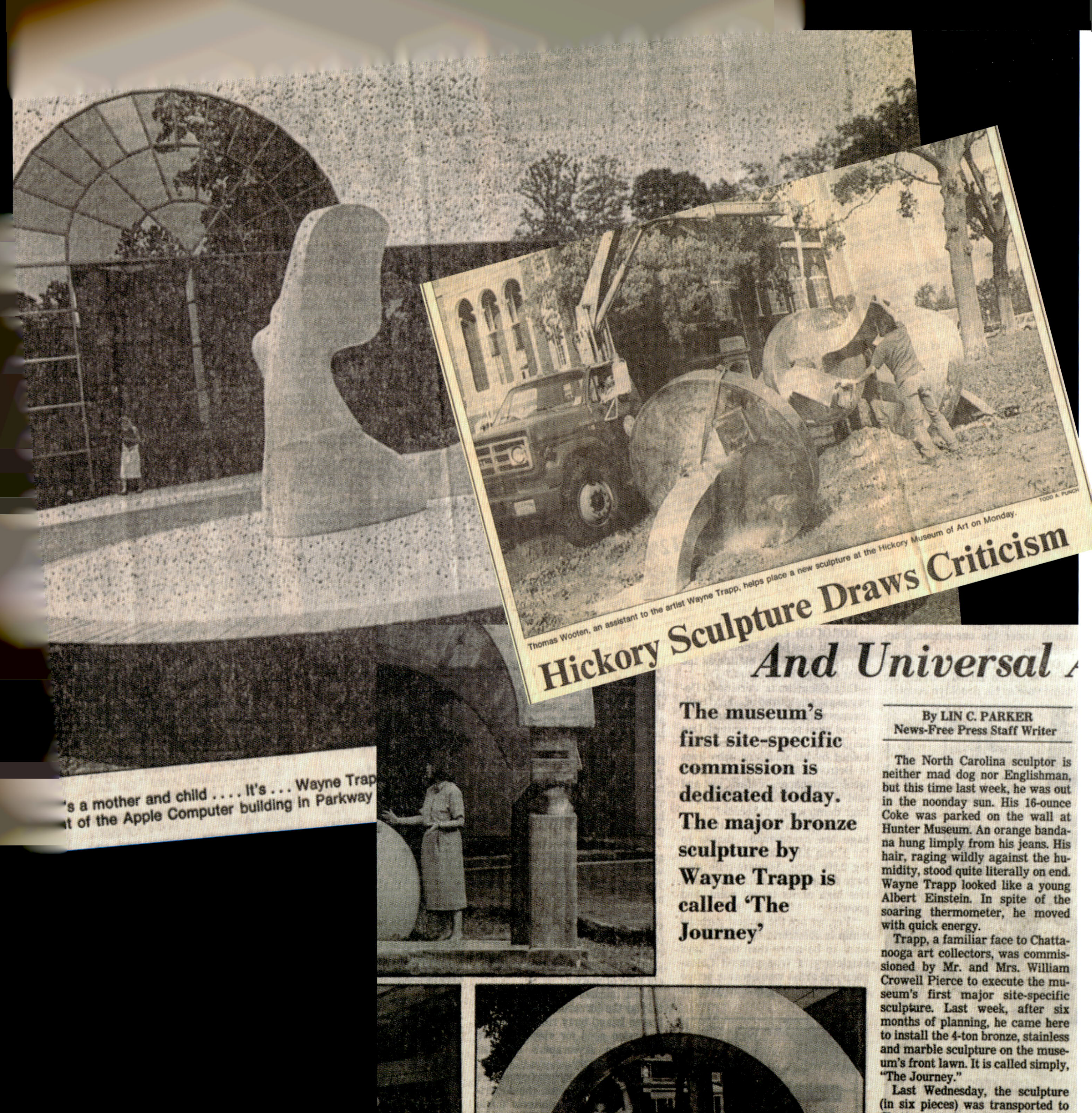

Hickory Sculpture Draws Criticism And Universal

The museum's first site-specific commission is dedicated today. The major bronze sculpture by Wayne Trapp is called 'The Journey'

By LIN C. PARKER
News-Free Press Staff Writer

The North Carolina sculptor is neither mad dog nor Englishman, but this time last week, he was out in the noonday sun. His 16-ounce Coke was parked on the wall at Hunter Museum. An orange bandana hung limply from his jeans. His hair, raging wildly against the humidity, stood quite literally on end. Wayne Trapp looked like a young Albert Einstein. In spite of the soaring thermometer, he moved with quick energy.

Trapp, a familiar face to Chattanooga art collectors, was commissioned by Mr. and Mrs. William Crowell Pierce to execute the museum's first major site-specific sculpture. Last week, after six months of planning, he came here to install the 4-ton bronze, stainless and marble sculpture on the museum's front lawn. It is called simply, "The Journey."

Last Wednesday, the sculpture (in six pieces) was transported to Chattanooga from his North Carolina studio on two flat bed trucks. By noon Thursday its base and four columns were set in place on a

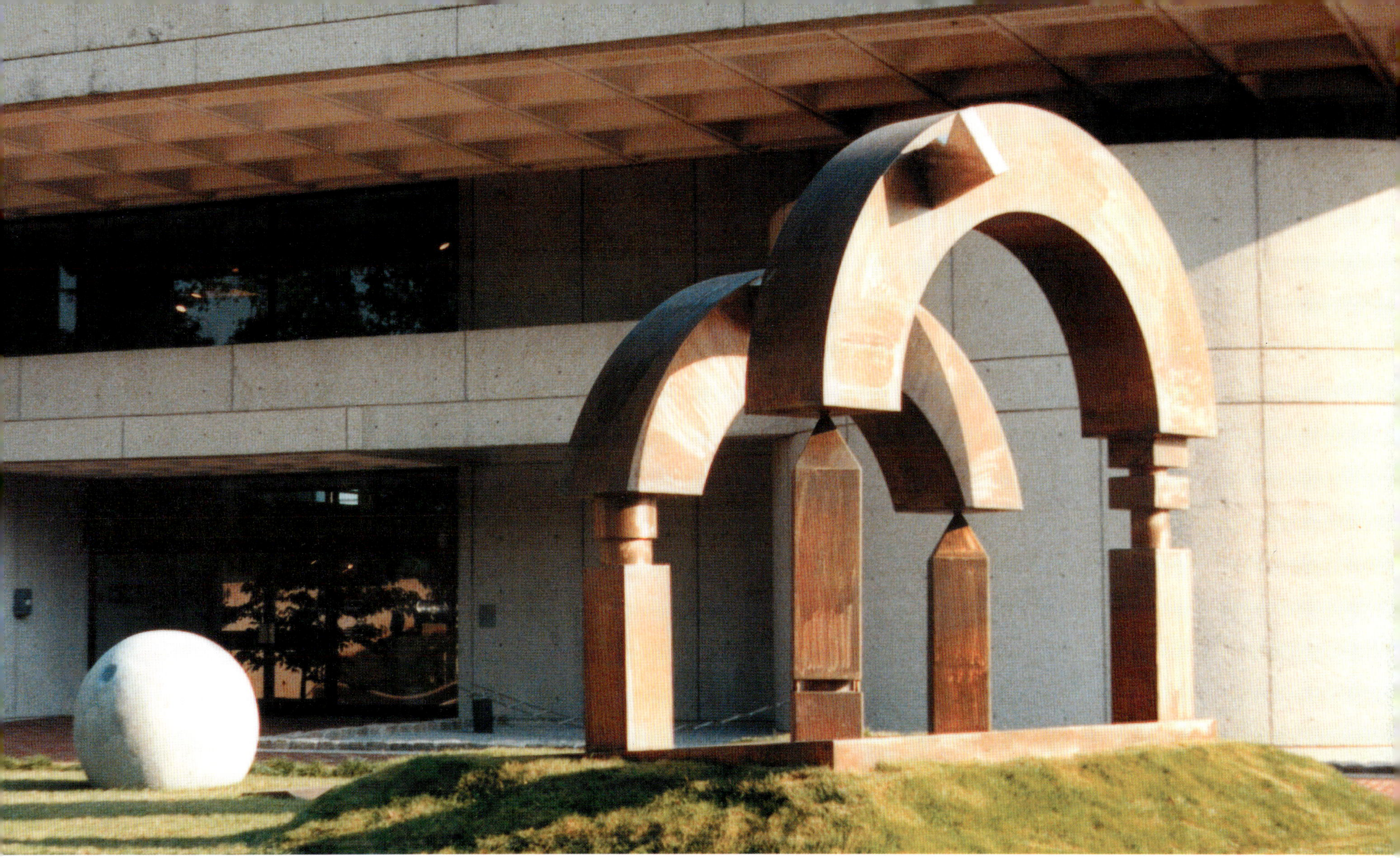

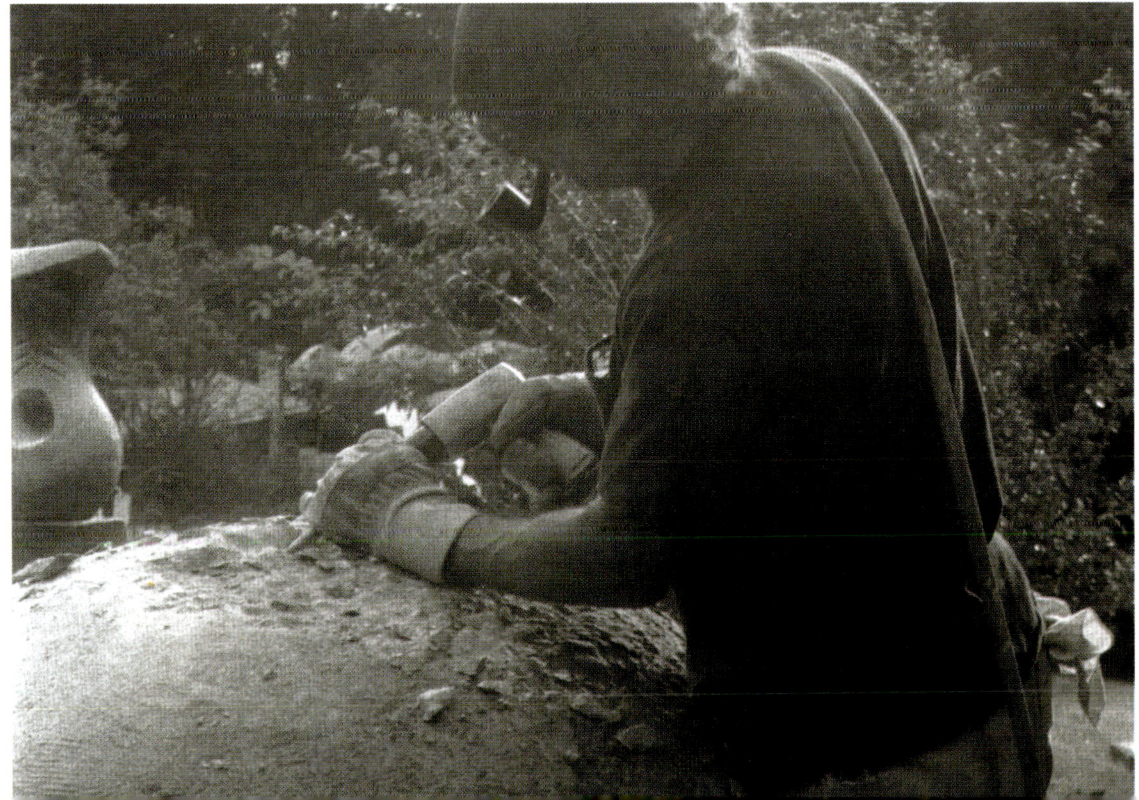

Everyone's Art

Corporate
Museum
Public

Cost Wrong Yardstick

"Linkages," the contemporary sculpture at the Hickory Museum of Art, is the subject of a disquieting misconception.

The sculpture, on the southeast lawn of the Arts Center of Catawba Valley, is the creation of Wayne Trapp, a noted sculptor of Vilas.

"Linkages" is worth approximately $75,000. It did not cost the Museum of Art $75,000 as many people seem to believe. A patron of the arts donated the material for the highly regarded work. Trapp himself donated the design and supervision. The labor costs, which were minimal, were absorbed by the museum — easily within constraints of the museum budget.

That's how the museum could afford to acquire the sculpture. People who love the arts helped considerably. Thus, "Linkages" is basically a gift — a wonderful acquisition of a major work from a major sculptor.

Indeed, generosity is the driving force behind Hickory's incredible wealth of art at the Arts Center and the museum. Without patrons large and small, without the attitude that art is an investment and not an expense, there would be no exceptional Arts Center and no Museum of Art.

"Linkages" is a noteworthy addition to Hickory's grand array of art. It — as all the art works — cannot be thought of in terms of dollars and cost, but in light of the benefits and enjoyment it will provide in years to come.

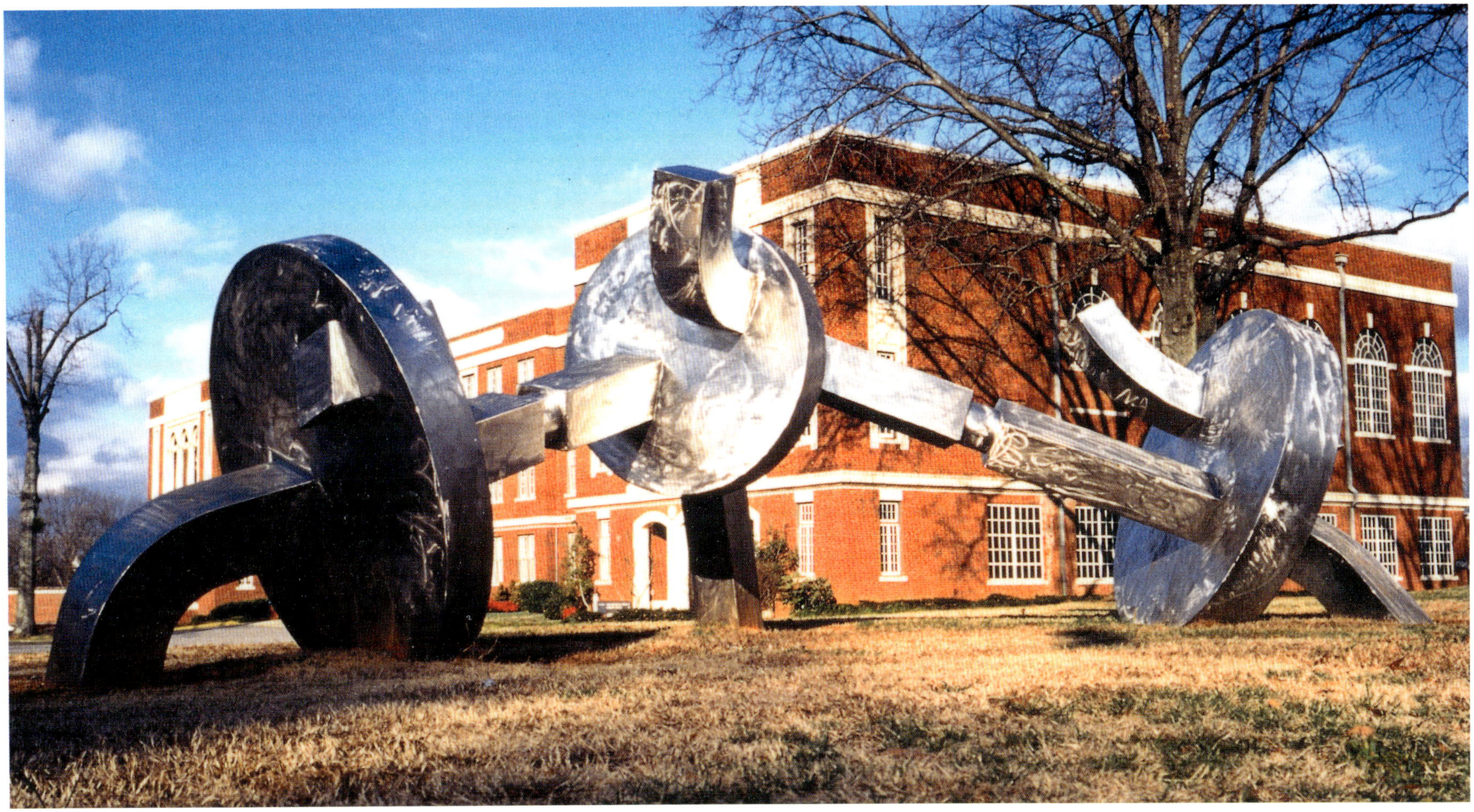

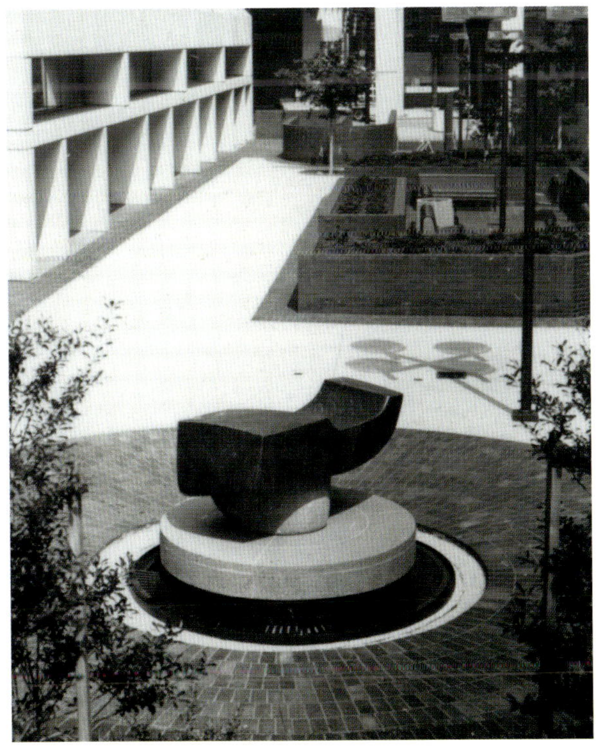

156

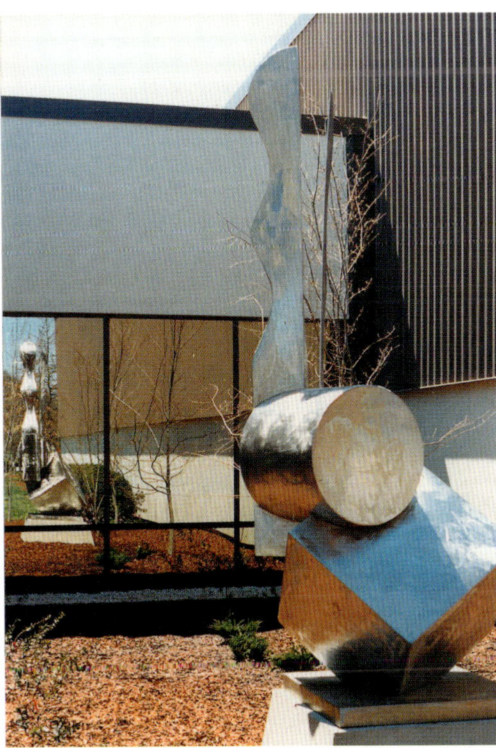

157

158

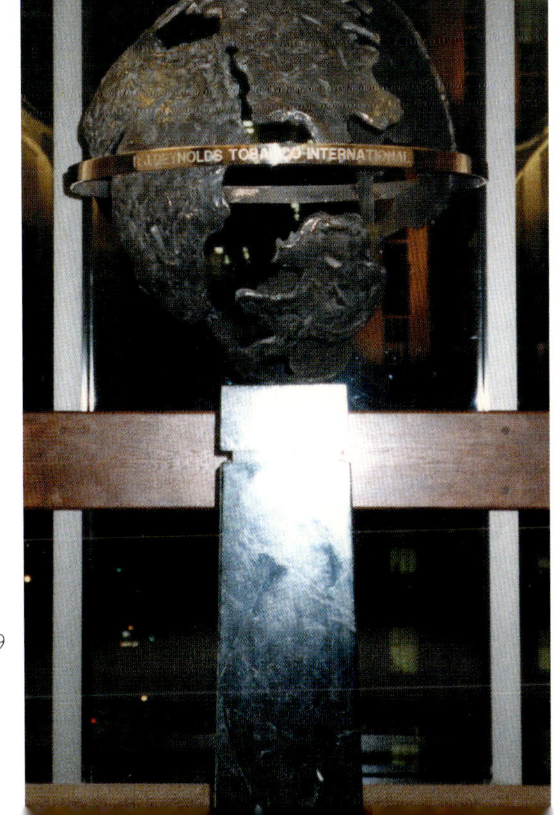

159

It is a complex thought process to anticipate man's future

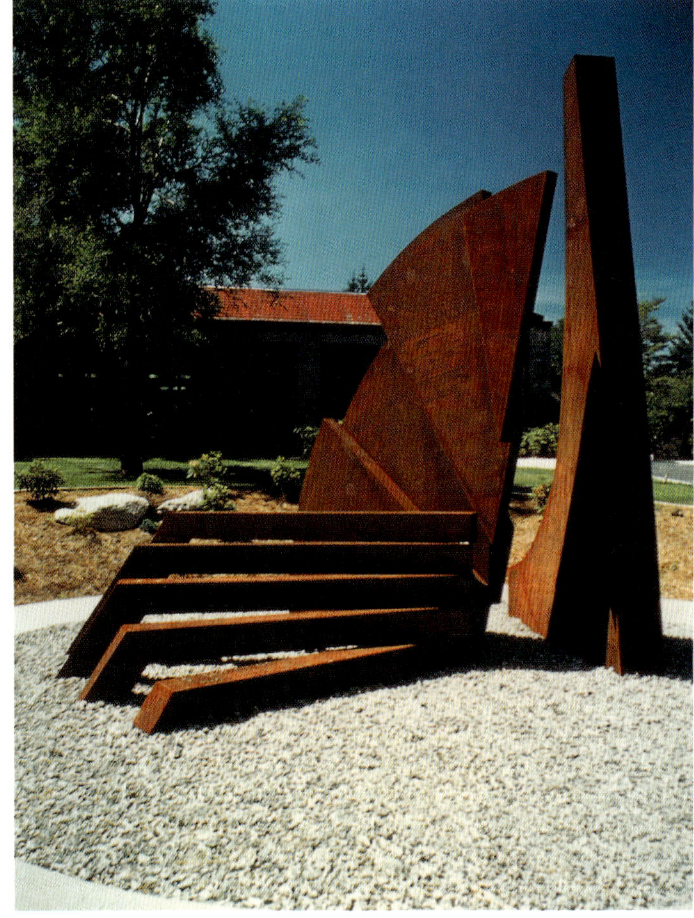

160

"Art is an essential part of
keeping ourselves humane."

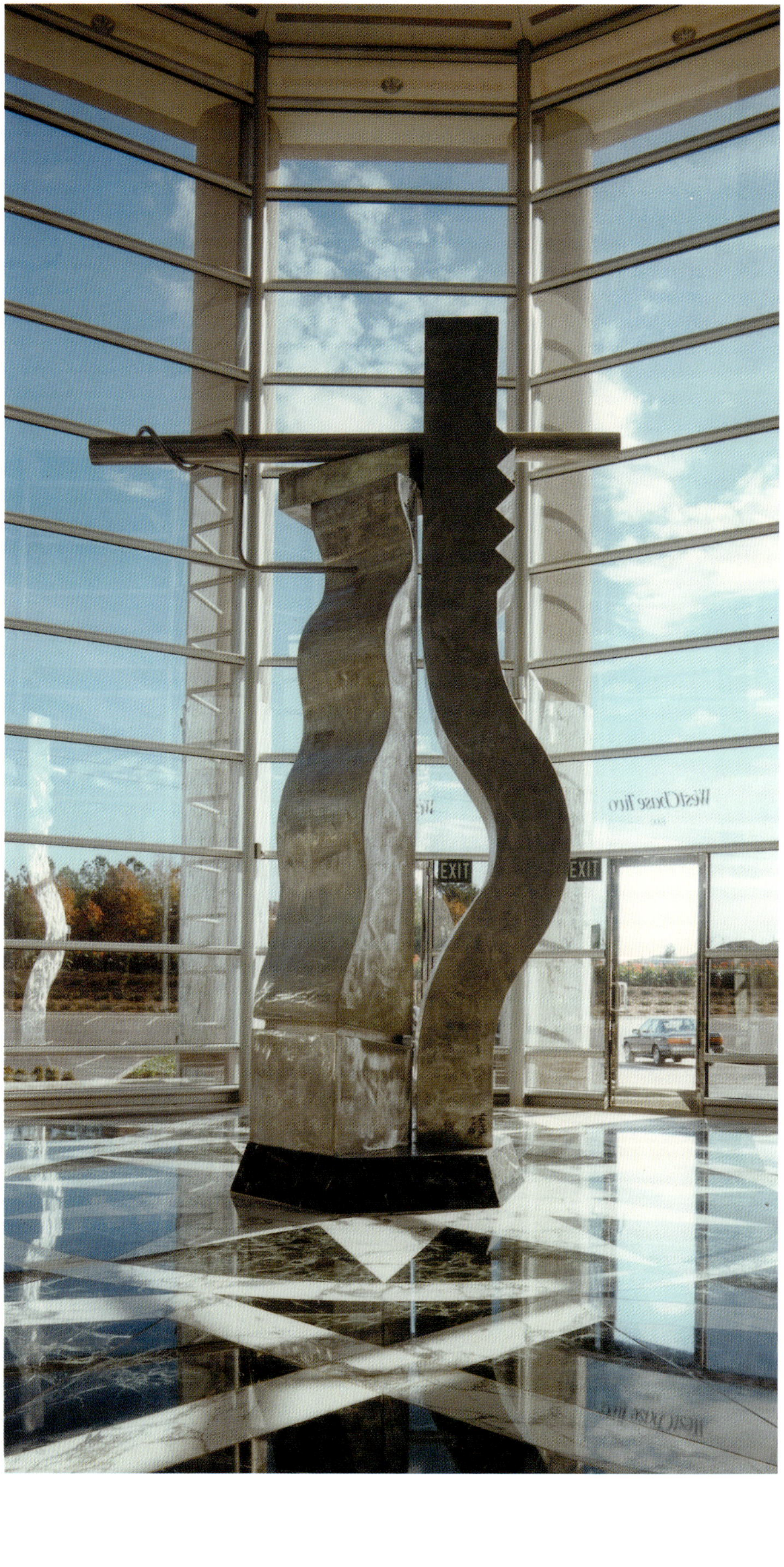

161

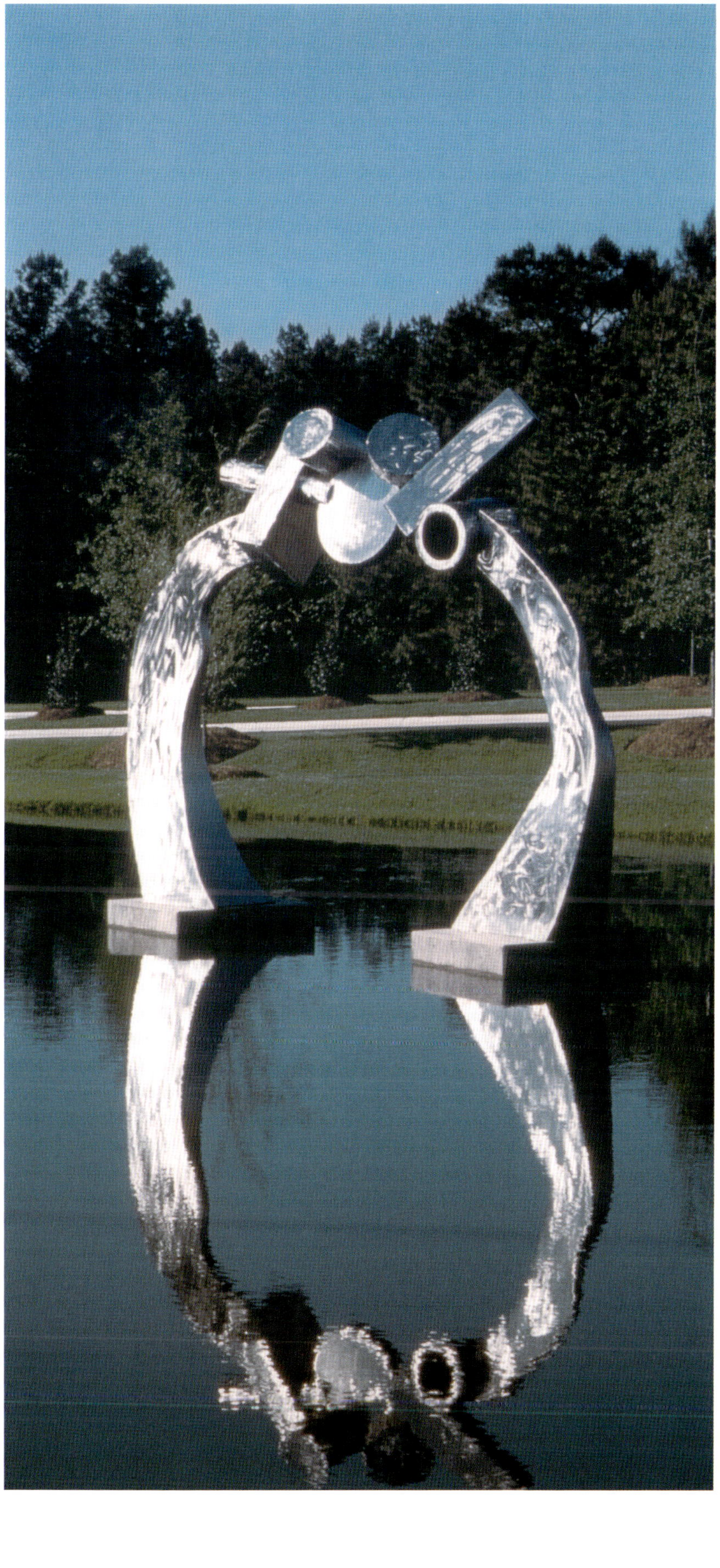

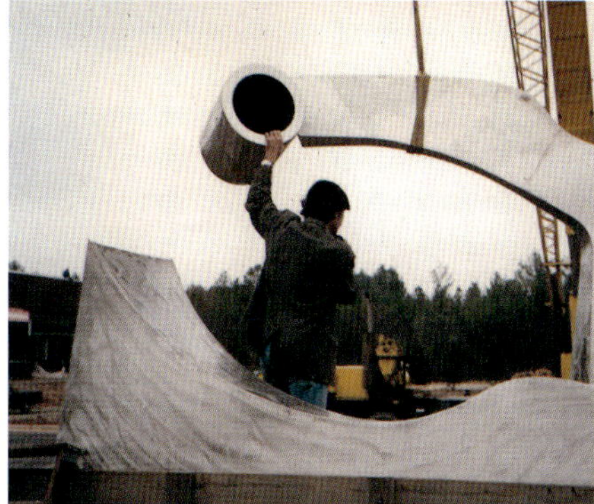

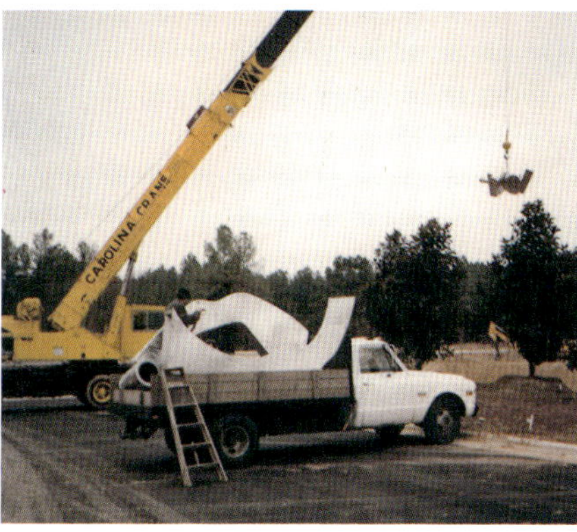

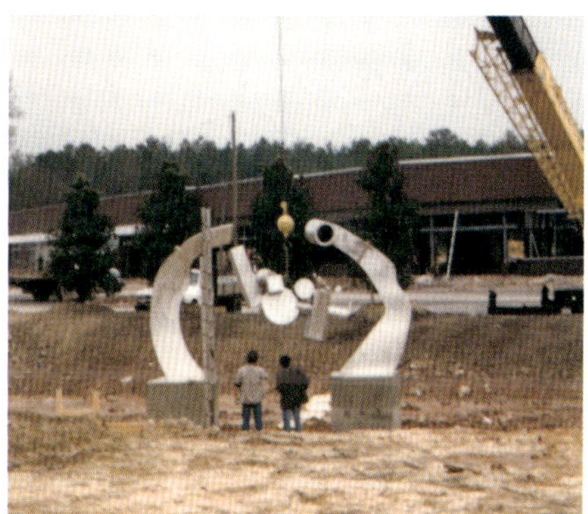

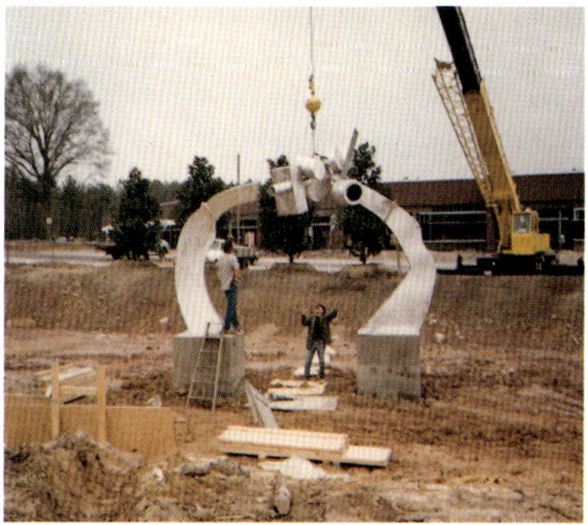

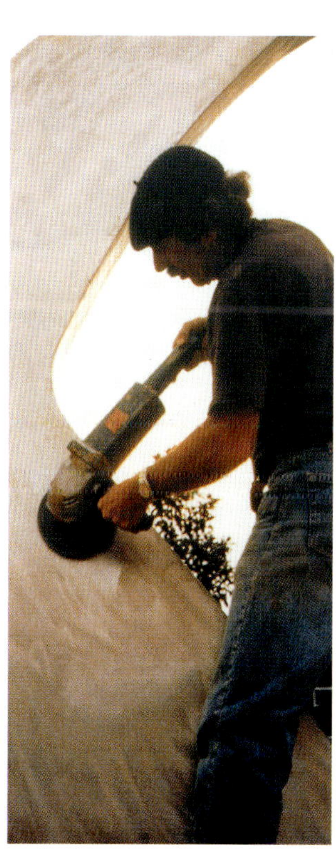

Lotus? Phoenix? Growth?

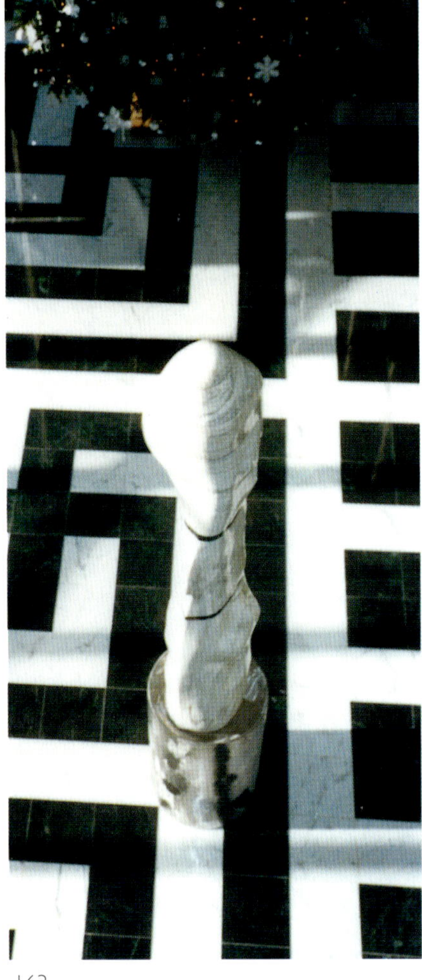

163

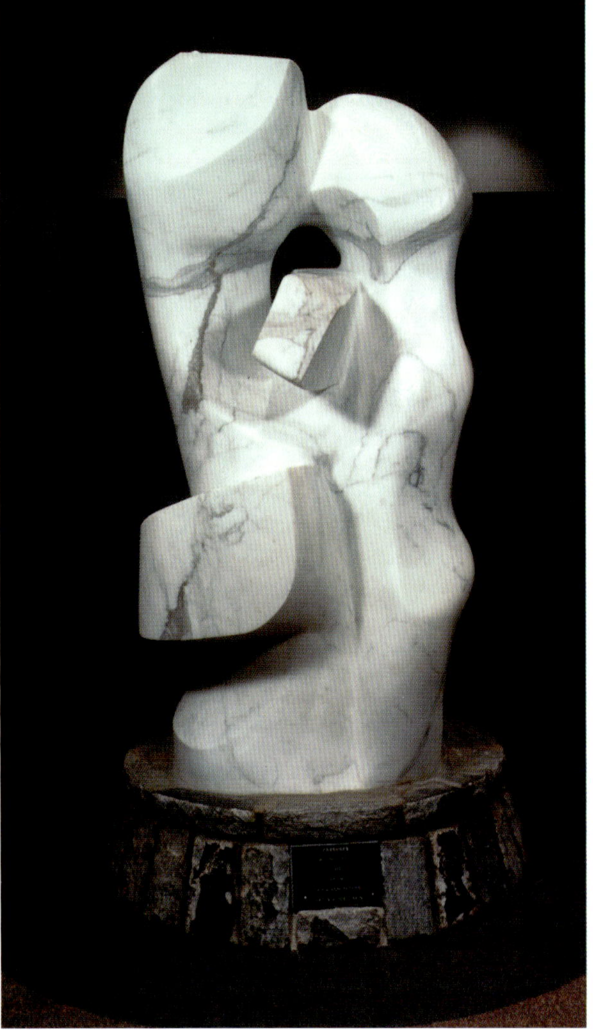

164

The essence of man is not man, but simply a gesture . . . That is more man.

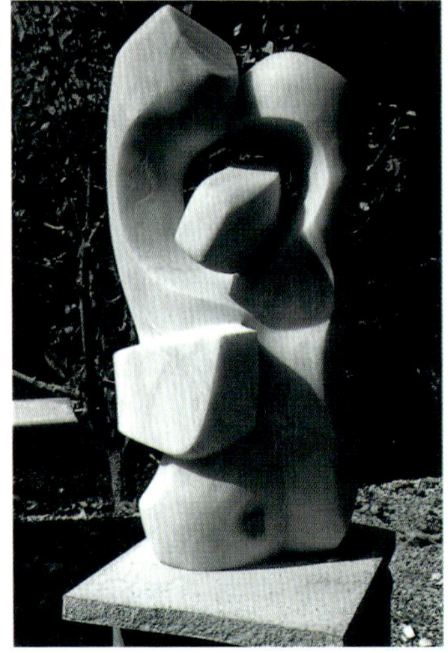

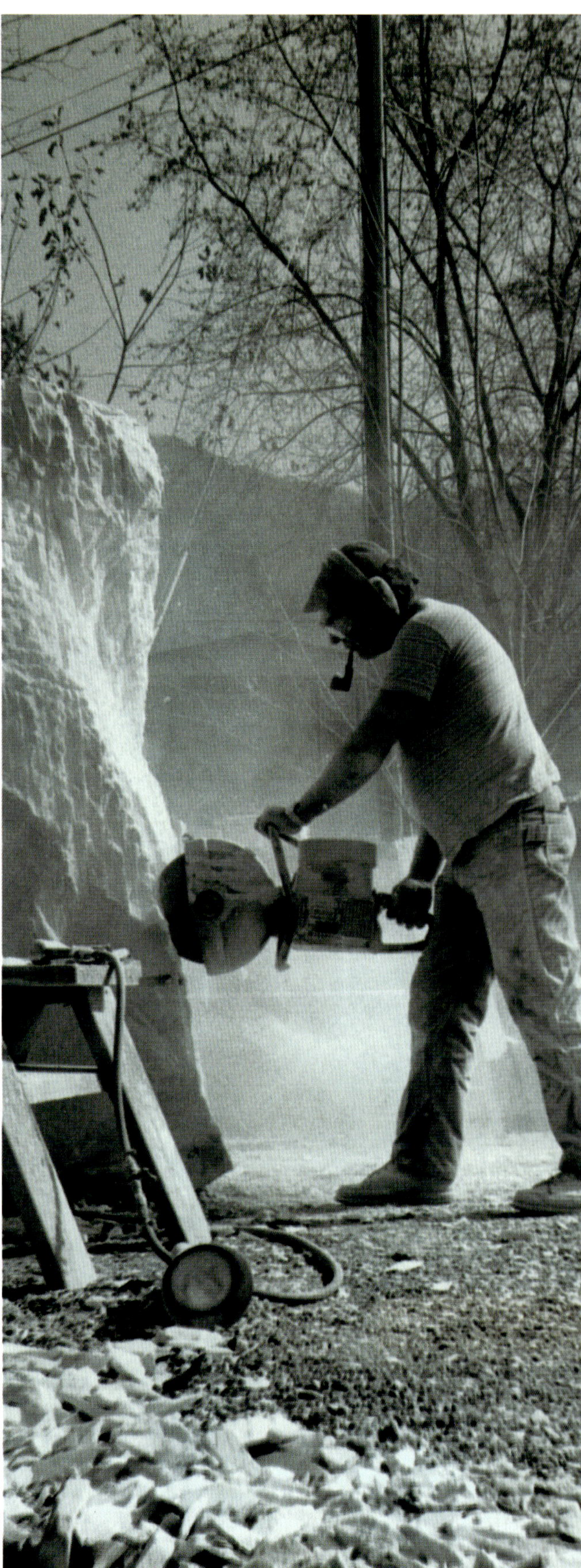

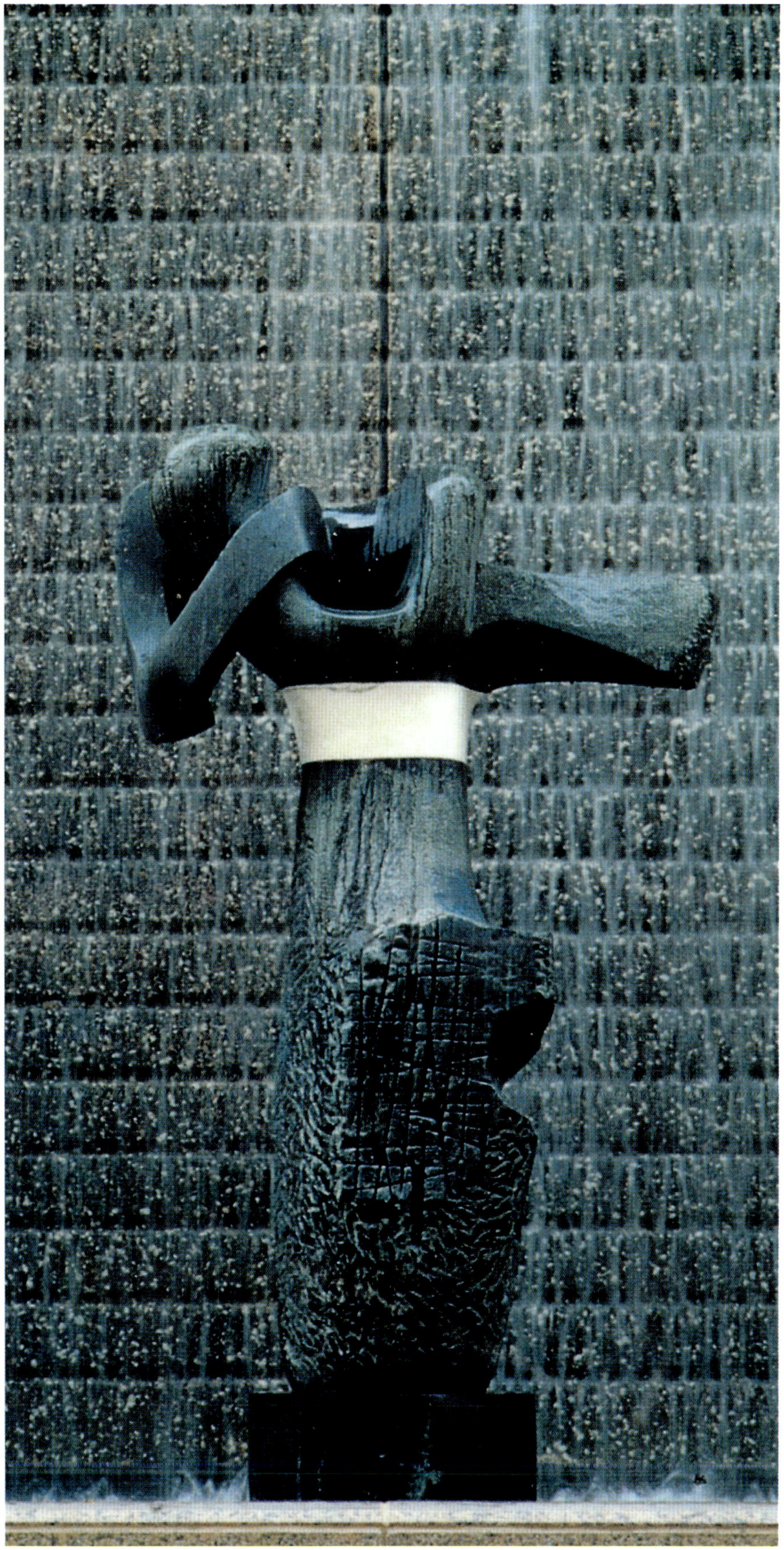

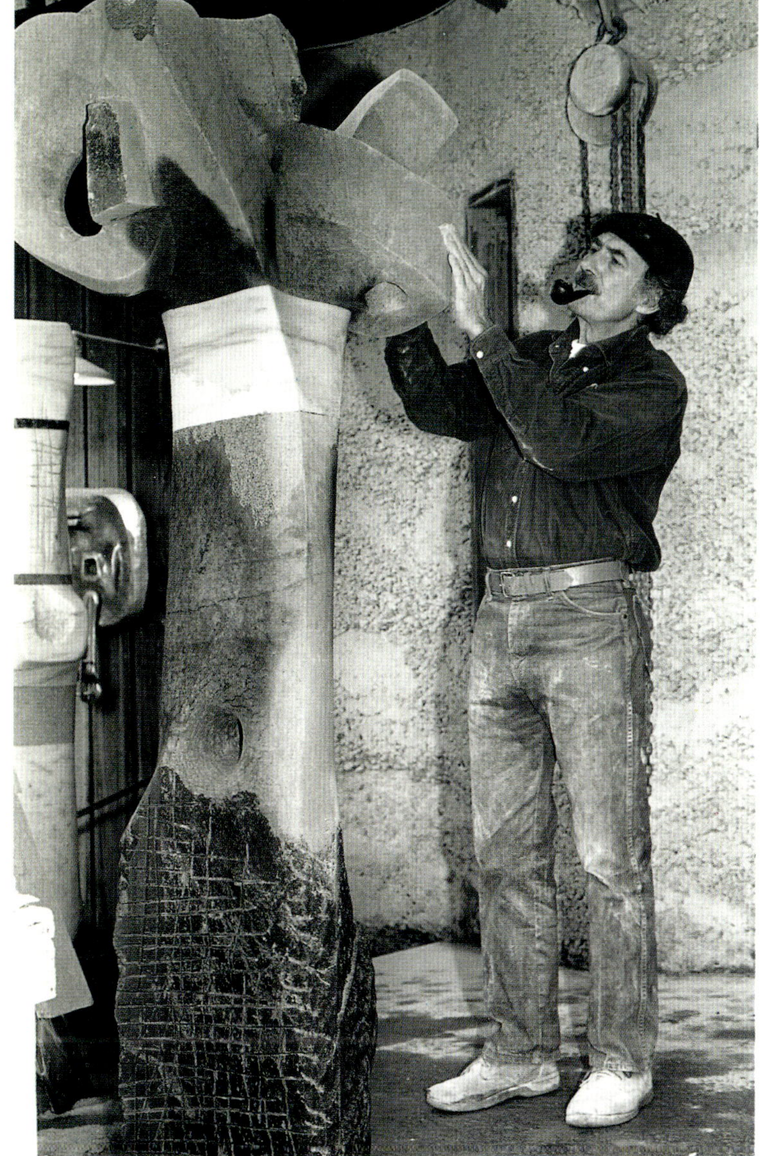

I want everything . . .

I need everything . . .

I squeeze that last second out of each day stopping only when I can no longer do any more. I continue to search and bring in all things, visual and otherwise, and then the sorting process (selective destruction) begins . . . I force people to become the very best they can be. I push some of them. Few pass my standards – and I know only time will judge me accurate or foolish.

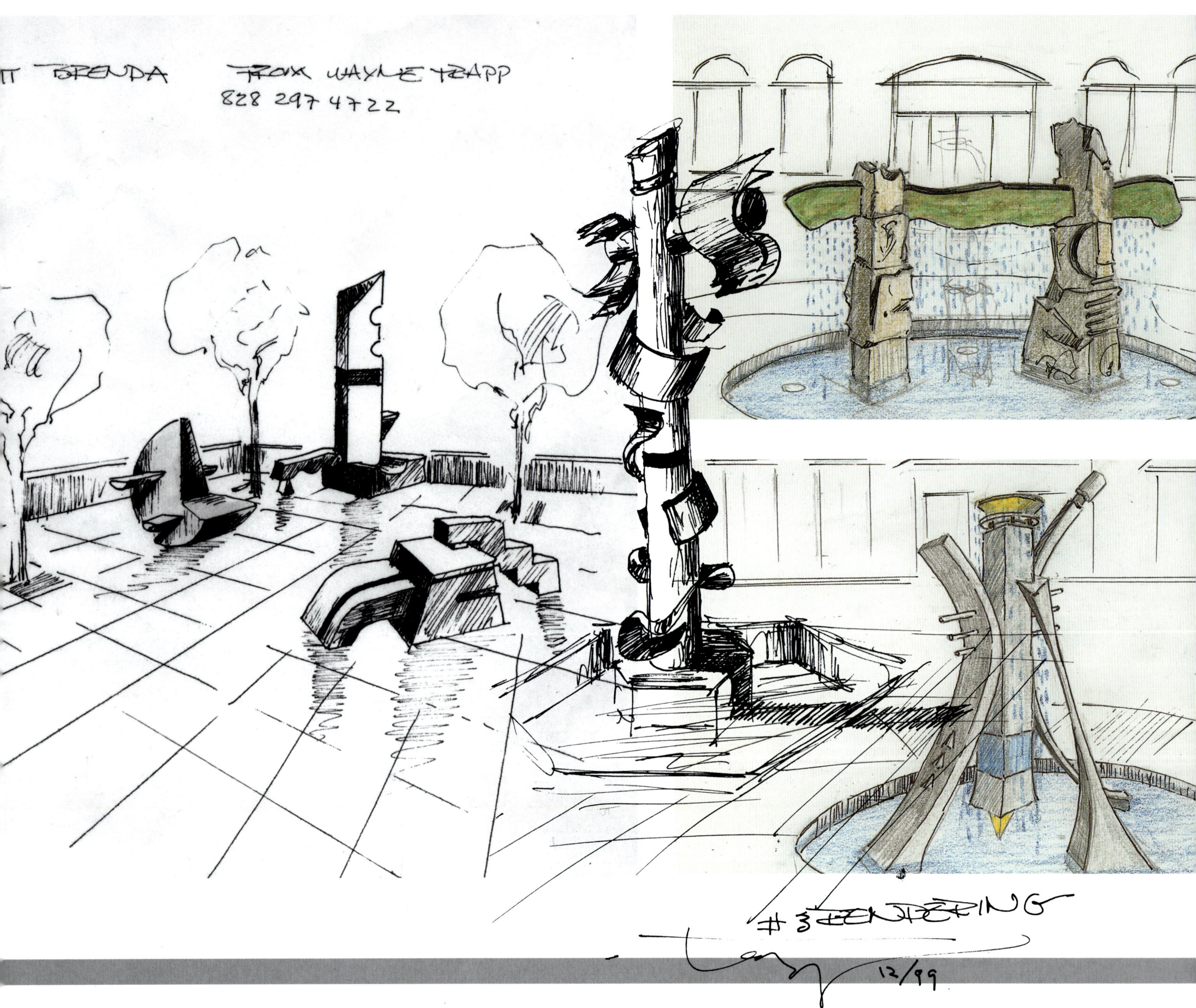
TT BRENDA   FROM WAYNE TRAPP
828 297 4722
3 RENDERING
12/99

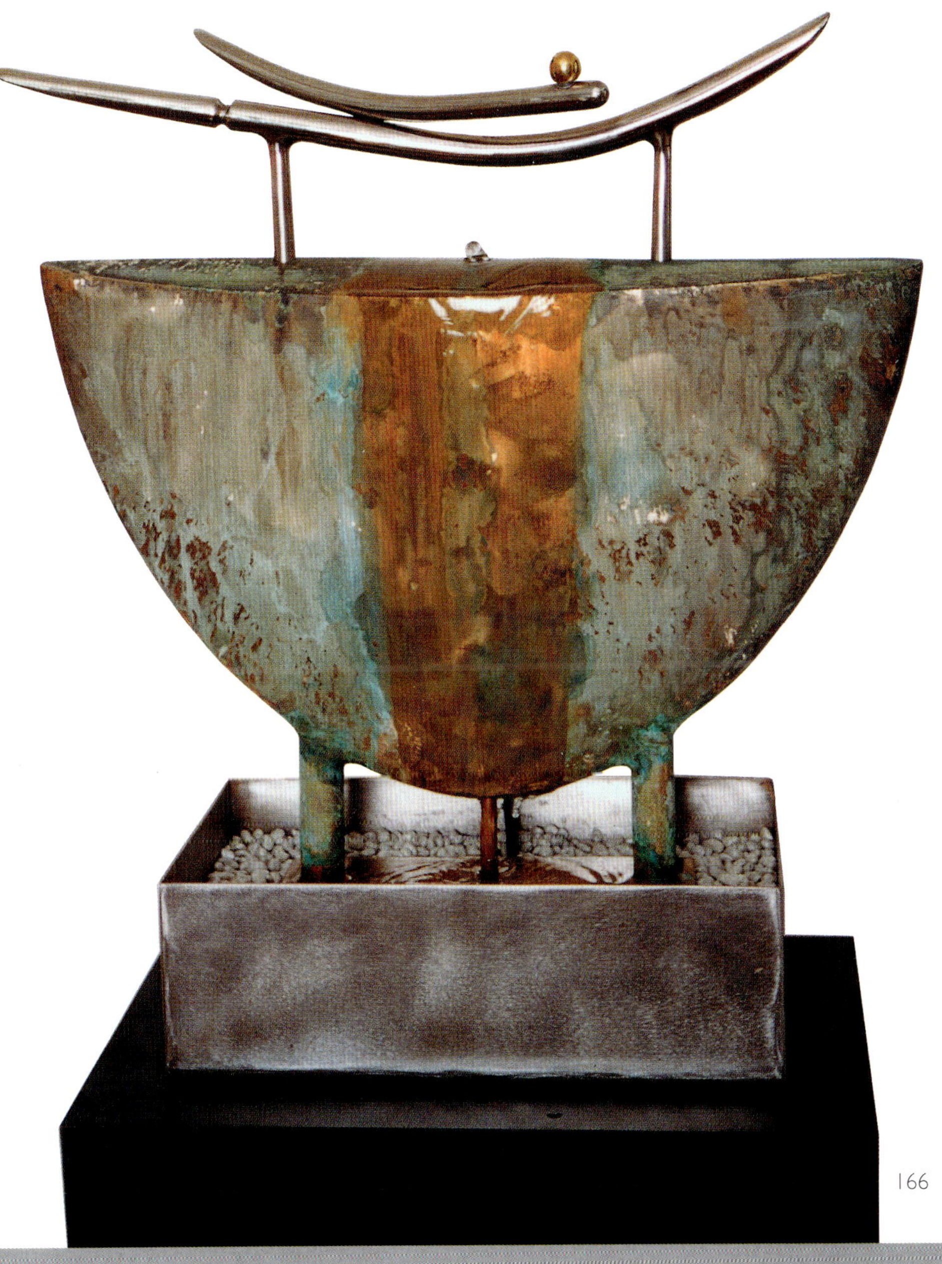

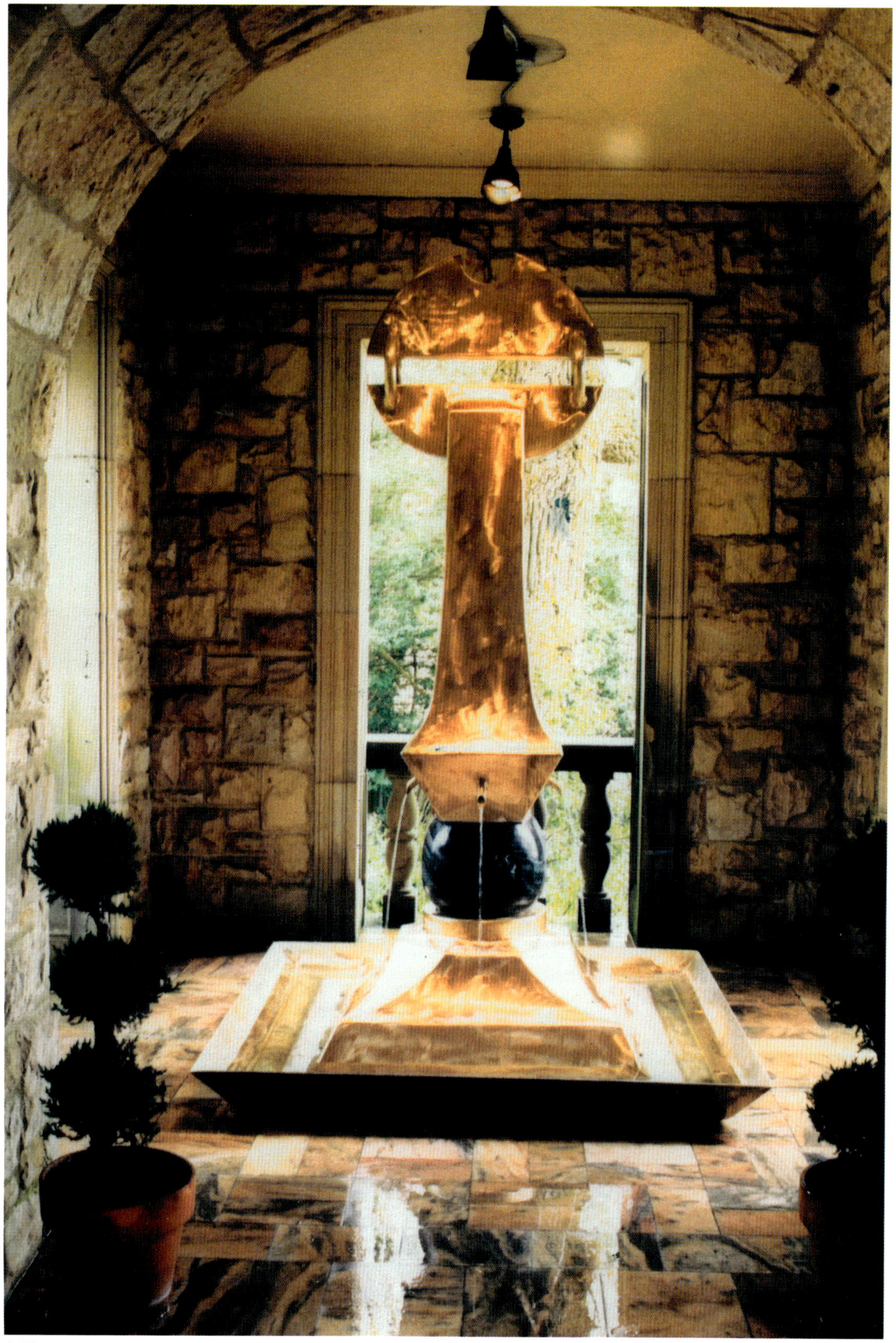

This evening I went to the beach — hoping to find it empty of people and disappointed to find it was not. I took Antoine (my dog) with me. The joy he experienced was like mine. He first ran with me, then swam, then tried to do both — full of the joy of the moment. Then the fog started to move in from out on the lake. There was no dividing line between water and sky. One large abyss. As people moved along the shore, they would fade in and out of sight, never really 'being' anywhere. Beautiful!

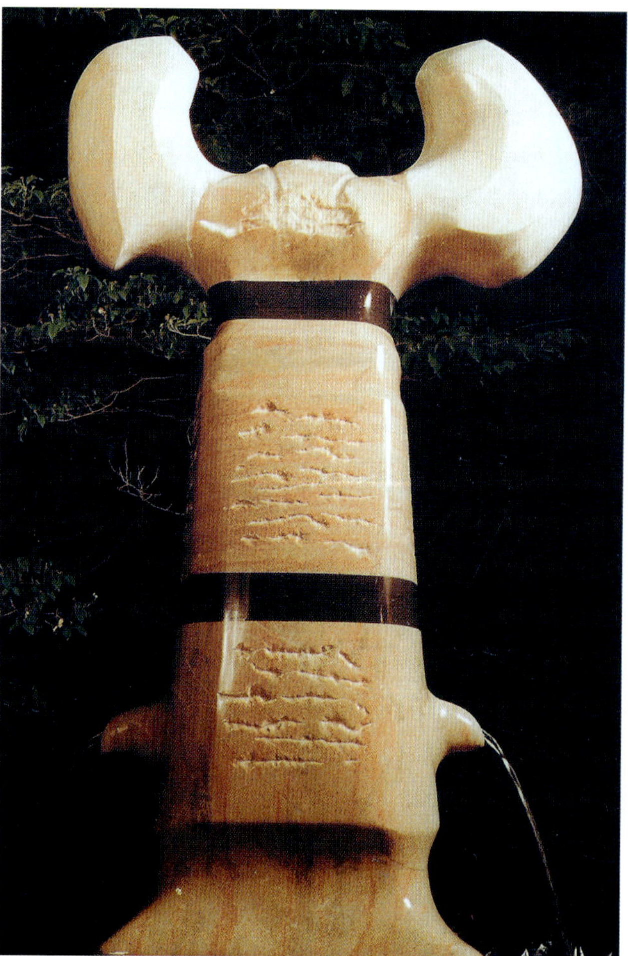

The invention of forms that beg to be looked at — that have that Noguchi magic — those are my final objective. East, West, and Beyond . . . a hard road.

I have finally recreated and destroyed "The Cry" by Noguchi. It is in wood. Had I invented it, I would have done it in bronze. It has that haunting magic that I keep speaking of. The dynamics are over-whelming. I only saw his piece once in 1969, but its impact has never left me. I've no idea how close our visions are, but having done it has satisfied something inside me, released me. Now I can go beyond.

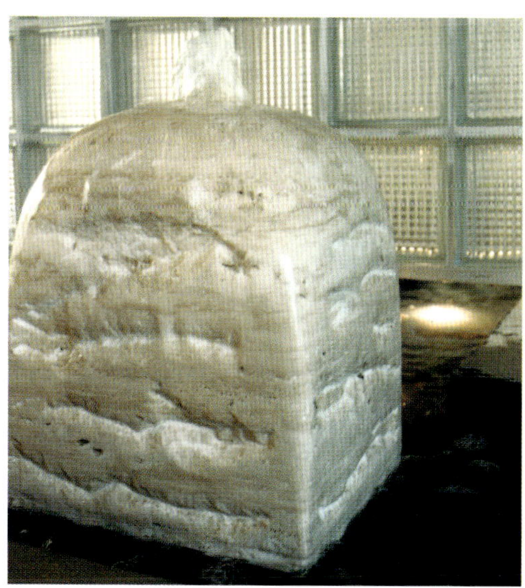

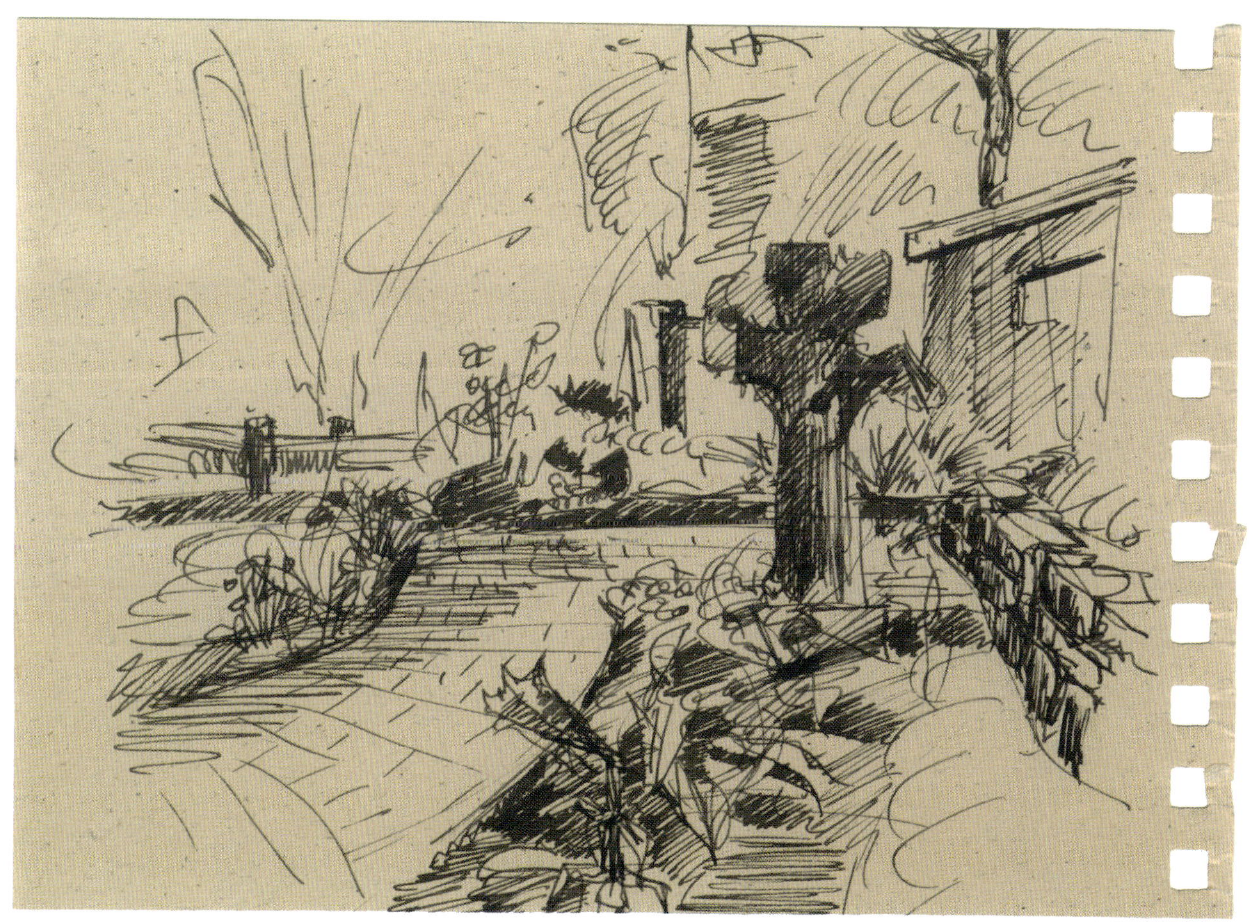

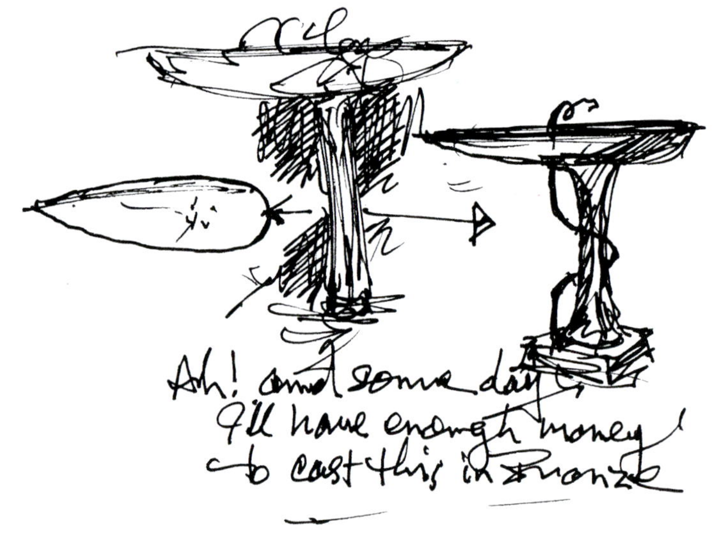

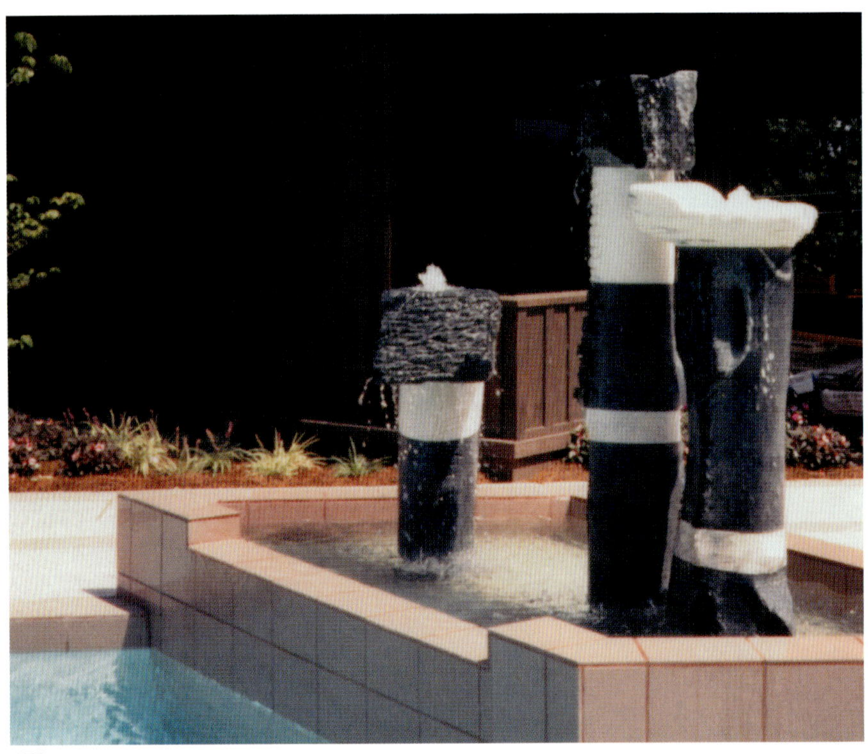

170

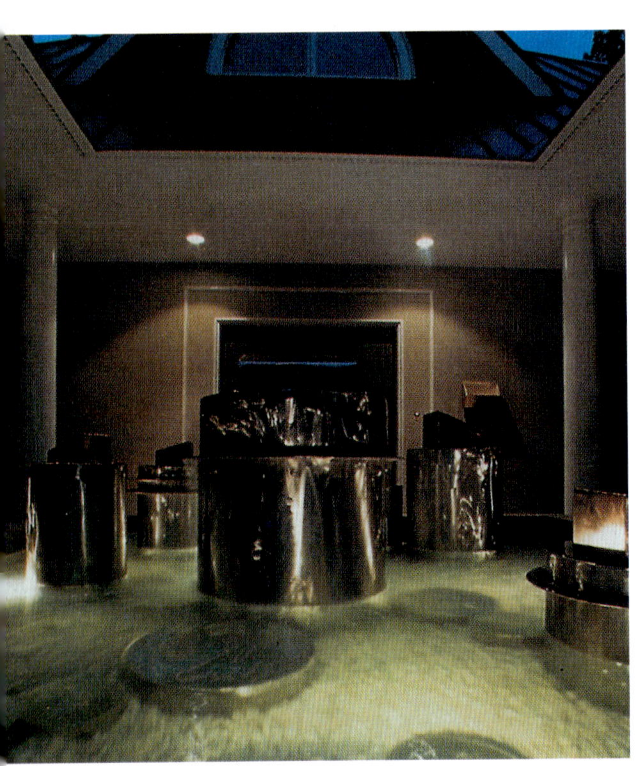

171

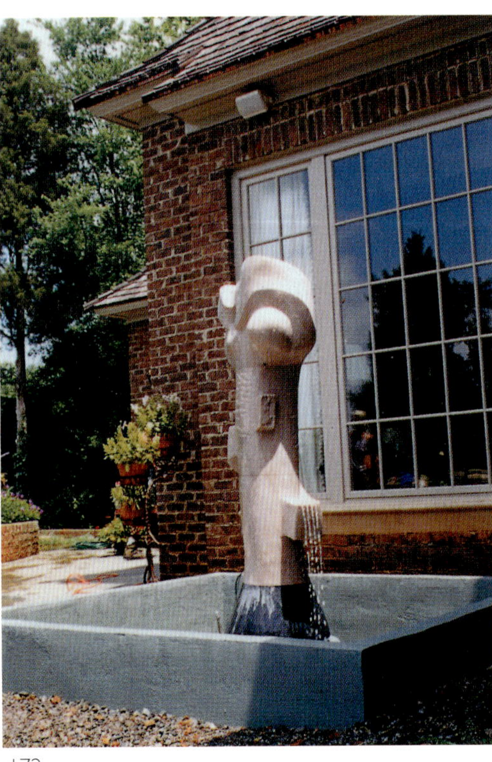

172

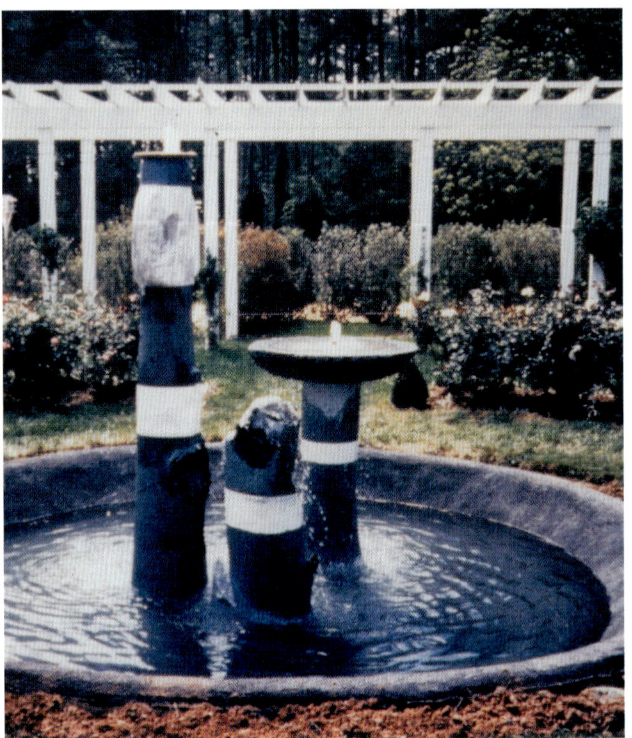

173

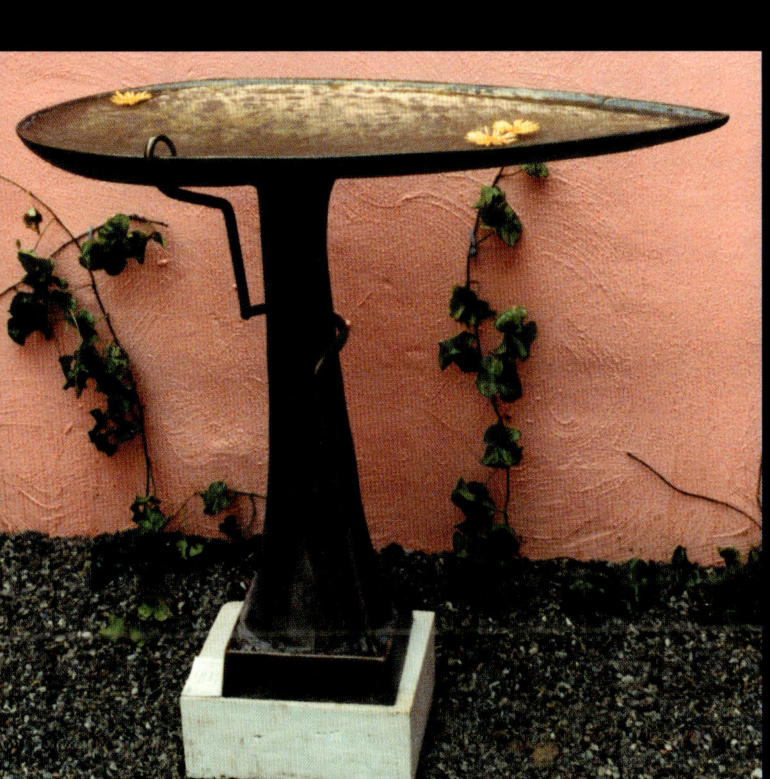

To purpose April, do you return?
Beauty is not enough.
You can no longer quiet me with the
redness of little leaves opening stickily.
I know what I know.

The sun is hot on my neck
as I observe the spikes of the crocus.
The smell of earth is good.
It is apparent that there is no death.
But what does that signify?
For, not underground are the
brains of men eaten by maggots.

Life itself is nothing.
An empty cup, a flight of uncarpeted stairs.
It is not enough that yearly, down this hill,
you come like an idiot, babbling and
strewing flowers.

— Edna St. Vincent Millay

Once again it is the first of April. How fast this
'year' flew by! Seems only moments ago that I
sought out this poem (my ritual for how many
years?), always struck in awe by its words that
seem to speak for me . . . that quiet scream for
Spring to be more than Spring.

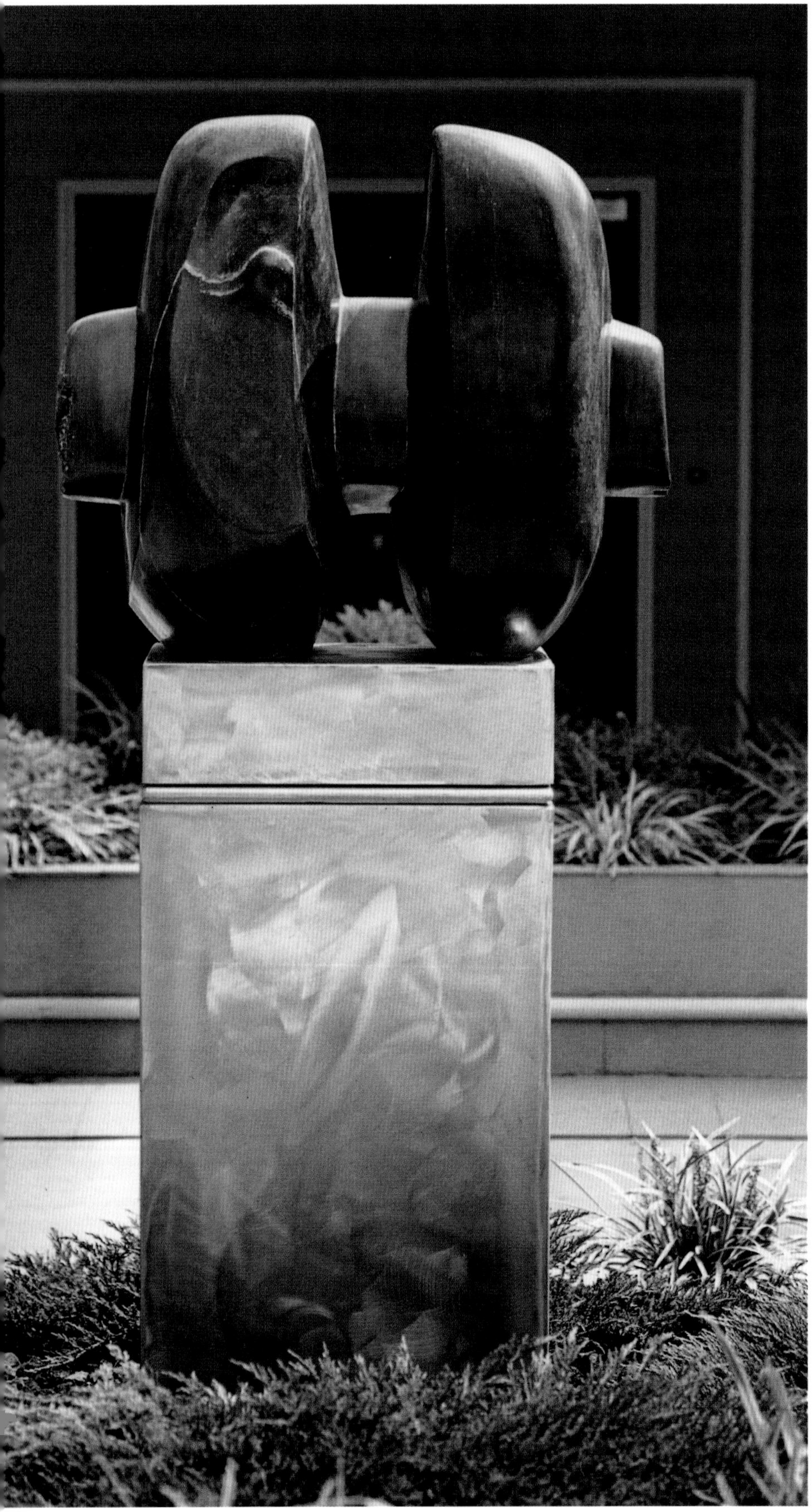

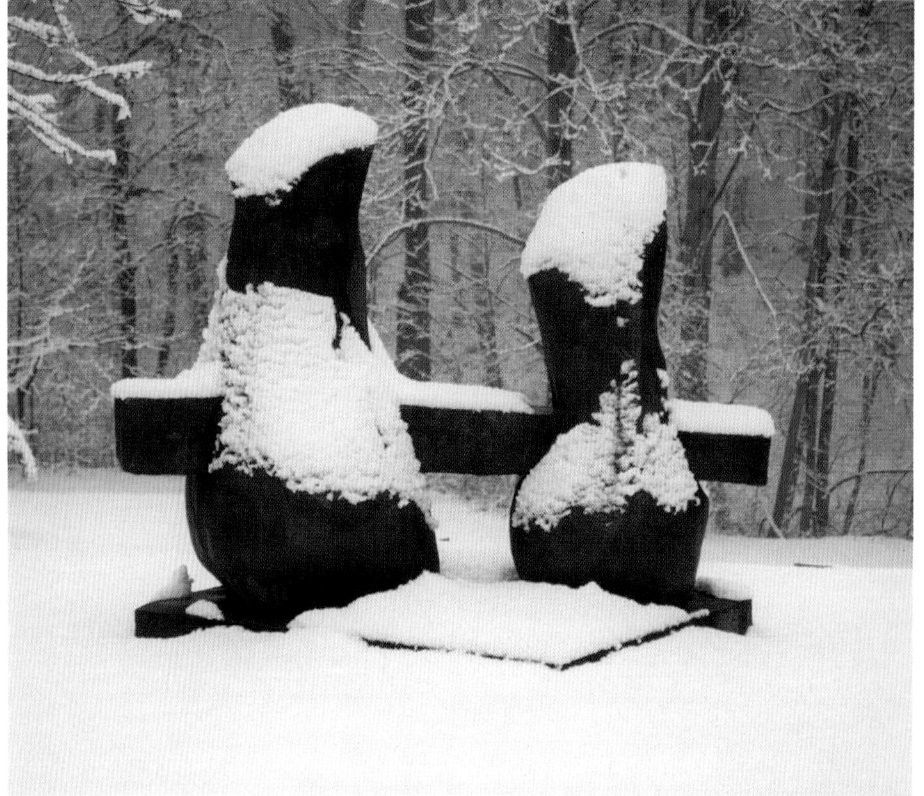

176

An oriental awareness of simplicity is perhaps the highest form of awareness. Knowing what little is needed. Knowing what must be illuminated to capture pureness. The essence of anything is not THAT thing, but a lie about THAT thing which destroys the actual and creates an even greater image.

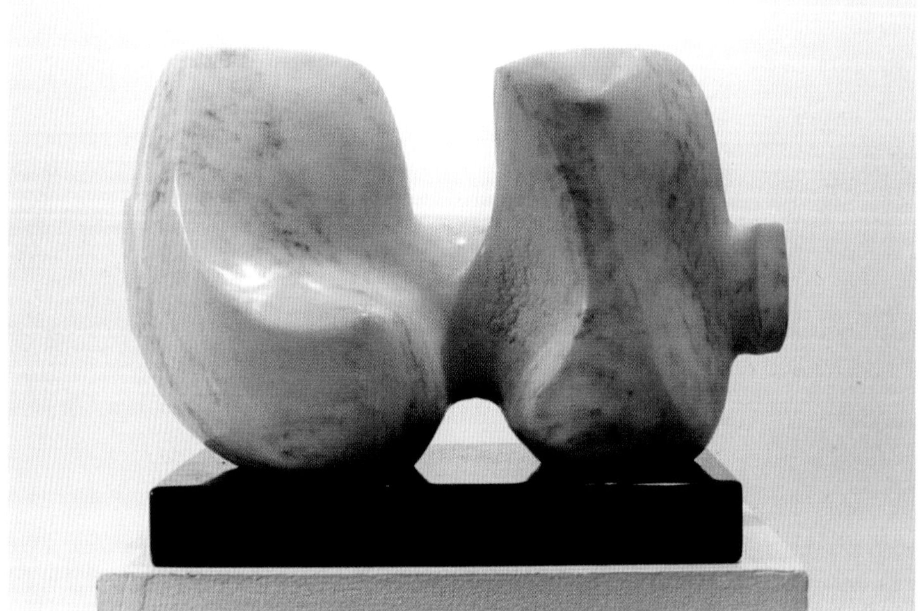

177

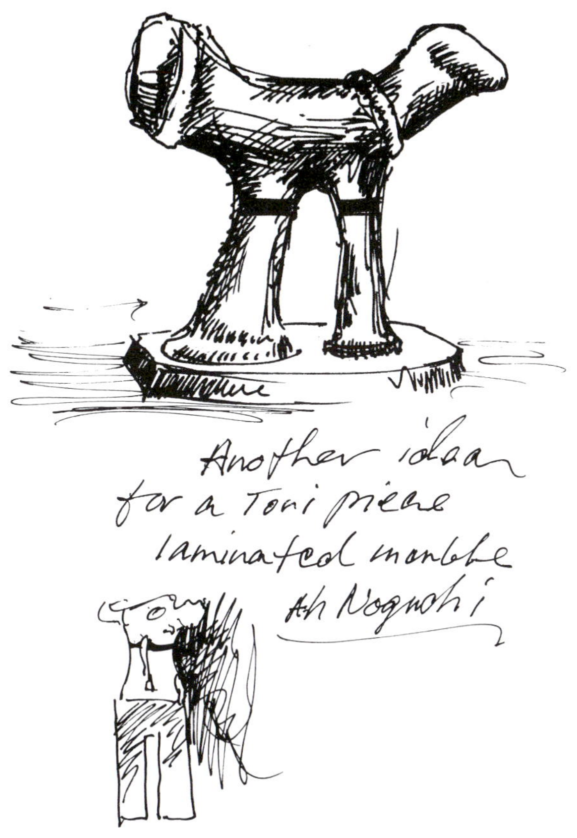

Another one of those joy-sadness days. It began at 5am doing soft, silent things in the studio so I could hear the rooster and bird songs. Slowly it became light – one of the more beautiful days followed. Coffee tasted better, the music, ah the music, and the blue cloudless sky and the slowly changing shadows always altering the sculptures. I completed many half done pieces, cut the grass, showered and sat alone as the evening shadows formed paintings on the grass. I sit by the stream now and am finally calm and reflective, the day still alive in my head and wanting to record it all and failing, except for words upon this page. Too much life sometimes – or perhaps it is all the noticing of so much life . . .

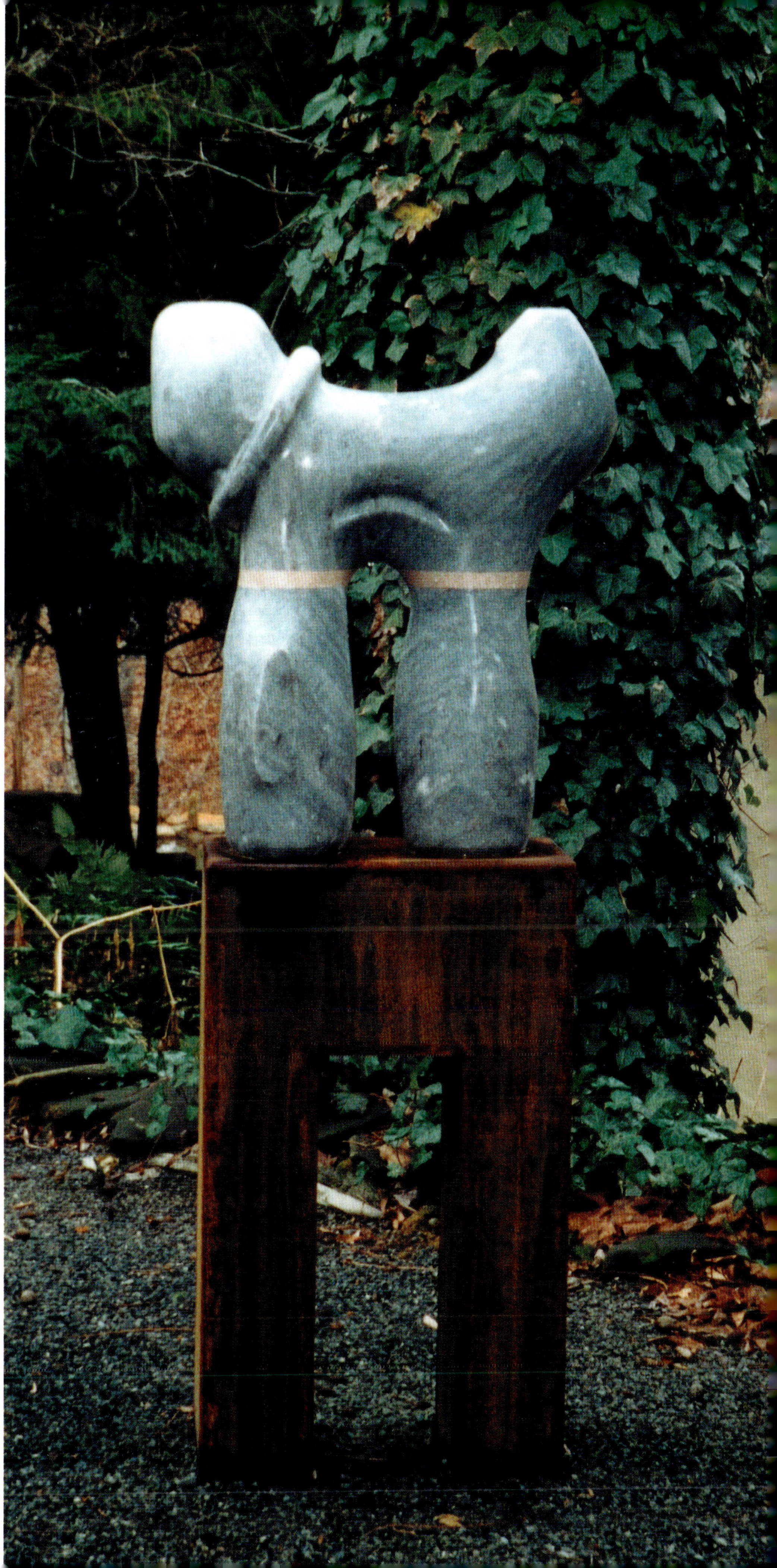

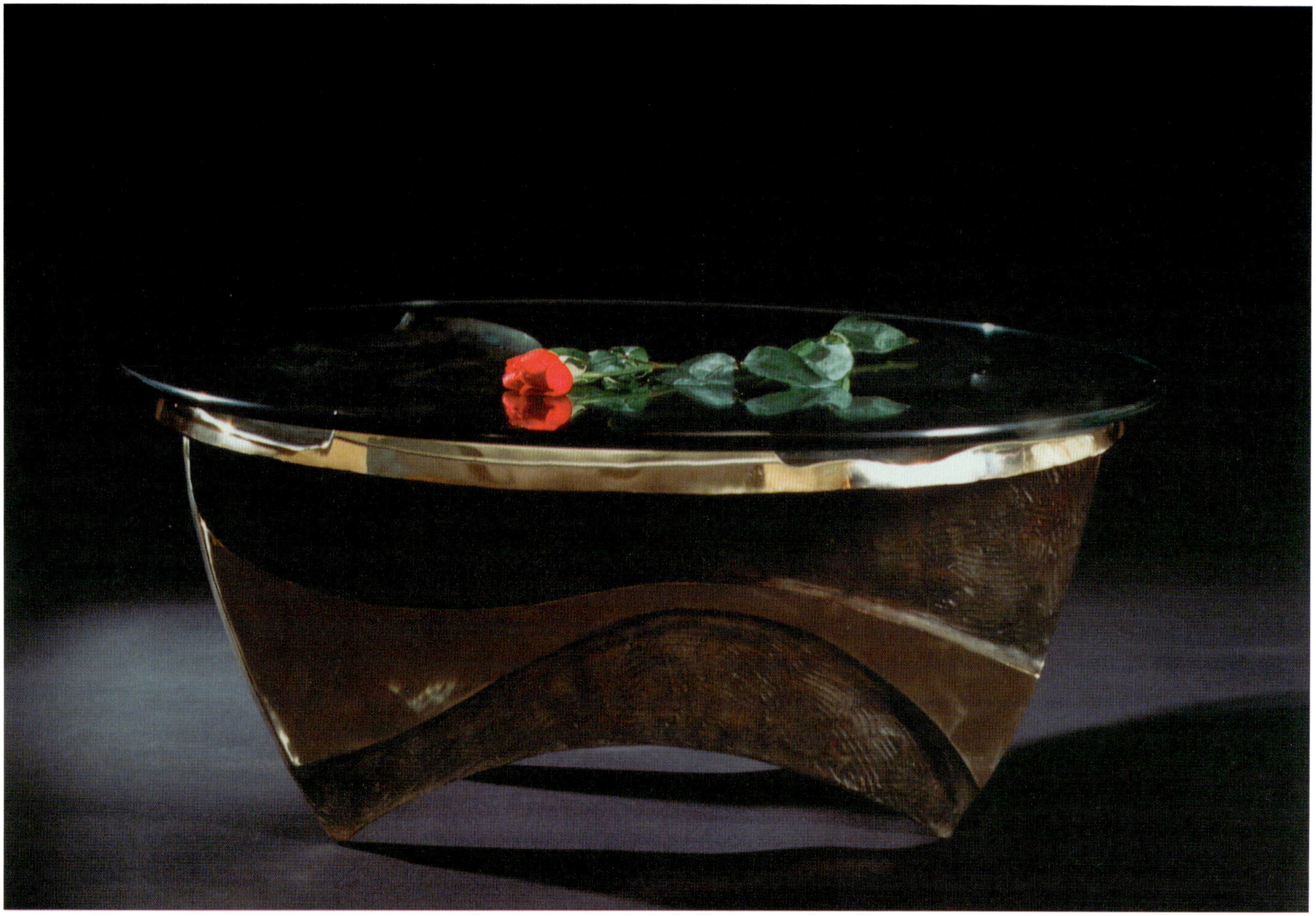

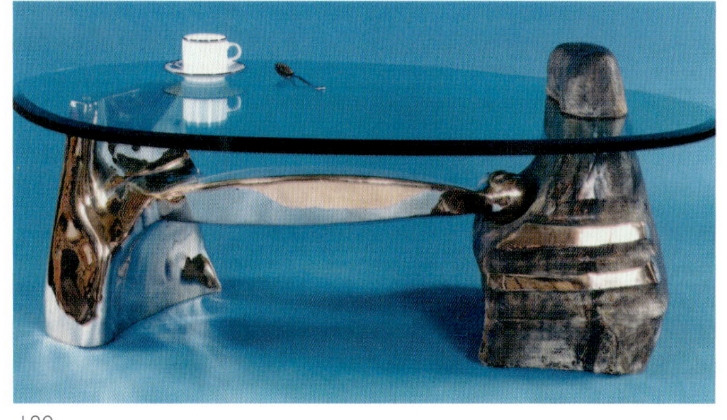

179

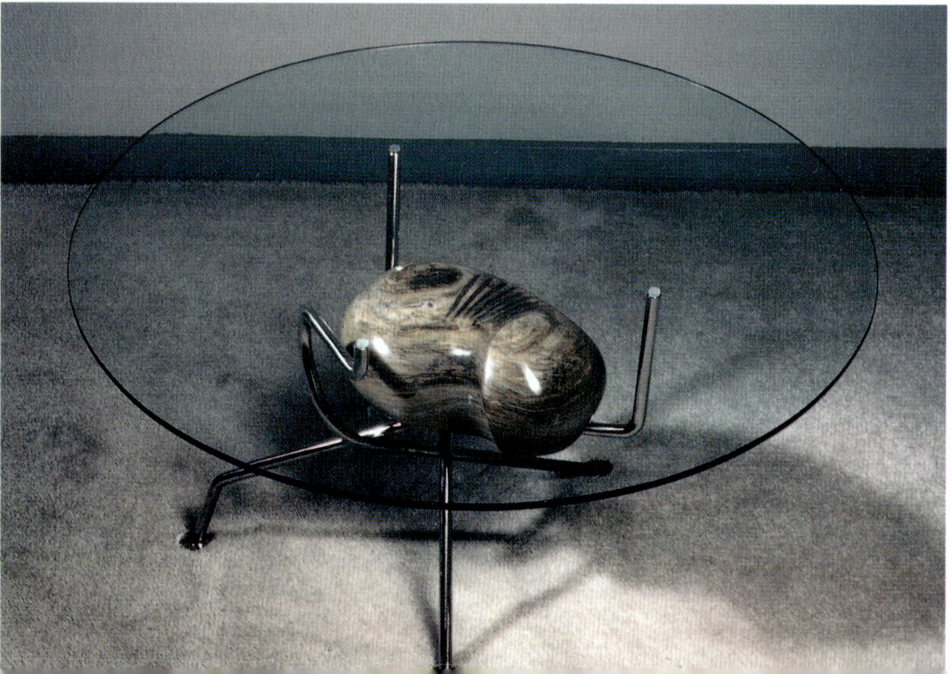

180

181

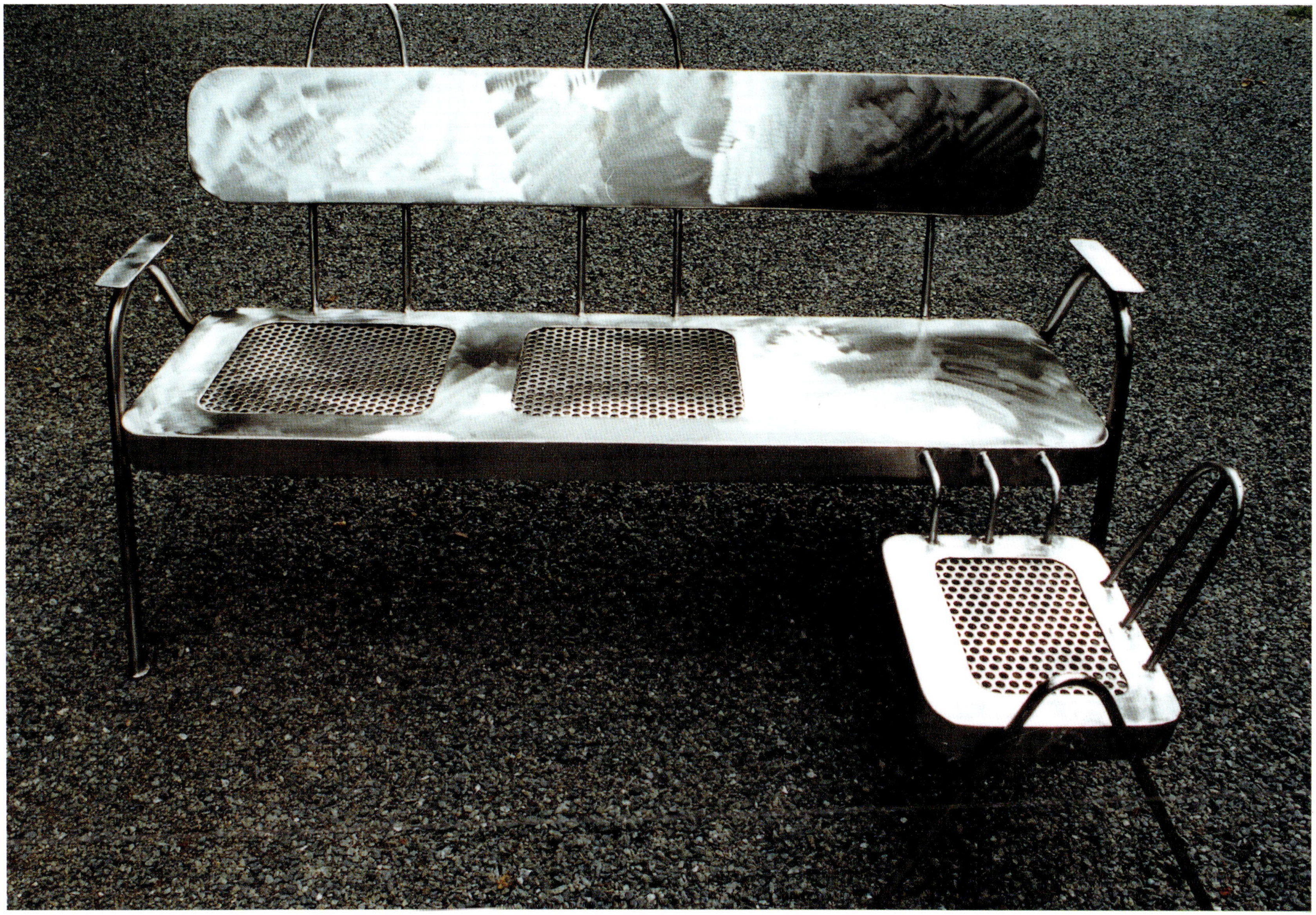

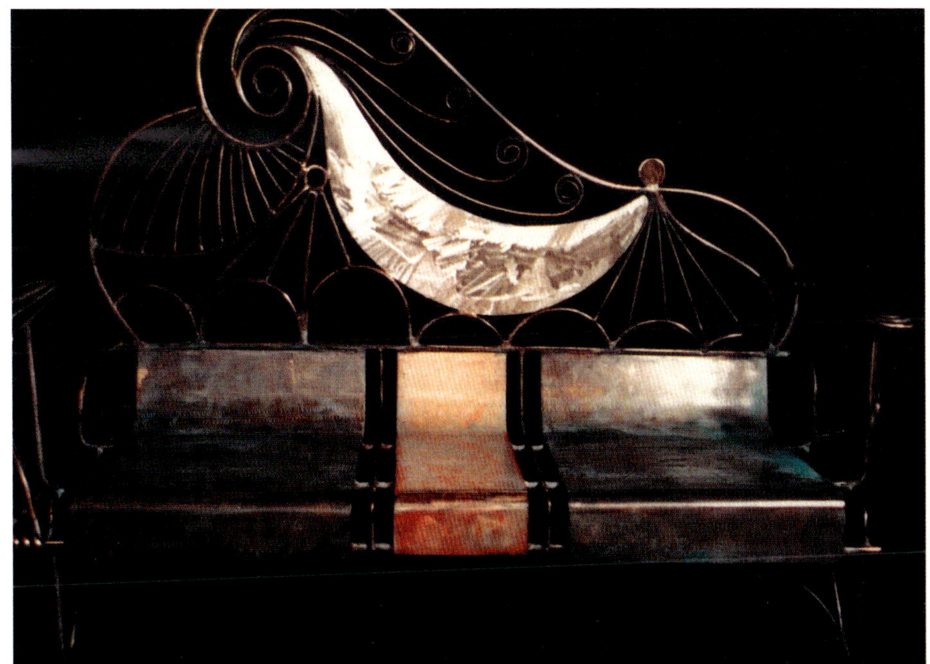

Calm and madness.
It is vital to have both.

I sit at my favorite spot – my desk – library table. As I read my new book (David Smith by D. S.) I know what the author is talking of when he talks about the pain and suffering he had gone through to achieve what he did. I know because my own existence is that of pain, loss of security, bills beyond hope of ever paying . . . Have spent almost a month with bad luck – the worst I've ever experienced. Have a pushing-pulsating desire to bust out of this fixed madness, to be liberated from this life and to see the freedom that will allow my world to be nothing but sculpture – to think, work, sleep, dream, DO sculpture. I have to get out from under this and DO. Time is passing by and I'm not taking advantage of its opportunity . . . I'm as if frozen in ice. I wait for the sun to melt my surroundings and free me. I can't move – even my mind is frozen. Have been sketching every day and night. That costs nothing. Am burning inside to put some of these sketches into works, but can't move. Christmas is near, want to at least travel and see works by other artists . . . don't have a car, money, nothing . . . what is the artist of this century to do? I ask for nothing more than being able to work 10-20-30 hours a day.

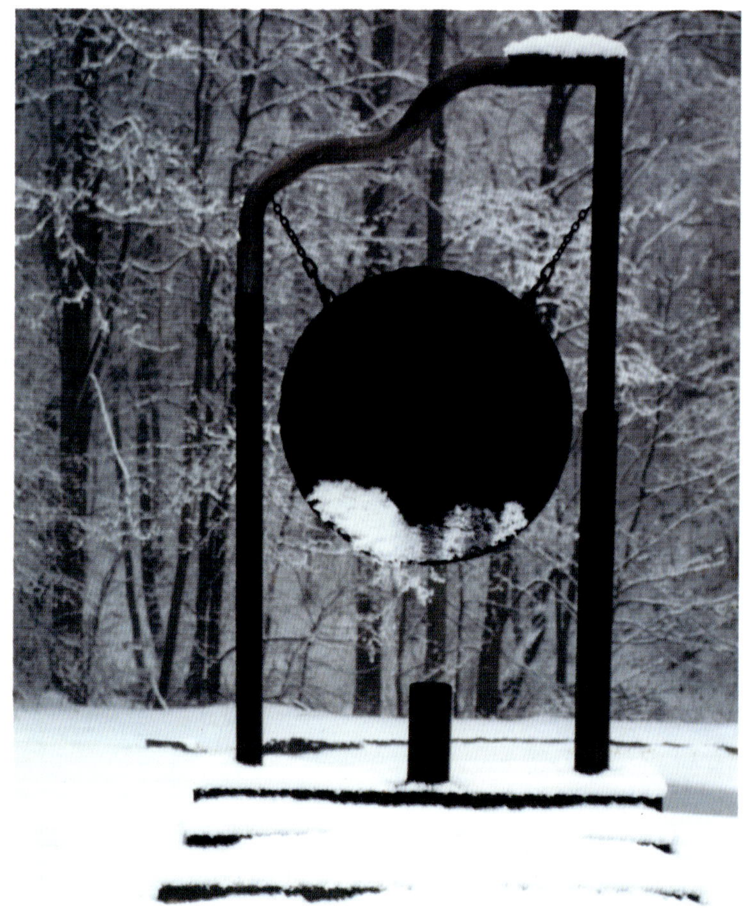

184

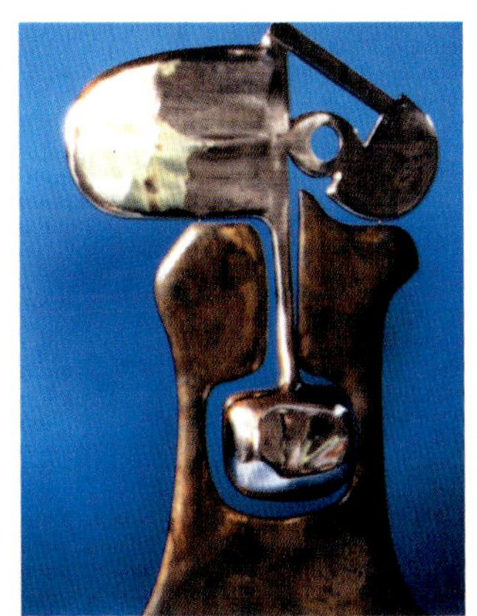

185

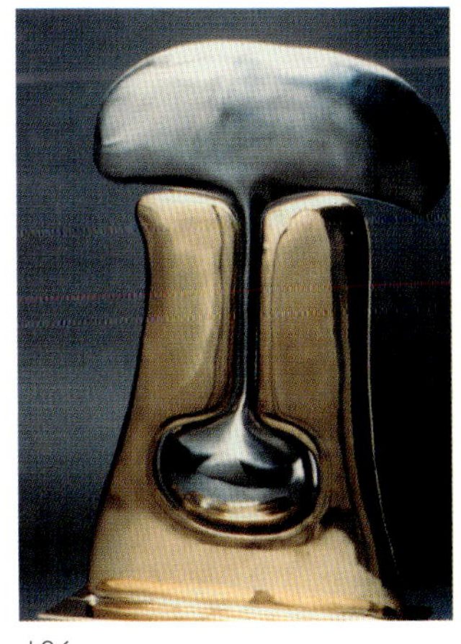

186

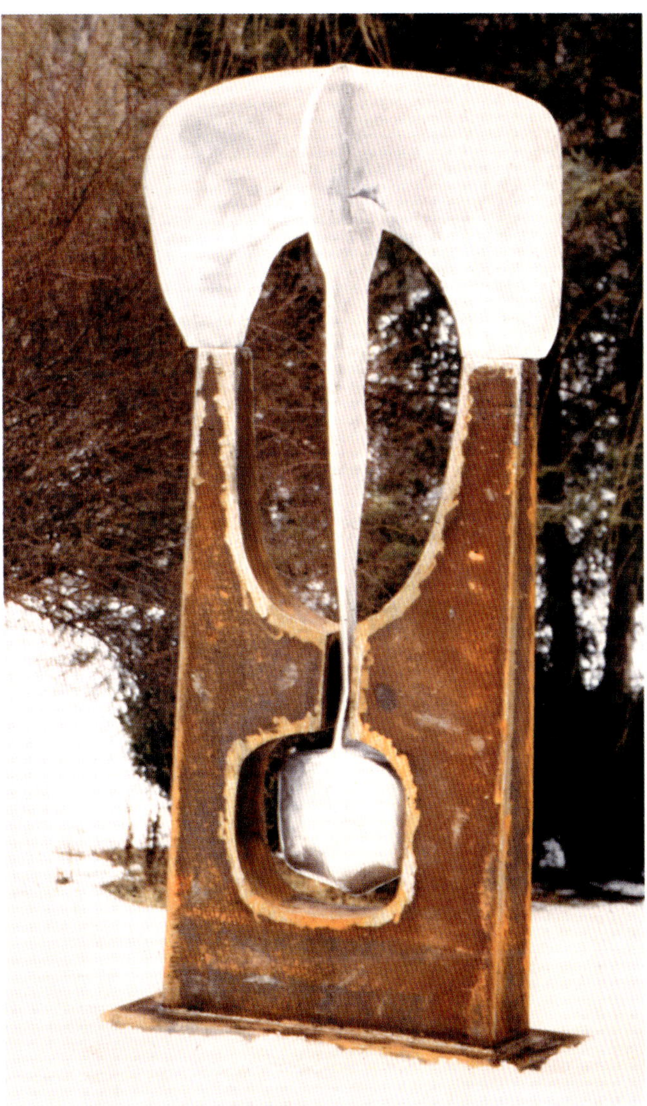

187

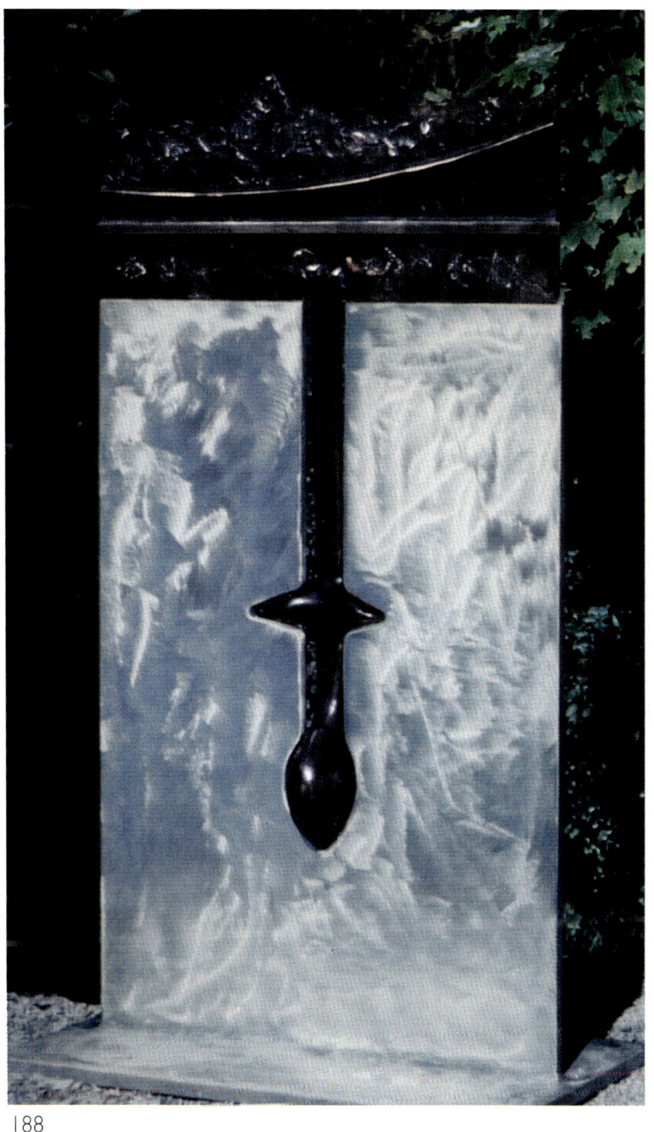

188

It all seems too new to me – each day a question. Is there something wrong with my mind? Shouldn't there be some kind of plan or routine that wouldn't surprise me as it unfolded? Maybe that's what art is about. The freedom to see things new. To be surprised always.

I absorb more now than I ever have. It takes little to fill my senses, to intoxicate me, to make my whole system dizzy . . . I don't need more stimuli. I need to put the mental images into solid form, to unleash the part of me that overflows and turn the overflow into creative energy, to work until I have drained my system, then rest . . .

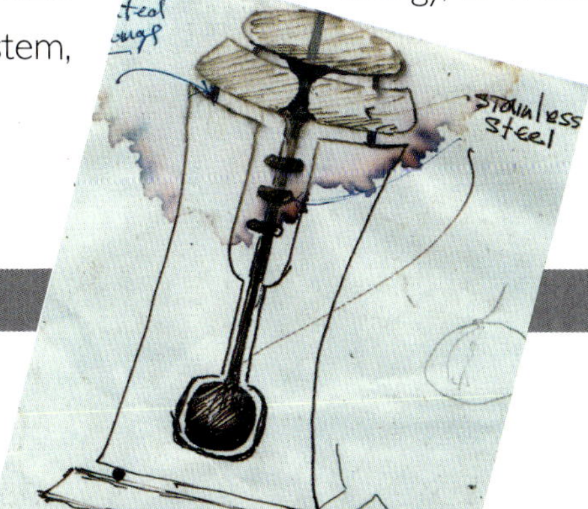

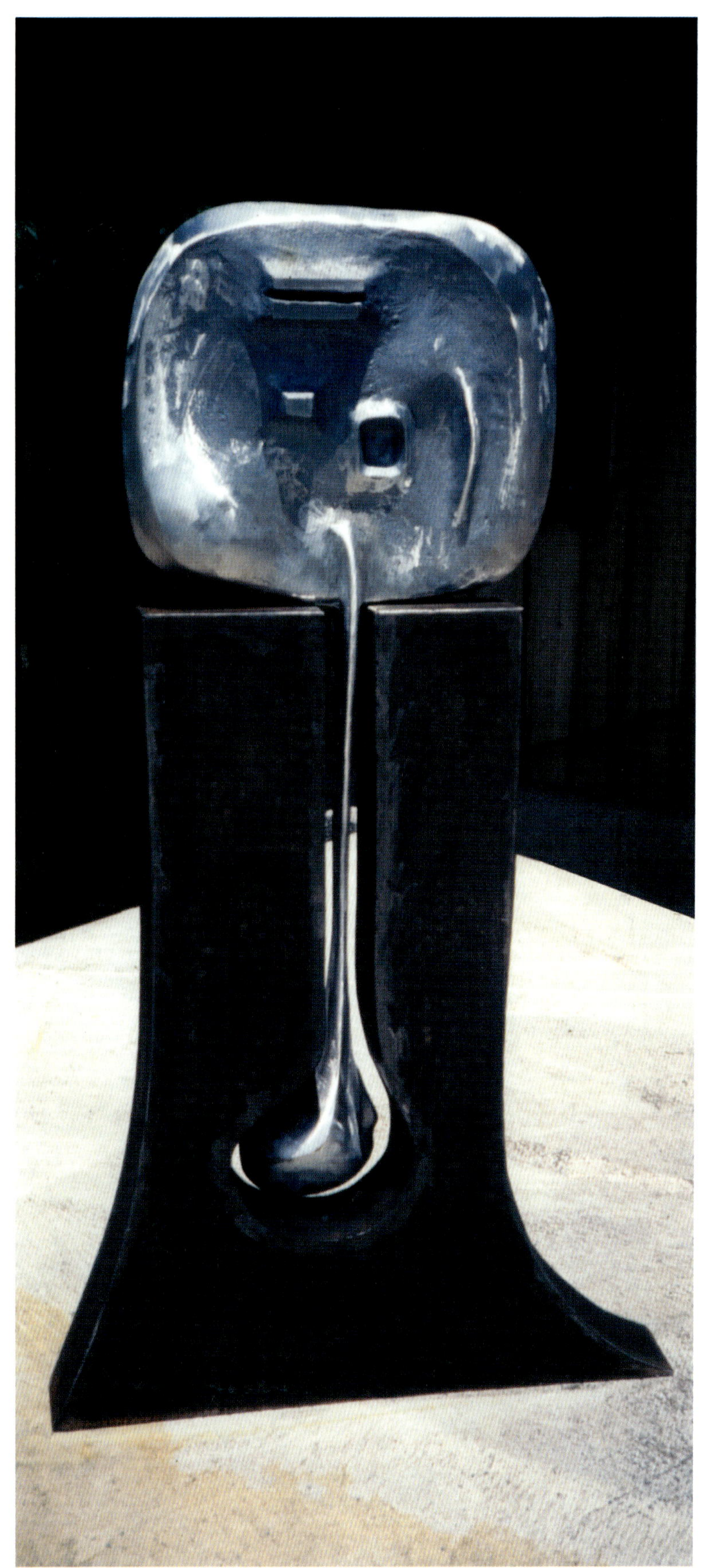

189

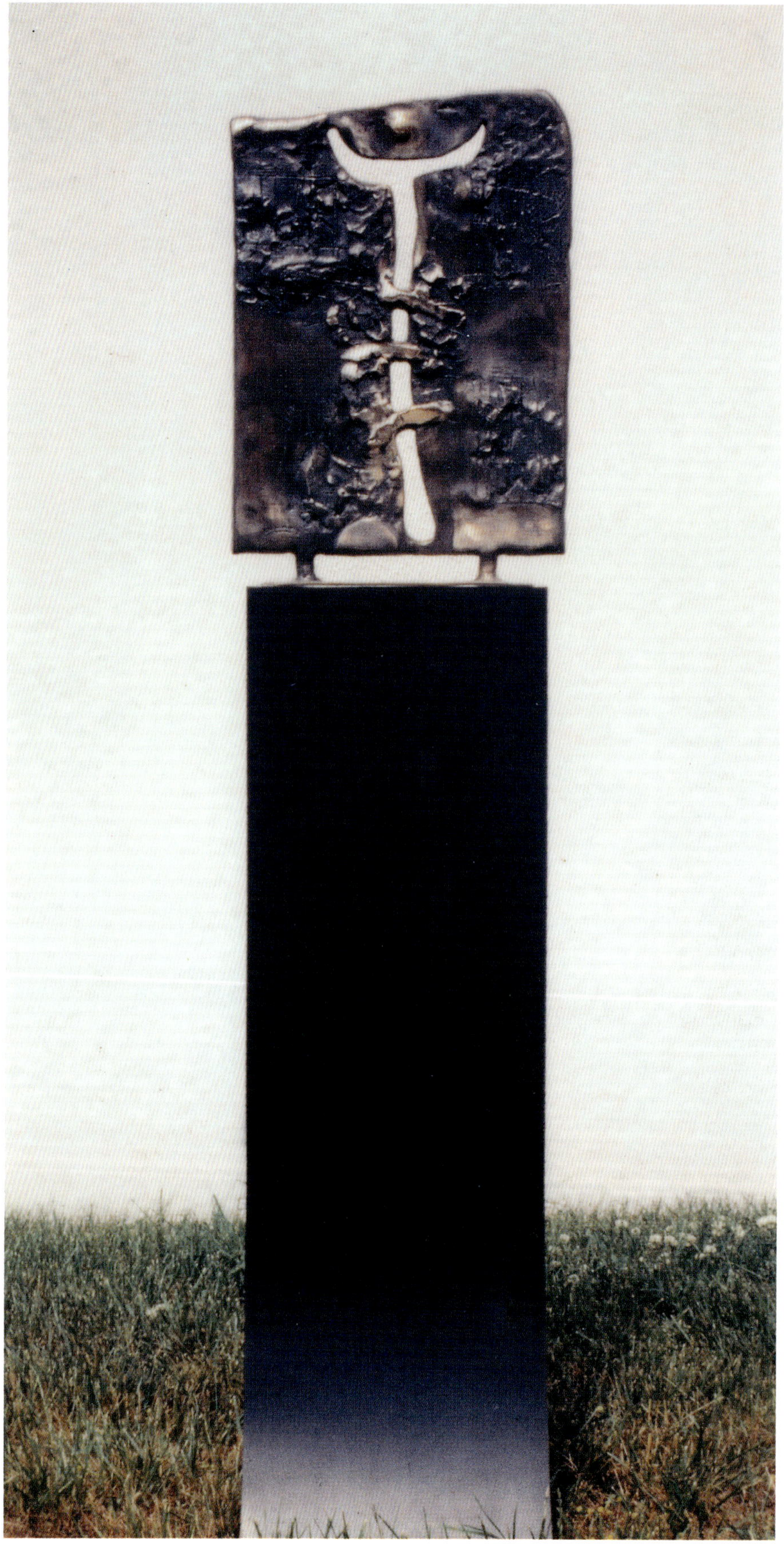

190

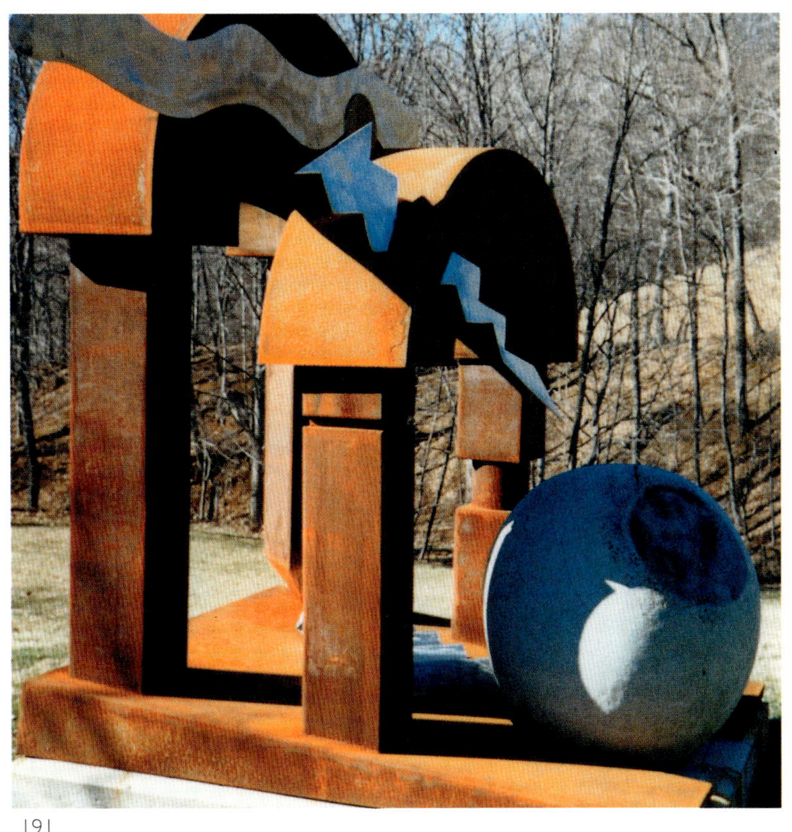

Made a rendering for a corporate client and even made a bronze model but never got the commission. However, ten years later was finally able to fabricate the piece for a private residence – what a joy!

191

Everything is a potential idea . . .

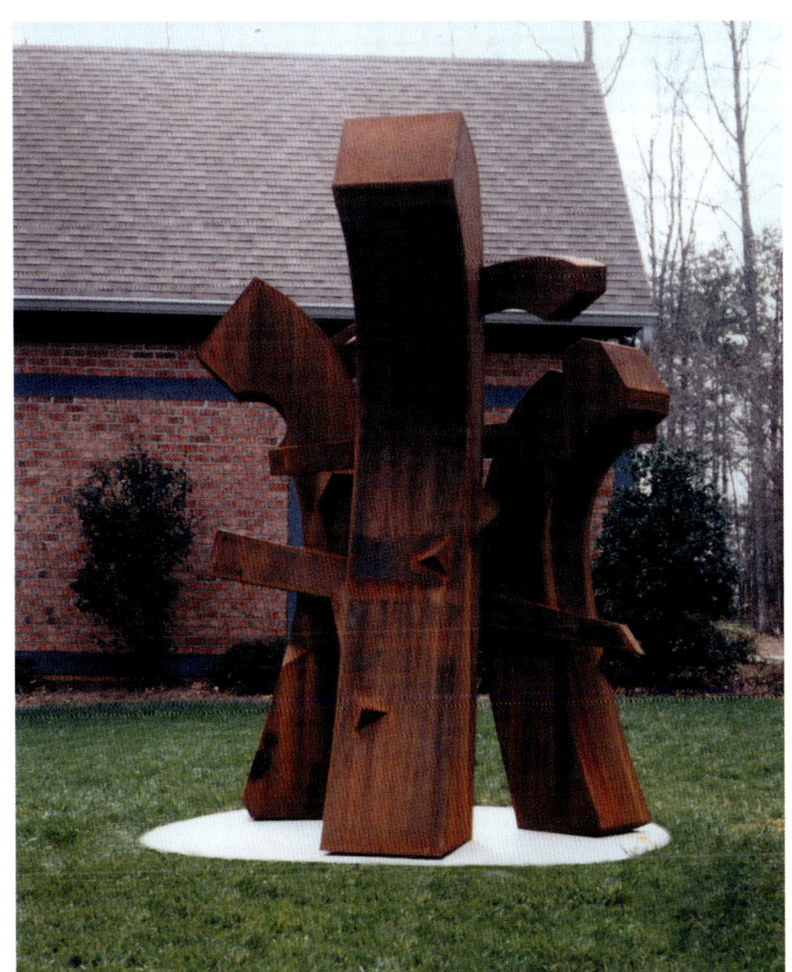

192

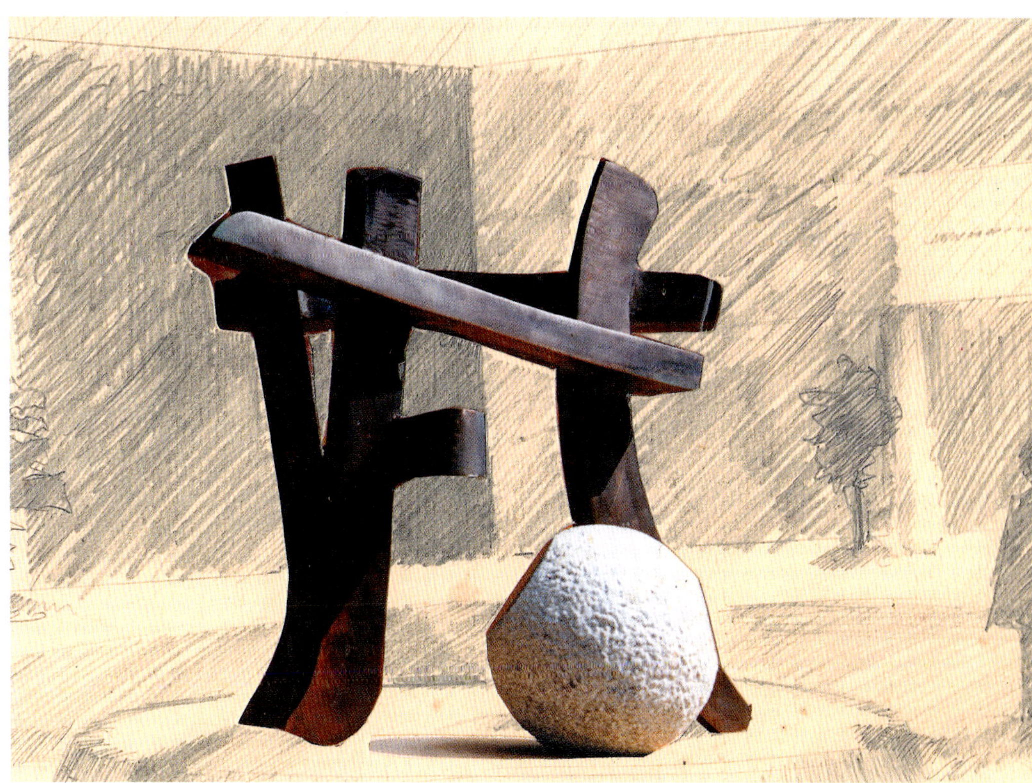

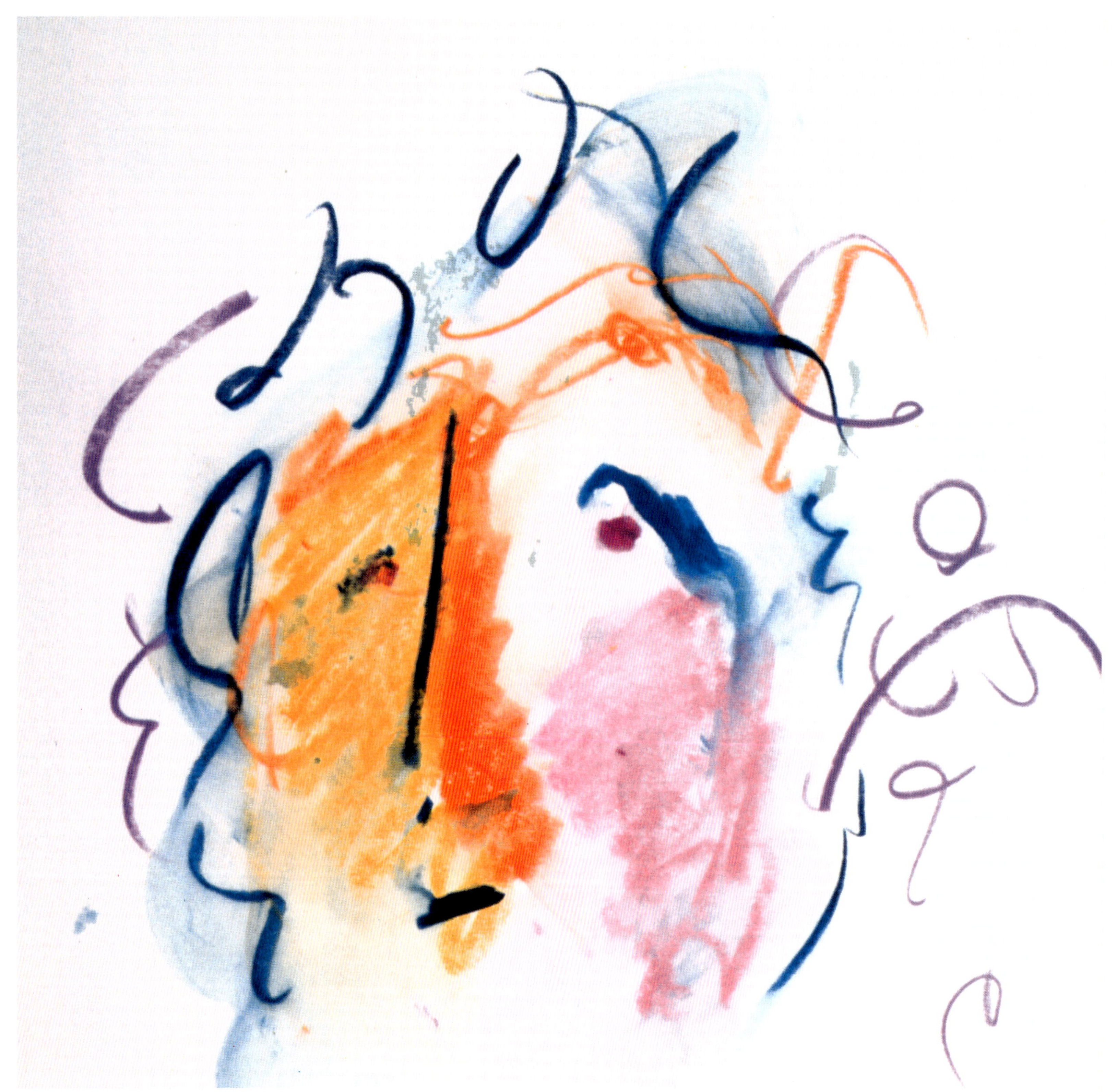

These eyes have seen too much . . .

I used to say that the only hope for man was learning to laugh at our own absurdity. I have tried to do this. Worked very hard at fully understanding this concept of life. Talked about it to others. Tried to explain it aloud so as to better know it myself. But alas, the reality is I'm too serious about life to laugh. Actually the pain is far greater than the joy. ____ finally admitted to his madness and committed himself. For what? To somehow justify his acts to himself — or to others? To substantiate his existence? To kindle the fire of hope (the only thing that keeps any of us going — that thing I'll never understand — that silent force that causes man to persist despite losing odds)?

There is no battle if one never wonders WHY? Without that question life is easy — moving as one is told, following the arrows, stopping at the red lights.

Must write. A strange evening. There is something unusually strange in the air. Like a feeling of death. The air outside speaks to me of dying — it calls softly. I know it is there and sit quietly here writing, not afraid — for I feel I know death well and am not afraid of it. But still, there is something else in the air — nothing with emotion, just a stillness and calm, and the silence of gently falling water. Is it the cold hand of guilt that clings around me, that reaches inside my rib cage and tries to pull at my heart — that Christian-bred guilt that I fight and push to the rear, that I say 'no' to — informing it that I make my own rules, my own laws, my own way. I am God. I create. I do. Therefore I am.

I have done a piece that came out of a meeting with an ex-alcoholic. It has to do with the struggle — with eyes that are at once calm and fearful. I've tried to capture the freedom that results from not drinking, but I banded the eyes because I believe that there is no real freedom. Never again can there be a moment of madness, a letting go, a scream — they are dangerous to the fine line that must be walked in sobriety. It's not too hard for the person who has never danced or yelled at the moon, but for the person who has, there is a chain around them from now until death.

**WE ARE ALONE AT BEST.
ANYTHING ELSE IS AN ILLUSION.**

A question: What is there? I sit at the big round table. Outside the home-made chimes ring as though they too are possessed by the stillness. The crickets' usual sounds are muffled and seem softer. It's too still to light anything more than a candle — as though time quietly stopped. The sound of pen on paper has become an audible 'scream'. I can almost hear my mind working. What is there? What part am I now of the nitrogen cycle? What part tomorrow? The dogs on the second ridge over sound as if they are under the chimes. The insects that normally move unnoticed are very obvious. I have grown. I ask better questions now. But who's to answer? I walk slower but more intelligently (looking first) but why go beyond the surface? Stillness — a time to ask better questions.

The old polarity again — this time spurred by the need to make art and sell art. 22 pieces out and no sales. Three galleries have my work and I have no money. What's going on? And yet I continue to do it. I can't believe it most of the time — sheer madness. Abandon all hope, ye who enter here.

Am reading P. White's Vivisection and finally understand many things about myself. One, the main reason I write in my journals is because I have never met anyone who knows what I'm talking about. I try to talk about some thoughts and as the words come out I see the expressions change on the face of the listening victim. I just now realized this has been going on throughout my whole life. For example, the things that most people find funny I find hard to laugh at. I find tragedy where they find humor. I don't like many people because I see in them more, or less, than they are aware I am seeing. I see it in the way they walk, or hold a cup of coffee — that they are one thing while they are telling me the opposite. The contradiction illuminates the lie. The person fails. Generally I am bored with most people. Few have enough honesty and mystery and energy and curiosity for me. Usually I find I'm better off by myself. White's book has been pointing these things out to me — each page illustrates another example of my relationship with others, and the constant problems I've always had in dealing with them at any level.

"I impose nothing on you. Take what you want, or trash it" – sometimes my students don't understand these simple words . . .

If you study art for one year you come away with baskets of imagery on your shoulders. You then have to transmit that to output. In your first attempt you have to be honest that the image in your mind came from somewhere/someone else. You simply need to imitate the form to make a decision about it. That is a process of growth. Once you get rid of all that you are free. Then there are two ways to go. One is "variations on a theme" – it is the easy way, however it is a gamble and the vision is narrow. The second is "sheer invention" – it is like the bounce between protons and electrons . . . the bounce giving you energy.

The year 84 is not what we'll remember; it's just a time marker along the road. The keeper was, we attacked the apple orchard late one night. Filled our pockets and shirts with life-challenging events. We reached out and grabbed, picked up from the grass, kept running, tripping, jerking them from branches, running, stumbling, falling. And once breathing slowly again, we sorted out the bruised and rotten ones and carefully polished the best of what we stole . . . laughing about the absurdity of it all.

Perhaps the major difference between the choice of art and any other profession is the reason one chooses . . .

At times I feel badly that I joke about all that I do when I see people so serious about what they do. I don't really know what is real about art, it is fun and continues to challenge all of my being – that's why I love it.

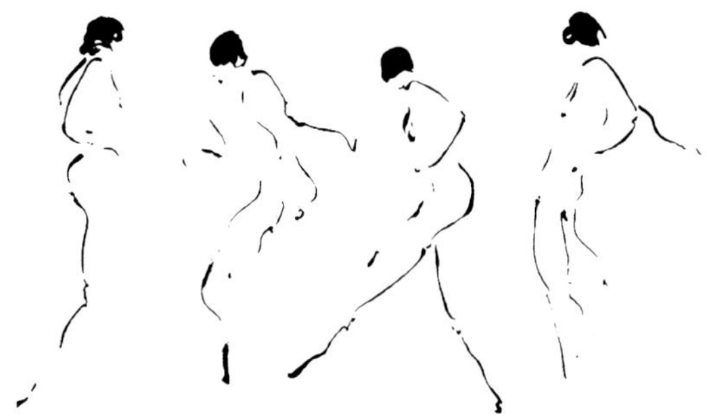

. . . just finished 80 drawings. Did the 'whole thing', did the erotic ones, satisfied most of my fantasies, and kept going . . . pushed my head far this time and now, just moments ago, I got ONE. Very Japanese, very stark. Was finally able to eliminate almost all of the lines. I can't believe the simplicity of the form! Keep taking away. Take away. Down to five brush strokes – each one elegant.

How can one never wonder or ask WHY? How does it feel to have no battle, to move on when told to, to follow the arrows and stop at the red lights? (Although it does seem that if man deals honestly with himself, he has to arrive at the conclusion that it's all absurd – and to make more of it than that borders on dishonesty.)

Detest writing in pencil. Visual image weak, not pronounced enough, lacks character, and I have no feel for it.

. . . this time I was very ill. The pain got worse through the night until I reached the point of SCREAMING for death to come and end it all. I finally passed out. Two days later here I am, awake, and still alive having survived my first introduction to death – and I find that I no longer fear it.

I must be free. Free to move as I must, to walk as I choose, a "yes" a "no" – doesn't matter as long as I CHOOSE. Must be free to find the truth with my being. Without this truth there can be no art for me.

No time for drawing right now. Sculpture commissions pouring in. I miss my drawing time. Would love to spend this evening naked and doing them.

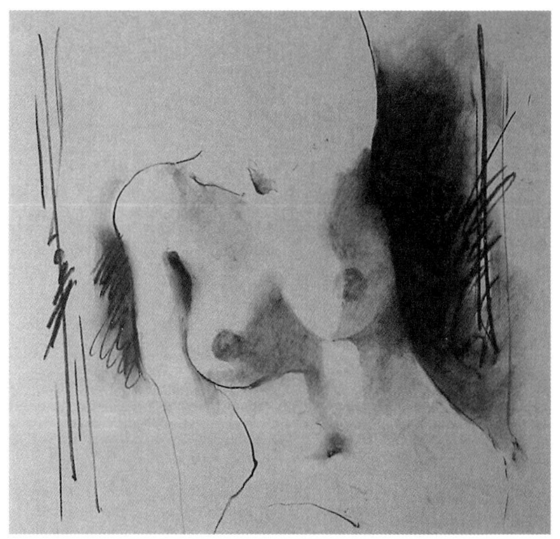

. . . I was in motion! Watch out! If you want to stop me you'll have to shoot me. Until then, I'll fight, claw, crawl, scream, laugh, dance, weep . . . this is SCULPTURE!

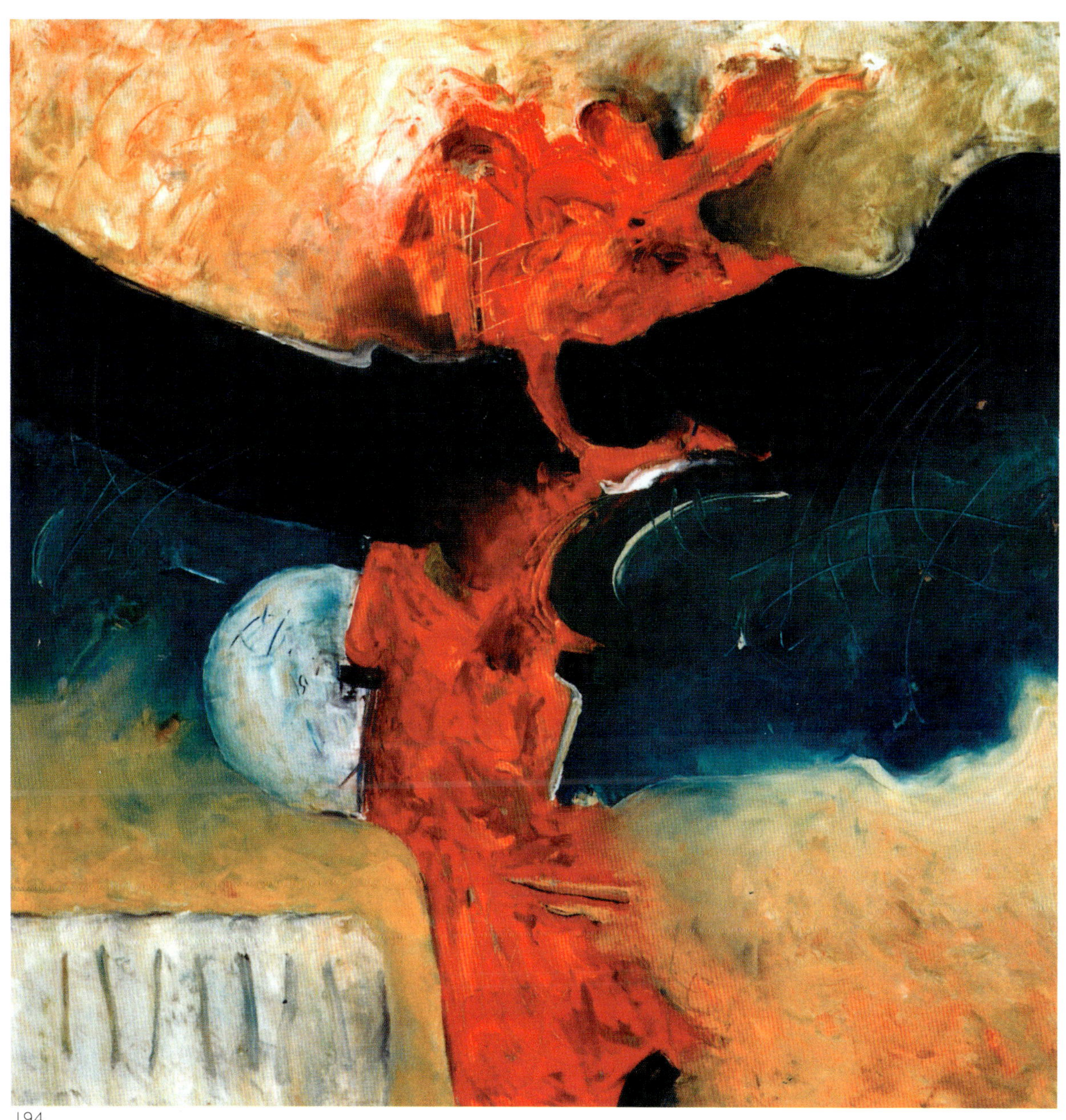

194

I have been painting almost every night now for the past 10 years. I had thought it would help me catch up in expressing all the images that pass through me — so much quicker are they than sculpture . . . now, some 1000 paintings later, I'm still chasing, racing, trying to keep up . . . perhaps Deborah will want to do another book?

106 – Forged Steel / Private Collection
107 – Forged Steel / Private Collection
108 – Forged Steel / Private Collection
109 – Forged Steel / Private Collection
110 – Forged Steel & Granite Custom Table
111 – Black Marble & Stainless Steel / Private Collection
112 – Black Marble / Private Collection
113 – Alabaster / Private Collection
114 – Alabaster / Private Collection
115 – Alabaster / Private Collection
116 – Alabaster / Private Collection
117 – Alabaster / Private Collection
118 – Alabaster / Private Collection
119 – Marble / Private Collection
120 – Marble / Private Collection
121 – Alabaster / Private Collection
122 – Alabaster / Private Collection
123 – Alabaster / Private Collection
124 – Alabaster / Private Collection
125 – Alabaster / Private Collection
126 – Alabaster / Private Collection
127 – Alabaster / Private Collection
128 – Alabaster / Private Collection
129 – Alabaster / Private Collection
130 – Alabaster / Private Collection
131 – Artist's Sculpture Garden / Vilas, NC
132 – "Untitled" / Corten Steel / Private Collection
133 – "Big Yellow" / Painted Steel / Artist's Collection
134 – "Clouds, Basenote, & Lightning" / Stainless Steel
        Private Collection
135 – "Full Moon Dance" / Stainless Steel / Private Collection
136 – "Half Moon Mountain" / Stainless Steel & Bronze
        Private Collection
137 – "Untitled" / Stainless Steel / Private Collection
138 – "Untitled" / Stainless Steel & Marble / Private Collection
139 – "Wind Harp" / Stainless Steel / Private Collection
140 – "Tribute To The New" / Stainless Steel & Bronze
        Private Collection
141 – "Mountain–Clouds" / Stainless Steel & Bronze
        Private Collection
142 – "Untitled" / Stainless Steel / Private Collection
143 – "Untitled" / Stainless Steel / Private Collection
144 – "Untitled" / Stainless Steel & Bronze Garden Screen
        Private Collection
145 – "Mariachi Band" / Painted Steel / Private Collection
146 – "African Bushwhacker" / Painted Steel / Artist's Collection
147 – "Delicate Balance" / Stainless Steel / Private Collection
148 – "Untitled" / Corten Steel / Private Collection
149 – "The Guardian" / Corten Steel / Private Collection
150 – "Kyoto and Beyond" / Corten Steel / Private Collection
151 – "Untitled" / Corten Steel / Private Collection
152 – "Untitled" / Corten Steel / Private Collection
153 – "Child's Toy" / Corten Steel / Private Collection
154 – Marble Fountain in progress

155 – "The Journey" / Bronze, Stainless Steel, Marble
        Hunter Museum, Chattanooga, TN
156 – "Linkage" / Stainless Steel / Hickory Museum of Art,
        Hickory, NC
157 – "River Wedge" / Black Granite / TVA, Chattanooga, TN
158 – Stainless Steel / Steel Case Corporation,
159 – Cast Bronze / R.J. Reynolds Corporation
        Winston-Salem NC
160 – "Roots & Wings" / Corten Steel / Lees McRae College,
        Banner Elk, NC
161 – "Tangible Tango" / West Chase No. 2, Raleigh, NC
162 – Stainless Steel / Private Collection
163 – Laminated Marble / West Chase No.3, Raleigh, NC
164 – "Passages" / Carerra Marble / Lees-McRae College,
        Banner Elk, NC
165 – "Water Wall / Laminated Marble / First Union National Bank,
        Durham, NC
166 – Bronze & Stainless Steel / Private Collection
167 – Bronze & Black Marble / Private Collection
168 – Laminated Marble / Private Collection
169 – Fountain, one of a series / Marble
        Dorado Beach Club, Puerto Rico
170 – Laminated Marble / Private Collection
171 – Stainless Steel & Bronze / Private Collection
172 – Marble / Private Collection
173 – Laminated Marble Fountain / Fearrington House
        Pittsboro, NC
174 – Cast Bronze & Forged Steel / Private Collection
175 – Black Marble / Private Collection
176 – "Linkage" / Fero Cement / Artist's Collection
177 – Untitled / White Marble / Private Collection
178 – Laminated Marble / Artist's Collection
179 – Cast Bronze / Private Collection
180 – Cast Bronze / Private Collection
181 – Forged Stainless & Alabaster / Private Collection
182 – Stainless Steel / Private Collection
183 – Stainless Steel & Bronze / Private Collection
184 – "Morning Song" / Stainless Steel & Mild Steel
        Private Collection
185 – Cast Bronze / Private Collection
186 – "Wind Song" / Cast Bronze / Private Collection
187 – Cast Aluminum & Corten Steel / Private Collection
188 – "Freeway" / Cast Bronze & Aluminum / Private Collection
189 – Cast Aluminum and Corten Steel / Private Collection
190 – Cast Bronze & Black Marble / Private Collection
191 – "The Journey" (small version) / Corten Steel & Marble
        Artist's Collection
192 – "The Entry" / Corten Steel / Private Collection
193 – "My Eyes Have Seen Too Much" / Pastels on Paper
        Private Collection
194 – "Thoughts of Ludwig" / Oil on Canvas / Private Collection

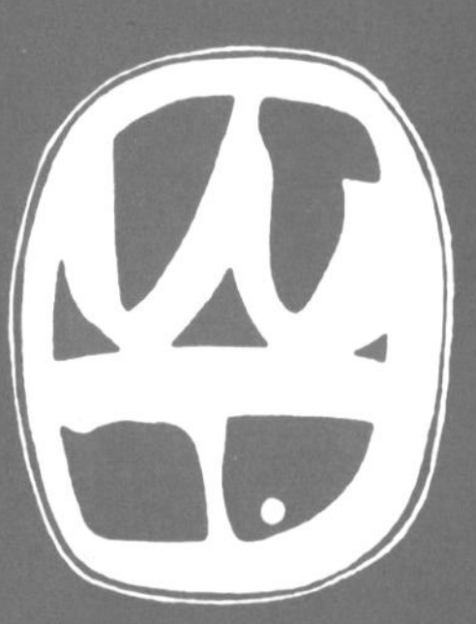